Although a child--one still in need of parental protection,
she was a plaything to any one of the thousands of sex-tourists
who came to Thailand and sought out
the youngest and most vulnerable.

Praise for Lon's life story

A highly-recommended read. It is informative, damning and at times touching. At the end you really feel like you know Lon.

Stickmanbangkok.com

...is actually an engrossing story of a girl who ran away from her home in Isaan at age 13 to come to work in Bangkok. I sincerely hope that this story will help focus more attention on the plight of disadvantaged Thai women.

Kurt Heck, GoodwillBangkok

She speaks with the powerful and determined voice of an activist making clear the injustice that she and many other girls have suffered. *David Reid, geocities.com*

...the first book, to my knowledge, that tells about how local (Thai) prostitutes view their profession in general, the sex tourists in particular. *Bernard Trink, Bangkok Post*

This book is well worth a read, even by Old Thai Hands.

www.bangkokatoz.com Mehkong Kurt

...this is the best book on THAILAND I have ever read. ...finest of its genre ... probably that will ever be written and I found the social commentary balanced, accurate, and particularly telling from the personal point-of-view of Lon. A fine book. *www.thaivisa.com*

Had me in tears on my flight back from BKK.
www.phuket-info.com

Only

13

The true story of Lon

A share of the proceeds from the sale of this book
will be donated to organizations dedicated to aiding young girls
who are at-risk for, or who have already become involved in, the
Sex-tourism or trafficking industries.

Only 13

Published by Only 13 Publications
Jomtien Beach, Thailand

Website: www.Only13.net
Email: Only13info@yahoo.com
Only13media@yahoo.com

Text and Photos Copyright
Julia Manzanares and Derek Kent

ISBN: 0-9772841-0-7

We wish to express our appreciation to Ms. Kusuma Mintakhin Bekenn,
Editorial Manager of the Bangkok Post,
for her generosity and assistance in allowing us to publish photos
from the newspaper's library.

We have made every effort to acknowledge all of the resources that
assisted with the development of this book.
If we have neglected anyone, it has been purely unintentional.
Please know how very much your contribution has been appreciated.
Printed in the United States of America

"Woman and child abuse is a rooted problem in Thai society. The inferior will always be the victim of the superior. It is the duty of all of us to 'keep our eyes open and to help prevent any kind of discrimination, physical assault, any kind of abuse to the inferior namely 'children and women' whom we consider vulnerable in Thai society."

Pavena Hongsakul
Pavena Foundation

"Pavena is my hero"

Lon

GOODWILL GROUP FOUNDATION

When I picked up Lon's life story in the airport bookstore in Phuket earlier this year, I did so with the expectation of learning something of a Thai woman's perspective of the sex industry in Thailand. In fact, I learned that and quite a bit more. Having directed the Goodwill Group - a Thai foundation for disadvantaged women - for the past several years, I thought I knew something of the plight of rural women who come to Bangkok seeking work, but Lon's story greatly improved my existing understanding of "the way things are" for rural women in this wonderful, perplexing and - at times - unjust country.

I've often wondered how it came to be that women born in the outer provinces of Thailand are handed such a rotten deal. From a very young age, female children are expected to start shouldering the burden of supporting their parents while their brothers are afforded the educational opportunities - such as they exist. A great many of these rural women leave school early to marry or get pregnant, then abandoned by their spouses they come to Bangkok to support their offspring. Others come to the city to support their parents and siblings, who in some cases pressure them into working in the sex industry, when in fact they are capable of much more. Bangkok is one of many places in Thailand which harbors a flourishing sex industry and therefore serves as a magnet for rural women seeking this seemingly "easy money"

I congratulate both Lon for having the courage to give such a candid account of her own experiences and Derek for putting it to paper in an objective manner. I sincerely hope that this story will help focus more attention on the plight of disadvantaged Thai women.

Kurt Heck, Managing Director
GOODWILL GROUP FOUNDATION
Bangkok, Thailand
October 11, 2005

FONDAZIONE UMANITARIA ARCOBALENO
Via Clemente Maraini 22, 6900 LUGANO, Switzerland
Tel. (41) 091.994.40.90 www.fondarco.ch info@fondarco.ch

Ban Naudom, September 15, 2005

Dear Derek,

I would like to sincerely thank you for writing Lon's story which did turn out to be greatly inspirational for me.

I did avidly read it in just two days, completely captivated by the story of this young Isaan girl and all her ordeals.

A book so sincere and honest that gave me more impetus and strength in my attempts to try to do something to prevent that many more Northeastern girls will follow Lon's unfortunate life and steps.

A small wonderful book, a must read for anyone, Farang or Thai, who cares for a better world, for better treatment of young and helpless people. An eye opener for every one, a book every farang in Pattaya, Patong Beach or Patpong shall be reading, and reflect upon!

I am starting a new project right now in Nepal, aimed once again at the welfare of so many distressed young girls and boys. Nepal as the Northeast of Thailand is a big provider of young poor girls for the sex trade and I really hope that soon I can find someone who can help me doing the same for Isaan, hopefully your book will provide a bit of awareness around the world. Once again, dear Julia and Derek, thanks a lot for your book.

Claudio Romano*

*CLAUDIO ROMANO, founder and Vice-President of FONDAZIONE UMANITARIA ARCOBLAENO, www.fondarco.ch

Dedication

This book is dedicated to my two sisters,
Ying and Sai,
who never had to see sex-tourists as I did,
and to my father,
the only one who truly loved me.

Forward

In the following pages, I will share my story and the stories of tens of thousands of other women and children, all who have found it necessary to follow my same path--through no fault of their own. It is one which females in my region of the world have been walking for centuries.

I will take you through my country and explain the simplicity of Thai economics, and the complex nature of Thai-Isaan culture, the latter steeped in the traditions, mores, and poverty of Northeastern Thailand. Just as these conditions affected my life, they continue to affect the life of every poor, young woman in Thailand. I will share the reasons it is the way it is, and the reasons I believe it will never change. We will travel together from the impoverished village where I was born, to the red-light districts of Thailand, to my several attempts at a new life in Europe from where I share my story.

This is not a pretty story as I detail the pivotal role my country, "The Land of Smiles," has in perpetuating human misery and human trafficking, both for the purposes of sexual slavery (where pedophiles find paradise in Pattaya, Phuket, and Chiang Mai), and in job slavery where children are held in human bondage. You will find that I use the word *"tragically"* frequently throughout this book because there is no other word to describe the suffering that we have endured, for no other reason than the disadvantage of being born female to extremely poverty-stricken families in the third-world. There will always be those who will use their wealth, status, and/or their power at the expense of the poor and powerless. This is the truth of my country where most young women who come from Isaan can never win—the deck is stacked against us—by virtue of our birth and policies of our government.

But I have won, although it has taken me more than a decade. I want everyone who has ever been down into the deepest abyss of life to know that they can win, too. We must come to the truth that deep down in the recesses of our souls, we are precious human treasures, even when it doesn't feel like it, nor look like it. We have value and are capable of making great contributions to ourselves and to the rest of the world. If we are fortunate, if we have even one single stroke of luck, and we add that to what we ultimately believe about ourselves, not what anyone else believes about us, this can determine whether we win or lose this game of life. I was one of the lucky ones! One of the lucky ones indeed!!!

Lon

Lon at 17

TABLE OF CONTENTS

GLOSSARY
Don't skip the glossary;
the language is necessary to understand the book

Bar-fine: The amount paid to the bar ($3 - $12) to take the girl out for a "short-time" or for the night.

Bar girl: A prostitute who works in a bar where she meets men.

BP: Bangkok Post, English language newspaper in Thailand

Brideprice: The price paid to the parents for marriage to their daughter.

Face: The degree to which your speech or actions adhere to Confucian principles of speech and behavior toward members of your social group. This language or behavior determines your perceived standing within that group. Your perceived standing is *"Face"*—or more simply, the receipt of respect.

Farang: This word may have been borrowed from the Persian word "farang" which means Frankish. France was one of the first European nations to establish ties with Thailand in the 17th century. All Europeans (Western people) were then referred to as farang.

Freelancer: A prostitute who is not employed by a bar or GoGo and instead meets men at singles' bars, discos, shopping centers, on the street, at the beach, or anywhere else.

GoGo: A Strip Club where the dancers may take off their tops and/or bikinis--or not.

GoGo-girl: A girl working as a dancer/stripper in a GoGo.

ICFTU: International Confederation of Free Trade Unions

Isaan: Northeastern Thailand; a person from Isaan; the language of Northeastern Thailand--also known as Laotian or simply Lao.

Karen People: Originated in Myanmar, fled government persecution, and settled in the mountains of northern and western Thailand, Laos, and Burma. Now the largest hill tribe in Thailand, numbering 350,000 people, divided into four sub-groups whose beliefs are Animism, Buddhism, or Christianity depending on to which group they belong.

Mama-san: The woman who manages the girls in a brothel, bar, or GoGo club

Patpong: Located in Bangkok, a red-light district full of GoGo clubs and bars for sex-tourists.

Pattaya: A Thai seaside resort, the major "Sex-for-Sale" capital of the world.

Short-time: A prostitute going with a man for an hour or so.

Soi: Street

TAT: Tourism Authority of Thailand

The Nation: English language newspaper in Thailand

The West: United States, Europe, Australia, New Zealand—anywhere that the Farang come from.

We: Bar girls and GoGo dancers in SE Asia

Throughout the book, you will see a conversion of Thai baht to U.S. dollars. The conversion rate has varied since 1997, so I have varied the conversion rate at the time of each episode in the book. To simplify, any way you look at it:

Isaan Girls are Poor;
Tourists are Rich;
I bridged the gap!

Introduction

Boontah's Family Tree

Grandfather

Boontah's maternal grandfather was born in Chiang Mai, the largest city in Northern Thailand, to a middle-class family who owned a large plot of land and many buffalo. His parents had produced a large family and his father had more than one wife. Once the wealth was shared among the many children--little remained for each. After her grandfather received his inheritance, he moved to Ubon and married a poor illiterate woman who was to become Boontah's grandmother. They produced nine children. The rearing of these nine children reduced the few assets he brought with him, and now he was also poor. Although he had basic literate skills, he spent his adult life in his room talking to the gods of the Karen people.

Grandmother

Boontah speaks little of her maternal grandmother because she was the one responsible for beating her tiny granddaughter with a stick for the first decade of her young life, or for reporting her to others who would. Little is known of her other than she appeared to be a hateful woman who took every opportunity to physically and verbally strike out at her grandchildren and forbid them every chance at happiness—especially Boontah.

Mother: **Bootsah**

It may very well have been due to being raised in a loveless home that Bootsah knew little about love. By the time she was born, her father was destitute—material possessions, cash, and love were nowhere to be found. She was the first daughter. As is customary in Thai culture, it is the responsibility of the eldest daughter to care for her younger siblings, and as her parents' age—to care for them as well. When she was only 15, she married Somphan whom she barely knew, and more importantly, did not love. Her earlier maternal tasks eventually led her to caring for her sister's baby, Sai.

Father: **Somphan**

A responsible, kind, and loving man, he seemed to be the only one who loved, understood, or cared for his oldest daughter. He would accept any offer of work, no matter how difficult or how far away, in order to provide for the needs of his family. When he worked in Bangkok, he wrote to Boontah often, knowing how she depended on him for her happiness.

Uncle: **Sakda**

The youngest son of her grandmother: When Boontah was 11-years old, it was Sakda who learned that she was the one who constantly stole from her brother, and as a result, he repeatedly hit her with a stick. With every beating, Boontah knew she was closer to running away and finding her father in Bangkok.

Siblings:

Her "twin" sisters Ulah (Ying) and Lampoon (Sai/Joy) were four years younger than she was. Boontah's brother Banya was two years older.

Ying

In Thai, "Ying" means lady. No other Thai name could have been more perfect. Ying was always a very vain child, and as early as six, she was afraid of getting fat. She would also spend a lot of time dancing in the bathroom—when later they had a house with a bathroom. Dancing may have been in the family's blood as eventually Boontah also became a dancer. Sai and Boontah would often sneak around to watch Ying dance. Ying also wanted to have long, beautiful hair. She would wrap a towel around her short hair to make it appear long and then pretend that she was a princess.

She chose to read books rather than go outside to play. She was never fond of animals either; as far as she was concerned, they were much too dirty and the thought of touching them made her flinch.

Ying rarely talked when she was small. When she did, everyone laughed. Her twin, Sai, was a chatterer—a talent that made Ying very angry. Ying's worst character flaw was her anger—manifested whenever she didn't get her own way, a flaw that appeared to pervade the characters of the entire family. When they played together, Ying always wanted to play the role of the princess. She refused to be the wicked character, a role that was always left to Sai. Although she hadn't yet been to a movie, cultural influence was strong in story books. Thai folklore and myth traditionally feature both a saintly and a dark character—roles played out in reality in every village and often in every family.

Ying continued to wet her pants until the age of six and would suffer the stick at the hands of her mother as a result. In spite of also being beaten, although not nearly as often as Boontah, her eagerness to learn was obvious. At only five, the year before she was due to start school – she would go to class with her older sister.

Ying was a very good dancer with natural ability and she demonstrated grace and poise beyond her years. Boontah taught her to sing and Ying learned quickly. Her talents soon gave her the opportunity to sing and perform at village parties in exchange for food and candy. She loved to wear skirts and she would borrow any articles from her mother and grandmother that she thought would dress up her simple and well-worn garments. Unlike Sai, she loved to play with dolls, and she hated most sports--except for running and volleyball. Also, very unlike her sisters, she always insisted on a kiss before going to sleep.

Ying won awards from school for writing, painting, running, volleyball, singing, and Thai dancing. Her teachers recognized her skills, talents, accomplishments, excellent participation in the classroom and in extra-curricular activities. She did well scholastically and she made her family proud, unlike Boontah and Sai.

Like her older sister Boontah, Ying loved her father more than her mother and she always kept a picture of him. When their father returned to Ubon from Bangkok, he would sell small sweets from a push cart. In the evenings, she would go with him under the pretense of helping him. But, he knew that she really just wanted sweets. She was a gracious little girl, responding to every gift from her father with the words "wonderful" and "beautiful"—no matter how insincere. Her behavior contrasted greatly to that of her sisters.

Sai (Joy)
Sai's natural mother was Bootsah's sister. Sai was left on Bootsah's doorstep when she was only three-months old. As she was barely three months younger than Ying, she was nursed and raised as Ying's twin sister. A year after Sai's mother had abandoned her; she returned and tried to kill her. Fortunately, Bootsah walked in just in time and stopped her. It was never learned why Sai's mother attempted so unthinkable an act.

Sai was a talkative little girl, scarcely stopping to take a breath. She was very different from Ying; she was a tomboy. Sai was happier to play with the boys and to catch frogs, fish, shrimp, and fresh-water crabs. She liked Kung Fu and she loved to play ball. She learned to swim and ride a motorbike before Ying. She was highly-competitive and took a lot of pleasure in beating her brother and sisters at sports. She didn't care about school, but cared a lot more about having fun. She also complained angrily about all nine members of the family sharing a one-room shack—a necessary fact of life in a poor village. She desperately wanted her own room--an impossible dream in their present circumstances.

As Sai got older, she would often wake up in the morning and go with Boontah to the pump for water. Some nights, she would go with her to graze the buffalo, sometimes walking as far as three miles in each direction--depending on the mood of the buffalo. She was also a very jealous little girl. She craved the attention shown to Banya at home and to Ying at school. Like Boontah, she wanted to be acknowledged. Neither would ever be so fortunate.

A neighbor (left) with Sai, age 6, and Boontah, age 10

When Sai was 10, her mother returned and wanted to take her back, but Boontah's mother refused to give her up. She didn't trust her sister to care for the child she had raised for a decade. This was the first that Sai, or her sisters, had heard that they were not blood sisters, but cousins. The realization that her mother didn't love her enough to raise her and had chosen to give her up—left her devastated. Her normal prankish childlike behavior changed immediately. She became hostile and defiant, changes that would lead her into acts of delinquency throughout the next 10 years.

Banya

Although in Thai, Banya translates into "Brain," it was far from an accurate description of her brother. He was never motivated to help out very much at home other than to avoid the threat of a stick wielded by his grandmother. He never intentionally hurt Boontah, but she frequently caused him a lot of trouble. In fact, Boontah, Ying, and Sai would always side against him. It is intentional that he has been mentioned last in the descriptions. He received what little extra their family could afford when they could afford anything at all, and it was always at the expense of his three sisters. At the age of 13, he received a bicycle from their mother while the girls always had to walk. He was never asked to share with his siblings and would never have considered doing so on his own. Although his bicycle gave him easy and convenient access to seeking out fruit from trees and vines along the roadside, it would never have occurred to him to bring something home for his sisters.

Banya, like Boontah, liked to take the buffalo out to graze, catch frogs, fish in the pond, and pick chili from the fields. He was never much of a student, but he was a happy child. When he was 13, his grandparents wanted him to continue his education, but he had other ideas. They were successful in keeping him in school until he entered the 8th grade. At the age of 15, he quit. He traveled to Chiang Mai to visit his paternal grandparents. He stayed there for several months and met a young Karen girl. She was just 16-years old--one year his senior. Not long after they met, they were married. It also wasn't long before they returned to his family's shack in Ban Jonejalurn. Even after he was married, his mother always considered his desires first, regardless of the most essential needs of the rest of the family—including the education of her daughters.

Boontah's Dog

Boontah's dog was her best friend and he could always be counted on to defend her when she would run from her family in fear. One day, her mother thought that the dog had rabies; she heeded an old wives' tale for curing this disease by taking a knife and cutting off its ear. This would become an act that Boontah would never forgive, nor forget.

Map of Thailand

My province of Ubon Ratchathani is highlighted.

Chapter 1

Thailand and My Isaan Village

Where It All Started

Boontah was born female into a desperately poor family living in a small, humble, and sleepy village in Northeastern Thailand, or more specifically, Ban Jonejalurn, Tamboon Nongsanooh, Amphur Boontalik, in Ubon Ratachani Province. In the West, her home would be considered not only shabby, but also primitive. It had little more than four walls, a rotten floor, and decrepit roof; all had holes large enough to see the stars when they sparkled and feel the rain during a downpour. This one-room wooden shack with dilapidated walls, no more than a shed, barely served as shelter from the scorching sun, stifling humidity, and tropical rainfall.

The furniture consisted of a few pieces of broken-down rattan and threadbare pillows. The toilet was a hole in the ground out back surrounded by four splintered wooden walls. The "shower" was a tub of water with a scoop for throwing the water over one's shoulders. Like all poor villages in this part of the world, Ban Jonejalum had dirt roads, little infrastructure, an inadequate school system, and no activities or facilities for children to play and to simply be children. Her village was this and far more, as her village was in one of the poorest rural provinces in Northeastern Thailand, better known as Isaan.

Some of the contrasts between Ban Jonejalum and the rest of Thailand are that the entire Isaan area is generally drier, has far less foliage with poor crop yields and either too much rain resulting in floods, or too little rain resulting in drought. So, although the village streets of the Northeast are often curtains of brown dust, and its inhabitants are besieged by the unrelenting heat of a tropical sun, they are also surrounded by the humidity of the tropics. In contrast, Thai villages in the central region of the country are set in a lush countryside, thick with vibrant green flora covering the landscape as far as the eye can see. The foliage at the tops of the trees glisten a golden hue as if kissed by the sun, and their outstretched leafy branches below, a dazzling emerald green, are drenched by summer rains.

Little has changed in Isaan since Boontah first opened her large brown eyes with those long silky black lashes, cried her first tear, and drew her first tiny breath over two decades ago. Ten-year old boys still ride motorbikes twice as old as they are--held together by rusty wire, electrical tape, and greasy parts scavenged from even older bikes. Their younger siblings seated in front or in back, hang on wherever their little hands can reach. The constant roar of motorbikes can be heard--often carrying a whole family and their dog, three or four astride, with smoke billowing from their exhaust pipes. Another constant, but more subtle clatter, is that of the farmer's lote tuk tuk--a long-nosed four-wheeled vehicle with a wagon securely attached above the rear tires. This modern version of the buffalo can be heard putt-putting its way through the mostly-unpaved roads. A combination tractor/family vehicle, it serves to carry rice and produce from the fields to the marketplace and as family-recreational transportation when work is done.

The venerable Tuk Tuk

The humble buffalo, symbolic of our Northeast and once the most valuable of all farm animals, can still be seen lumbering its way along the highway, dining on the tall, green grass surrounding the rice paddies just beyond. No longer part of a herd, it now labors alone. This once powerful creature, the backbone of the farming industry, has been replaced by automation. The smell of diesel fuel mixed with the stench of farm animals permeates the air.

Boontah's Early Life

In and around the countryside of Thailand, it was and remains commonplace for one or both parents to move to the major cities of Bangkok or Chiang Mai for work. Their children are left with family--generally a grandmother. Bootah's parents were no different. They moved to Bangkok and the children were forced to stay with their maternal grandparents in the one-room shack they all shared. Her father had no other choice; work was always in short supply in and around their small village, and he had accumulated a great deal of debt. A year earlier, in their first year of farming, they

3

had grown a successful watermelon crop. The following year, he borrowed money for insecticide and fertilizer to expand his yield, but his crops failed and he lost everything. Due to the unpredictable climatic conditions in the Northeast, it is not uncommon for farmers to suffer heavy farming losses that lead to financial obligations from which they will never become free. Frequently, these losses eventually lead to their ruin.

Boontah's parents lived and worked in Bangkok much of her young life, although her father sometimes worked there alone. She didn't see them very often because the cost and distance of this 500-mile trip made it prohibitive for them to return except during the holidays, or when emergencies arose. She always felt unwanted and unloved by everyone but her daddy, feelings that were validated by her family's frequent abuse. When she was feeling particularly blue, she would write to him again, and again. He was the only person with whom she could share her feelings and the only one who was proud of her and of her accomplishments.

On one occasion when Somphan went to Bangkok alone, he slept the first few nights on a bench at the Hualompong Bus Station while looking for work. In a matter of days, he had been hired by a metal factory near the Saphan Kruengthep Port. After working for only a couple of days, he lost a finger in an accident while using heavy equipment. He went to the hospital immediately, but there was nothing that they could do to reattach it, and even if they could, he could not have afforded the surgical fees. His company told him that after he had paid the medical fee for the suturing of his hand, they would reimburse him. They also promised to pay him his wage for that day of missed work. Instead, he was never reimbursed for his medical expenses, nor was he paid for the day he lost from work in order to go to the hospital—a common Thai employment practice, then and now.

4

Due to Somphan's abject poverty and his family's desperate need for money, he felt that he had no other choice but to continue to work at the metal factory. His poignant story is no different than the stories of millions of men and women, boys and girls--some as young as twelve, who leave their penniless families in their villages to seek a better life. They seek out employment far from their families to improve the quality of their lives and that of their families. Bangkok attracts workers from the countryside more than Chiang Mai or the attractive and enticing tourist resorts because it holds the most opportunities. Somphan stayed in touch with his family by writing letters as there wasn't a single phone to be found in the village. Even if a phone had existed, lack of money would have prevented him from making a call, just as lack of money would have prevented him from affording the surgery to reattach his finger—if that procedure had been possible.

Boontah's father was a kind man who loved his family very much and never refused employment. The first time he went to work in Bangkok, Boontah cried as if her young heart would break. Whether she was born a difficult child, or became one after being beaten time and again, she was certainly unwanted and definitely unloved; she was also the first, and sometimes the only child, to suffer the sting of a large stick to her tiny body when anything went wrong.

Work Starts Early and Never, Ever Ends
Everyday, she awakened at 5:00 A.M. to the sounds of roosters crowing. It's probably not a lot different from the way many American farm children wake up, but this is where the similarity ends. Her home, which rested on stilts, had a broken wooden floor with holes in the slats through which she could see and hear chickens cackling directly beneath the room where she, her brother, and sisters slept. Shortly after she awakened, she went to work--even before she had left for school.

5

Sometimes she went with her grandfather to the mountains and hunted. They grew enough rice to meet their needs, raised chickens that supplied food, and owned a buffalo. Boontah worked hard with little help from her brother. Her daily chores consisted of taking care of their small plot of land and of the animals. Like most children in the province, she had few toys. As they were relatively isolated from the "big city" and modern society in general, they had never seen very many toys. She had little time to play anyway as it seemed that there was a never-ending list of chores--chores that rested mostly on her tiny shoulders because she was the eldest daughter.

On a typical weekend, the jobs of gathering firewood, bamboo, and chilies, and of grazing buffalo belonged to Boontah. Her sisters were too young to help, so she usually went alone. Once in a while, Banya or Sai would go along, but never Ying who would avoid doing anything that would dirty her hands. The only responsibility that Banya ever really had was to help Boontah take the wheelbarrow and the water tank to the pump in order to get water for the family. On the way to the pump, Boontah would push the wheelbarrow and Banya would ride. On the way back, when the tank was full of water, Banya would push and Boontah would ride. One day, they broke the tank and their grandmother went after them with a stick. They never received anything extra for this backbreaking chore. But, when something went wrong with the old tank, it was entirely their fault. It was always Boontah who suffered the greater punishment.

Can't Stay Out of Trouble

Boontah was always up to something; she was never willing to leave anything alone. She and several friends frequently went to the temple to help themselves to mangoes from the trees—an activity they engaged in as often as possible. As usual, because she was the most agile, she volunteered to climb the tree while the

6

others stood watch for the monks. On one occasion, when she reached the top of the tree within reach of the luscious fruit, the monk came out with his stick and chased her friends away. Luckily, he didn't see her. She had climbed so high that he would have had to look almost straight up. She waited and waited with her heart pounding faster every second. A few moments later, he returned to the temple. She took her ill-gotten treasure and ran home. She was not about to leave empty-handed after risking life and limb, and maybe even a beating, for those delicious, tart, apple-green mangoes—a delicacy of the Northeast—especially when eaten with a blend of chili, salt and sugar.

On one of her many lonely days, Boontah took her father's turtle to the monks for a blessing. Most villagers didn't keep turtles and even fewer had them blessed, but it seemed like a good idea at the time. So, she picked up the turtle and happily made her way to the temple to see the monks. After the blessing, she placed the turtle into the moat around the temple because she thought it would like to play in the water. When she returned, she found it motionless. She used a stick to tap its back so that it would move through the water. When she brought it close enough to see it well, she realized that it was dead. *"Some good the monks did him,"* she thought. *"The water must have been so dirty that it killed him."* She allowed her family to believe that the turtle had simply crawled away from the house one day, never to return.

Boontah was six-years old when she started to attend school. On weekdays, she walked about three kilometers--about 40 minutes to school. After school, she played a little with her friends and then walked home. The school bus didn't provide transportation because the road to her house was unpaved. The children from the poorest of families--the ones living on the rough and primitive roads didn't receive transportation. It wasn't unusual for a school to be located as many as seven or eight kilometers from

7

one's home. On her way home from school, in torrential tropical rains or under a scorching sun, she would always pick a mango, banana, or papaya from a tree so her sisters would have a snack; they had little money to buy anything from a store. Although they were only three-years old, they would always run to the front of their yard and yell out her name *"Boontah, Boontah,"* eagerly anticipating the treat they would soon gobble up. They would squeal with delight as it dribbled down the corners of their tiny mouths.

Boontah liked school a lot and earned good grades--even when she began to get into trouble. Her teacher once told her to remain in school because she thought that she would do well. Unfortunately, Boontah's mother had other ideas. It was only her brother who would be afforded an education. She and her sisters would not be as fortunate until she went to work, *not only to provide for her mother, but in order to send her sisters to school.* This is a lesson in "Isaan Family Values," pervasive throughout the rural provinces of Northeastern Thailand. Boys always come first. If there is a financial investment involved, as in education or in providing gifts, boys are most often the *only* recipients--as in Banya's bicycle. Girls are frequently denied benefits of any kind. This is a very simple fact of life in Thai society, particularly in the provinces.

Boontah was about eight-years old when she told her mother that she needed new shoes; her only pair was too small, full of holes, and hurt her feet. Her mother's response, *"It's not my problem."* Although her mother found money to buy shoes for her brother, there would be no new shoes for her. *She was much too young to understand that as a daughter, she was of little value to her mother.*

When boys at school mistreated any of the girls, Boontah

would hit them and then run away—as fast as she could. She could always be expected to come to the defense of the underdog. Her "Acting out" didn't earn her any girlfriends, although the girls were always glad that she would attack when they didn't. Her teachers knew that she was "Trouble" and out-of-control. What they didn't understand was that she was a troubled child. They also had no idea how to handle her, nor how to help her.

On one occasion when Boontah's parents left for Bangkok, she was barely 10-years old. She had been a good student, but with her father away, she had to deal with the adults in her family without his protection. Her young life, difficult enough as they were so poor, quickly deteriorated. Her problems in school were clearly a direct result of the pain and anguish she suffered at home.

Boontah's uncle would hit her for the slightest infraction. The adults in her family seemed to take pleasure in abusing her and beatings with a stick occurred often. The more she was punished, the more she acted-out, often stealing and destroying Banya's possessions. She was terribly jealous of her brother. As the only son, he was the first and often the only child to receive any of the normal toys of childhood.

Boontah was born a "Free spirit;" but there was no room for "Free spirits" in Boontah's family. The truth is that there was never any room for young Boontah in her family—even if she had done everything asked of her. It certainly wasn't that she didn't try—at least, initially. Feeling angry and desperate, and not knowing how to deal with her feelings, she lashed out at the easiest target, her teacher's daughter. Boontah stole her books, ruined her drawings, and interfered with her success at every opportunity. She wanted someone, anyone, to feel the pain that she was feeling and to suffer the anguish that she lived with--every waking moment of her life.

9

A Music Teacher

Boontah was only 11-years old when she began listening to Apeechaet, a teacher from school, play the guitar and sing. Each night at 8:00 P.M., while her parents were working in Bangkok, her grandmother was asleep, and her grandfather was talking to the Karen gods, Boontah would sneak out of the house. Apeechaet lived on the bottom floor of the teachers' housing accommodations. The buildings were made of wood with large slats in the middle, so she could speak to him and see him from the outside. He knew better than to open the door for her because he knew that people would talk. She really enjoyed listening to him sing and watching him through the wooden slats. She sneaked away to listen to him for many months—until she could keep her secret no longer.

On one balmy night, Boontah took a friend with her to listen to Apeechaet's sweet melodies. The next day, her friend told everyone. Boontah was very angry; she knew that she would be in trouble, once again. This was to have been their secret and keeping this secret was as important as "Life and death" in her young mind. When their rendezvous came to the attention of the principal, Boontah was expelled from school. Apeechaet was fired or transferred; Boontah never learned which punishment had befallen him, and she never heard him sing again. He was dismissed because some of the villagers claimed that he was sexually-involved with her. There were no questions asked, nor was there a hearing held. He was simply and matter-of-factly dismissed. Ignorance and closed minds symbolize the attitudes of the uneducated of rural Thailand.

Immediately after Apeechaet was terminated from his teaching position, Boontah quietly returned to the ramshackle building that housed his room. She peered through the holes in the slats and saw him playing cards and drinking with other teachers. That would be the last time that she would ever see him.

10

Half of the teachers at Boontah's school thought that she was the problem and the other half thought that Apeechaet was the problem. It didn't occur to anyone that there might not be a problem or that the entire non-encounter was innocent. It wouldn't have occurred to anyone that an artistically-inclined little girl simply wanted to listen to the lovely voice of the music teacher. If by chance that thought had occurred to someone, no one would have risked giving it voice for fear of being ridiculed. Nearly everyone firmly believed that she was a very bad little girl--destined for a life of wickedness. She was the ill-fated one in her community to be ostracized as a witch—a common theme of Thai movies. When Boontah walked to the store, the shopkeeper and others would yell, *"You are only 11-years old and already want a boyfriend for sex. You are just a little prostitute."*

Boontah lost the few acquaintances she had as their parents told them to stay away from her. Village people can be mean, a cruelty stemming from ignorance and superstition. She still hears their hurtful taunts in her nightmares. But, when she closes her eyes and allows her thoughts to drift back to one of the few sweet places of her childhood, she hears Apeechaet's beautiful voice. She remembers watching him sweetly singing soft Thai melodies and gently strumming his guitar while she peered through the splintered slats.

Expelled

After being expelled from school, her grandfather had finally had enough. He wrote to her parents in Bangkok complaining that he was tired of the problems she created. He wanted no further responsibility for her. Her father knew that she was treated badly by everyone in the family. He also knew that he was the only one who could protect her. He arranged to bring her to Bangkok where both he and Bootsah were working. She had only been living with her parents a few months when it appeared that her life might be turning around—that she might be receiving a chance to move in a direction that would give her a real childhood—one that would finally allow her to be a "little girl." Her former principal had approved her readmission to school. She returned to her village and to school where she learned to dance--an omen for her future.

Returning to School

After Boontah returned to Ubon, she began to dance with other girls in musical shows that traveled around the neighboring villages. She earned between Bt 30 and 50 ($1.20-$2.00) for a couple of hours of work each night, two or three nights each week. This was a lot of money for an 11-year old--money she shared with her sisters. For a brief period of time, she was very happy to work and be self-sufficient. She even taught Ying the standard Thai dance, "Luk Tung." Their grandmother didn't approve of Boontah's dancing because she wore a very short skirt and danced on stage—both considered rather provocative in rural Thailand.

Electricity and running water arrived to their village about this time. Her grandfather thought that these amazing conveniences were magic and sent by the spirits. They couldn't believe that something so wonderful could come to their seemingly poor, forsaken village. Although her grandmother was now very fortunate to have these conveniences, she couldn't fully-understand their benefits, nor appreciate their value. As a result, she banned music from the house claiming that it was a waste of electricity. The girls learned to dance in silence. *Today, there is a music video that presents a similar short-story; a girl of 14 dances in local shows and is snubbed by her teacher until her teacher eventually agrees that her dancing and her outfit are socially-acceptable.* Boontah was not so fortunate 14 years ago.

At the age of 10,
Boontah painted the happy home she always wanted.

Boontah eventually made an agreement with her grandmother that if she couldn't earn money by dancing, she could earn money by cleaning in Dae Udom City--very close to her village. Dae Udom was a short 20-minute ride in a rickety old pick-up truck. Her grandmother agreed. Shortly after she began working, she told her grandmother that she also wanted to go to middle-school in Dae Udom City. She no longer needed anyone's help to pay the illegal fees demanded by the public school; she could now pay for them herself. Her grandmother refused, claiming that she didn't have to go to school, nor could she work any longer in Dae Udom.

Boontah was bewildered and angry. She could never understand why her grandmother was hostile to her every request— to anything that would offer her money, education, independence, and most importantly, happiness. Her grandfather had sent her

13

away and her school had expelled her. When she returned to school, her grandmother had not allowed her to dance with other girls in order to earn money. Then after a short stint as a cleaner in a nearby village, her grandmother also forbade her to continue to work or to attend school even though she could pay the school fees herself. Her grandmother refused her anything that would allow her to live the life of a normal happy child. Boontah's life with her grandmother was intolerable; she was a prisoner and her grandmother was the warden. Boontah did what most anyone would do when they have been imprisoned; she ran away.

Running Away

At the age of 11, Boontah ran away for the first time and began a 500-mile journey on-foot to Thailand's capital of Bangkok. On the way, she met a 17-year old girl named Loong who warned her against the dangers of running away and took this small and determined 11-year old home with her. Three days later, when Boontah awakened at Loong's home, she saw Loong's mother speaking to her family. They took Boontah home. As could be expected upon their return, her uncle Sakda hit her again and again. She refused to talk to anyone or to go to school. The only activity this sad and tormented little girl would allow herself was to write letters to her father.

By the time she had agreed to return to school, she had become a relentless troublemaker. She was a seriously-troubled child filled with unbridled rage and unbearable pain over which she had no understanding and no control. At school, no one liked her, not her peers and not her teachers. One day, shortly after she returned to school, her teacher came to her home and told her grandfather that she could no longer attend school; she was difficult and a nuisance. Boontah was expelled once again!

Running Away, A Second Time

Boontah was 11 when she fled to Chiang Mai in Northern Thailand. She had only the money that she had saved from working as a dancer and a cleaner, but it was enough to get away from her family--as far away as possible. When she arrived in Chiang Mai, she saw an advertisement for a job as a waitress. She met the owner of the restaurant who saw that she was very young and had arrived without family. Rather than give her the job, he called a government officer to come and pick her up. The officer arrived with two policemen. They asked her a lot of questions, but she didn't give her real name nor did she tell them the truth about her home. They also tried to find out what she had in her bag, but she resisted. After 20 minutes of questioning, they took her to a psychiatric hospital until she could be sent to Bangkok. At the hospital, she talked to the Social Worker and told her that she would never return home. The Social Worker agreed to help her find a new place to live.

One month had passed and Boontah was still in Chiang Mai; she had not received a new place to stay as promised. She hated being in the hospital; the environment was hostile, patients were fighting, and the food was nearly inedible. In the hospital, she called herself Kumai. When she realized that the Social Worker might not help her after all, she decided to write a letter to the nurse and tell the truth about her name and her family. Upon receiving the letter, the nurse called her father in Bangkok. When he reached the hospital, Boontah hugged him and cried uncontrollably. He said that although he understood, and he knew there were very serious problems at home, he pleaded with her to promise that she would never, ever, run away again. They returned together to the shack their family shared in the village.

15

Immediately upon her arrival, she faced the wrath of her entire family—all of whom yelled at her and accused her of being the source of their problems and an embarrassment to them. Her father realized that she was obviously not safe without him to protect her. In order to spare her any further abuse--he would have to stop working in Bangkok and return to the village at whatever cost. He also couldn't afford to send her to school. He tried to get a job in Ubon at a building site, but it didn't pay enough money for the family to survive. Instead, he borrowed money from his neighbors to start his own business--a push-cart that sold candy, while Boontah's mother sold noodles--carrying food from a harness on her shoulders. They rented a room in Ubon City for Bt 680/month ($27). The entire family, including her grandparents, stayed in this single room, one that lacked running water and electricity. They drew water from the community well, used sunlight by day, and candlelight by night. With this move, the family had taken a giant step backwards; once again, they had returned to a room without the modern conveniences of electricity and water—a situation they blamed on Boontah.

Boontah's mother screamed at her husband and children all of the time. Her father was a soft-spoken man who only wanted peace in his family and to earn enough money to support those he loved. Boontah couldn't stand to see her father treated so hatefully by her mother and her grandmother. It was more pain and pandemonium than any child could be expected to endure. She decided she had to run away once again. She stole Bt 200 from Ying's piggy bank—candy money saved for over a year that her father had given to her. Her two younger sisters had been able to save all of their money because Boontah spent her money on them.

Running Away, Once Again
This time when Boontah ran away, she headed for Bangkok once again. She was 12-years old when she walked to the train

station in Ubon. She always saw her father's face telling her to do the right thing. She hungered for a new life, and she would risk anything to give herself that chance. She had Bt 200, the equivalent of $8. This small amount of money was her only hope. On the bus, she told herself over and over that she had to be strong.

While traveling to Bangkok, she told her story to the man sitting next to her. He said that he knew of a job selling food and goods in a Chinese shop--to which she quickly agreed. Her salary, Bt 1,500/month ($60). She worked from 5:00 A.M. to 7:00 P.M., 14 hours/day, 7 days/week. At the end of her workday, she was not allowed to leave the premises and her Chinese employer never paid her all of her earnings. Once again, she found herself imprisoned. She had become a victim of the unmerciful exploitation of underage and illegal workers that remains common in Thailand, even today. At the tender age of 12, she decided to quit; she had fled one intolerable situation for another.

Boontah had saved about Bt 400 while working at the Chinese shop, but she didn't know where to go or what to do. While wandering around the city, she became tired and hungry. Seeing a noodle-soup stand in the Patawun Police Station near the bus station, she had a bite to eat. Nit, the owner of the noodle shop, noted that she was carrying a plastic bag with what appeared to be all of her worldly possessions. Curious about this little girl, she asked her if she were looking for work and offered her a job selling noodles. Her offer was readily accepted. When Boontah went to Nit's home that evening, Nit's husband, Boontanh, a policeman, refused to allow her to work for them. Instead, he placed her in a holding cell at the police station and called the local social service agency to pick her up.

Boontah was taken to an orphanage where she again faced more fighting. It was no different that being at home with her

17

family, except that the orphanage provided training for making paper flowers, cutting hair, sewing clothes, and other skills that would give the girls a vocation. On one particular day, one of the girls was bullying some of the other girls. Boontah struck her. She had seen so much violence in her young life that she would do whatever she could to stop it. But, she knew of no other way to stop physical violence than with more of the same.

Boontah was questioned following the altercation because she was always accused of starting fights. In turn, she manufactured stories to hide the truth of her involvement. The truth was she couldn't stand to see others fighting, but she was not against starting her own. It was decided that she would be sent to Ban Kunwitiying in Pratumtani City. The purpose of this facility was to care for females of any age who had been diagnosed with psychiatric illness. If no one came to pick them up, they would remain there until they died. Her transfer took place on September 7, 1993; unbeknown to the social workers, that was Boontah's 13th birthday.

At this new facility, Boontah was friendly and cooperated with other patients and the guards. For the first time in her life, many people loved her; she was talkative and made people laugh. One of the guards allowed her to stay in a nice room with her. The room had many amenities that Boontah's dormitory room did not--a mattress, fan, pillow, and sheets. One evening, when the guard fell asleep, Boontah stole the keys and ran away from the hospital. But, when she arrived at the surrounding wall, it was far too high for her to climb. By this time, all of the spotlights shined on her tiny figure and the alarm had sounded. She had been caught; she was not going to gain her freedom that night.

As punishment for trying to escape, Boontah was chained, shackled, and placed in solitary confinement without food. She still bears the scars on her ankles from where the shackles dug into her flesh. After a few days, she was released and the chains were removed; she was warned that if she tried to run away again, she would suffer a more painful punishment.

Boontah finally slept; several hours later when she awakened, she was surprised to find so many people peering into a nearby room. Curious, she also peered in, around, and underneath to see what everyone was looking at. She saw an old lady lying on her bed; she had died the night before. No sooner had Boontah reached the door to the old woman's room, when Pookum, the supervisor, said that she needed four people to carry the body to the vehicle that would take her body away. Many people volunteered to carry the body, including Boontah. After the body had been carried to the vehicle, Boontah prayed that the woman's soul would go to a better place. She hoped that if a ghost could rise from this dead body, it would help her to escape from her own involuntary confinement.

It was only a few days later that she was released from the locked ward and allowed into the normal population of the facility. She participated in all of the group's activities without any further acting-out. One day, when everyone was busy with a meeting, Boontah stole street clothes from the employees. By rolling up the sleeves and the cuffs, she made the clothes look as if they belonged to her. The security guard, without a word or a second-glance, opened the door for her. She casually made her exit and never looked back.

Boontah had remained angry at Boontanh, the policeman who was responsible for sending her to the psychiatric facility. She was a very bold 13-year old and didn't think twice about going to see him at the police station. She wanted to know why he had sent her to the facility. While waiting for him, Kak, another policeman, asked her if she were hungry; she admitted that she was and he took her to his house to eat. Kak was Muslim and had two wives. One of his wives asked who the little girl was. He suggested that she could help sell food. Boontah thought that she had a new home and believed that Kak had come to rescue her. She had worked at his apartment for less than a month when one night while sleeping, he came into her room and tried to rape her. One of his wives heard her screams and stopped him. The two wives immediately agreed to send her away, blaming her for the attempted rape. They gave her Bt 1,000 to survive on the street. Although they didn't want her in their home, they also worried about her. They didn't want anything to happen to her, while they also wanted her to go far away from their house, and more importantly, from their husband.

Boontah had only walked a short distance when Kak arrived on his motorbike. He told her that he loved her very much and that he would find her a place to live. Foolishly, Boontah believed him and hopped onto his motorbike. He took her to a hotel. Young Boontah thought this was to be her new home. As soon as she entered the hotel room, Kak tried to rape her again. She screamed as loud as she could. Fortunately, the receptionist came running in the direction of the screams and Kak ran away.

The receptionist told Boontah that this kind of thing often happened to girls who ran away. Everyone in the hotel advised her to return home; they believed that she must have a loving family who was worried about her. They all contributed money to assist in her return. And, that she did--with great reluctance.

It had been three months since Boontah had last run away. Upon her arrival home, she found herself most unwelcome. This came as no surprise. But, when she learned that her father had died in an automobile accident while searching for her, she was heartbroken, filled with grief, and overwhelmed with guilt. Her

20

pain and anguish only intensified when her family blamed her for his death. She knew in her young heart that it was time to leave again, and returning to Bangkok seemed like her only option. She had always been aware that she was unwanted, but now her family couldn't have made it more clear just how much they hated her. Boontah asked her mother for money. She was given Bt 300 and told never to return; Bootsah never wanted to see her daughter's face again. This was the largest "Gift" Boontah recalls ever receiving from her mother. Her sisters, who had been the only ones to greet her, were also the only ones to say *"Good bye."*

Boontah was now truly an orphan in every sense of the word. Her father had died while looking for the little girl that he loved, and her mother had banished her from their family home— such as it was. She could never return until she had somehow made amends for causing the death of her father. She had to find a way to become a part of her family, once again, no matter how truly despicable a family they were. Thais are not like Americans, nor Europeans, people who are comfortable with being alone and who often welcome solitude. Thais are family-oriented and need to have others around all of the time. To Thais, solitude represents pain and loneliness.

The death of Boontah's childhood occurred when she was banished from her home and blamed for the death of her father. She traveled to Bangkok to seek a better life. She had run away from home on numerous prior occasions to seek a life free of beatings and burdens most certainly undeserved. Now, she also knew that she would have to find a way to earn the love of her mother, regardless of the cost to her own life, in order to ever return home. The sex-tourists havens were awaiting her with open arms. Her life as Lon began. *I was only 13.*

Chapter 2

Bangkok, My New Home

My Arrival

At the age of 13, I had known only housework and farming. I had no idea what I was going to do in Bangkok and I was very, very frightened. I had no idea what lie ahead, but I had already decided that I would not allow it to be further poverty.

Although I was young, I wasn't going to allow my mother's ignorance and prejudice to slow me down. I knew somewhere deep inside that I had potential. I knew that I could have a better life than that offered by remaining in my village of poor peasants. My mother only cared about giving my brother every opportunity, while also demanding that my sister and I remain home, care for the animals, and the little land we had. The heavy work and the physical and emotional abuse were more than enough impetus for me to run away one last time. I was not going to be a deprived and abused little girl in Ubon all of my life. I was not born to be a farmer, nor was I born to be beaten and oppressed. *Most importantly, I was not born to be poor!*

I bought the cheapest ticket available at Bt 95 ($4) on a fan-cooled bus for the 10-hour trip. It would have cost the equivalent of three days work in Bangkok to pay for a seat on the air-conditioned bus. It had been only on a few rare occasions that I had ever felt air-conditioning anyway, when I strolled through a few stores where I couldn't afford to buy anything. I had very little money and I considered each and every baht like gold.

My mother had given me Bt 300 and told me never to return. Everyone blamed me for my father's death. I had no desire to return—at least to the dire circumstances from which I had run

22

away several times before. As far as I was concerned, I deserved the meager money she gave me—and much more. I had begun working before I began attending school. I couldn't remember ever not working. I was also determined that I was not going to live in Ubon the rest of my life. No one had any future to speak of in Ubon. *Most importantly, I had no future in Ubon!*

I arrived in Bangkok in the evening. I had only Bt 205 ($8.00), that was all that separated me from hunger. I couldn't spend my few precious baht on a cheap room. On that first night, I slept at the bus station; I remember feeling that the mosquitoes that buzzed around me were my only friends. I ate discarded food and drank water from bottles left in trashcans. I had nowhere to go and I knew no one. I was very much a little girl lost and alone in the very large, busy, crowded, and cosmopolitan city of Bangkok—a city that I would soon learn was the major sex-capital of the world. Before long, this city would also become my new home.

Until that very moment of my arrival in Bangkok, I had never seen an elevator, nor ridden an escalator. The department stores and office buildings were the tallest I had ever seen. Streets were highly-congested with thousands of cars, pick-up trucks, rickety-red fan buses, and shiny air-conditioned blue ones--all packed bumper-to-bumper and creating bedlam everywhere. Gray and black smoke polluted the air while the deafening noise from thousands of horns shattered my eardrums. Motorcycles by the dozens led the traffic at every intersection, while the multitude of pedestrians bravely put one foot in front of the other and quickly dodged both stopped and moving traffic to make their way across the street. Neither the drivers nor the pedestrians gave much heed to the traffic lights. Thais seemed to move ahead with tunnel vision and with little regard to safety while Farang were more cautious.

I had never seen such huge crowds in one place, nor had I ever seen so many people from so many different countries. There were African women dressed in colorful, floral, ankle-length costumes, each wearing a matching head-dress; East Indian women in their sexy, native, silk saris with pants tapered at the ankle and baring their tan midriffs; Sikh Indian men in their traditional white turbans; Arab men in their crisp, button-down, long white thobes and gutrahs; and American and European tourists in their casual jean shorts and tank-tops. Then there was me, in my provincial shirt and baggy pants, looking as if I had just arrived from the backwoods of Thailand—which of course, I had.

Boontah, Age 13

24

I had also never seen so many people moving so quickly through crowded shopping streets, nor had I ever heard so many languages spoken. There was nothing that a quiet but busy farm life in a remote Thai village did to prepare me for this new life, one filled with so many unknowns. I had seen Bangkok on television while in Ubon and I had seen the outskirts of this city while staying with my parents. But this was not television; this was real life. I was much too young to understand the significance of this moment. I was standing at the threshold of my new life in the middle of the hustle-bustle of this exotic city. At this very moment, my feelings could only be understood by another who was also the product of a small, primitive, and impoverished village in a third-world nation; one who had just entered the center of a modern metropolis for the very first time. *I was anxious, excited, fatigued, and hungry, but most of all, I was scared!*

I had very little money, no friends, no family, and no place to live. In order to survive, I began begging for hand-outs; I was barely 13. I learned that there was a lot more money available from tourists than there was in actually working. While sleeping on the street, I met a woman who found work for me as a nanny for a high-ranking policeman. He also happened to own a bar in Patpong-- Bangkok's largest red-light entertainment district. I began to help out cleaning in the bar when I wasn't working in his home. He insisted that I choose between cleaning at the bar or in being a nanny to his children. I chose to work in the bar as I made more money cleaning and washing floors than I did working as a nanny. I was in Bangkok to make enough money to gain my family's forgiveness for causing my father's death. I was Boontah no longer; I, Lon, had come to be. *I would find a way to redeem Boontah to her family for causing the loss of her father. Only then, could she, and I, return home.*

The Cockatoo Club

I began working as a full-time cleaner at the Cockatoo Club--a GoGo bar and popular hang-out for Farang men. It was also full of girls from Isaan--speaking my dialect. I mopped and cleaned up after sex-tourists. I earned Bt 1,500/month ($60), plus a share of the tips--Bt 1,000 ($40), for my 28 days of work each month. That was far more than I had ever earned in Ubon. I was able to send Bt 1,000 or more to my family each month. This is one of the reasons that I came to Bangkok.

Thais and many other Asians do not think of themselves so much as individuals as they do members of a family. The attachment is part of our "individuality" or lack thereof. We are not just members of our family; we are integral to one another. It is only as a family that we can be individuals. *We are individuals together; it is only as a family that we can survive.*

I was earning a total of Bt 2,500/month ($100) in salary and tips--a good start, but my family was desperately poor. My father had died and I had two younger sisters whom I wanted to support. I wanted them to be able to go to school; I wanted them to have a better life than I did. I had to earn more money.

Age 14

Patpong's "Other" Workers

Bangkok's Patpong, the most popular "Red light district" in the entire world, is difficult to accurately describe to the uninitiated. It is two very long blocks: "Patpong 1" is about 200-meters long; "Patpong 2" is about 100-meters long. Each is bordered on both sides with open-air bars, GoGo strip bars, discos, and sex shows. In these two blocks of "Sex-for-sale," nearly 3,000 young women wait to meet a man for an hour, an evening, or as some of them hope-- forever. *"One girl from Patpong marries a foreigner every week."*[1]

The GoGos and bars vary in size from employing as few as 10 girls to as many as 100. In each GoGo, there are also other workers. This is where I began my new life. We are the cleaners, bartenders, waitresses, and door-girls. *Officially, we haven't yet begun to go with men.* We survive on the Bt 1,500/month ($60) salary plus Bt 1,000 ($40) in tips from the tables. We are not part of the "Asian Economic Miracle." *Unofficially, after the bars close, some girls have unknowingly begun to walk this path to self-destruction, although by no means--all of them.*

For some of us, the day started at around 2:00 P.M. and ended at Midnight. Other girls came in at 7:00 P.M. and worked until 3:00 A.M. We came to work and began cleaning up from the previous night's activities. We would spend an hour or two cleaning the spilled beer remaining from the night before. Then it was time to make the beds in the "Short-time" rooms and clean the bathrooms. After that, it was time to go into the bar and move hundreds of beer bottles, slice pineapples and lemons, wash dishes, and perform every other menial and distasteful job that needed to be done. Customers would get drunk, spill beer, and vomit anywhere. It was my job to clean up after them. I wouldn't have minded cleaning up normal dust and dirt, but this was a disgusting job—one that often made me sick to my stomach. The dancers made a lot of money, sometimes as much as 20 times more than I did, and they didn't have to clean up anything. It didn't take long for me to learn that the "Real" money at the bar was not made in my line of work. I knew that I also wanted to make the kind of money that the dancers made and I was willing to do whatever I had to—to earn it!

I was barely a teenager from a rural and rustic village, and I couldn't believe my eyes. Attractive and sexy girls in bikinis--and out of them, seductively dancing around the stage, and behaving in a way I had never seen before—not even on television. No one in Ubon would ever dress--or undress, like they did. No one in Ubon ever wore bathing suits. Instead, we wore cut-off jeans and T-shirts into the river. No one in Ubon would ever slither up to a pole and slowly caress it to her naked body. I couldn't understand how these girls could take off their clothes in front of all those male customers and dance so provocatively. I was shocked! I couldn't believe that girls from my village, my province, my Isaan "sisters" --could behave in such a forbidden manner. But there they were--hugging their beautiful and tanned bodies around a pole, performing titillating routines, lap dancing, and making a lot of money. GoGo girls worked about seven hours each day and had one day off each week. They danced for 15 to 20 minutes each hour; they spent the rest of the hour talking to customers and trying to persuade them to buy their services for the night. For those who didn't land a client for the evening, after the bar or GoGo closed, they went on to Thermae.

There are roughly 30,000 Thai girls in Bangkok, Pattaya, Phuket, Koh Samui, and Chiang Mai who seek the tourist trade. There are tens of thousands more in the Philippines, Indonesia, and Cambodia; they are the ones who have been "fortunate" enough to see foreign men instead of locals. There are about 400,000 prostitutes in the brothels of Thailand, and millions more in other Southeast Asian countries who see local men for pocket change or simply to pay-off family debt--plus the massive interest charges that accrue. Their parents may have received $20 to $200 in exchange for their daughters working as prostitutes for several months or far longer; sometimes, it is for the total of their short and tragic lives. I was extremely lucky not to have this fate befall me.

Thermae

Thermae looks like a sleazy bar out of an American movie. It is not like the typical bars you see in the U.S. or Europe. It is noticeably different. One of the differences is that the ceiling is extremely low. It is only about eight feet high. At only 4' 7", this was certainly not a problem for me, but the low ceiling kept the smoke lingering lower than at the GoGo club where I worked. Both tourists and Thai bar girls smoke a lot. The smoke is sickening and debilitating. In Ubon, girls didn't smoke, but Isaan girls were smoking here. Thermae was filled with attractive, young, sexy women, mostly from Isaan--women who had come for the sole purpose of meeting male tourists.

Thermae is best described as an "after-hours" bar. The massage parlor upstairs is open from the afternoon until Midnight. When it closes, the bar becomes busy. Later, about 2:00 A.M., as the GoGos close, many of their dancers come to meet a tourist or an ex-pat for the night. This is the camp that my friends fell into. They all worked as dancers at the GoGo club from 7:00 P.M. until 2:00 A.M, and if a tourist didn't pick them up from there, they would go to Thermae to find one.

On my first night there, I watched as my friends would catch a man's eye, give him a shy smile, slowly but deliberately move in his direction, snuggle-up close, cross their slender legs revealing their beautiful thighs, and attempt to entice the potential buyer into taking them home. I had seen girls going through this same seductive routine at the GoGo at which I worked. The difference at Thermae was that I wasn't working—at least as a cleaner. I came to have fun and attract male attention myself, but I wasn't following in the steps of my Isaan sisters. I couldn't wait to finish work each day so that I could go to Thermae. There was certainly no place like this in Ubon.

30

Why would sweet, young girls want to go to a place like Thermae? The reason is simple; they are the result of Asian Poverty–and they are not alone. Their behavior is the direct result of the low value placed on women in Thailand and throughout Southeast Asia. Even now, in this 21st century, *"Six baby girls are abandoned every day in Bangkok."* In my case, my family's poverty, and my need to win back their love were more than enough motivation.

Who would be interested in a 4'8", 75 pound, 14-year old girl?
My First Customer: The Sale of My Virginity

After working as a cleaner in the GoGo for about one month, a man came in looking for a young virgin. *"A Young untouched female"* was his stated objective, and his cash offer was more than I could ever have imagined. I learned that he was not the only man to come to Thailand looking for a child. I learned that it was not uncommon for sex-tourists to ask for someone like me. The *mama-san* asked if I was interested. The sexual encounter would earn me Bt 30,000 ($1,200), more money than I had ever dreamed possible. I didn't think twice about accepting his offer. She arranged for the sale of my virginity. I was barely 14-years old. His name was Hans, and he said he was a 35-year old Swiss national, although in the photo he gave me of himself, he appears to be closer to 50.

About 30 minutes after he negotiated the price with the *mama-san* and received my approval, Hans returned to the GoGo with cash. I spoke almost no English and did not participate in my own sale. My only response was "Kha," or "Yes" in Thai. He paid the *mama-san* the price of my innocence. It was more money than I had ever seen in my entire life, and it was soon going to belong to my family.

My heart raced for joy over the money I was about to receive, and in fear over what I would have to do to earn it. I had never even held a boy's hand; an act frowned upon in Thailand's rural countryside. In fact, a boy and girl were sometimes made to marry if they were caught innocently brushing against one another. Now at 14, I was about to have sex with a Farang whom I had never seen until moments earlier. He was about 6-feet tall--nearly a foot-and-a-half taller than me. I was terrified and *I would do anything for that money.*

We left the GoGo in Patpong and took a taxi to his hotel on Soi 26, Sukhumvit Road. The taxi driver didn't cast a second glance when he picked up an adult Farang who was hand-in-hand with a tiny 14-year old girl--who looked even younger. He knew exactly why we were together--and what we were about to do. Still, we made a very strange pair, this tall, fair-skinned European and a tiny, bronzed-skinned little girl. Hans spoke to me slowly in English; he also used the few Thai words that he knew during the short ride to his hotel. I continued to smile, regardless of the terror I was feeling deep within every cell of my body. He could never have known what was in my heart. Thais are raised to always smile, never show anger, and keep their pain hidden, *"Jai yen"* or *"Keep a cool heart!"* I was exceptionally good at it!

We arrived in front of his hotel; he hurriedly paid the taxi driver and pulled me alongside him. He was in a very big rush. While he went to the front desk and picked up his key, I sat in the lobby. The front desk clerk looked at me, then at him, then at me again and said nothing. A very young girl—really just a child, with a grown man, must not have been too unusual a sight for her to see. I walked beside him to the elevator and went up to his room. This was the first time that I had ever been in a nice hotel.

After a few minutes, we finally reached his room. My heart started to pound. Reality was beginning to take hold. Only then did I truly begin to understand what I had gotten myself into. I wanted so much to turn around and run away, but I wanted the Bt 30,000 even more. We entered his room and walked towards the bed. I sat on the chair furthest from the bed. He motioned for me to take a shower. I didn't respond. He took a shower instead. I sat in the chair contemplating what was about to happen. I hoped that he would stay in the shower forever, but I knew that eventually he would reappear.

I thought about running away. I had enough time to get out and race back to the bar. I wanted the Bt 30,000 so badly, but I didn't think the *mama-san* would give it to me if I returned to the bar too soon. I even considered going back to Ubon a failure--a girl unable to send money to her mother. So many thoughts ran through my mind that I was ready to faint. Hans emerged from the bathroom wearing only his towel. I stopped thinking about how to escape and started worrying instead about what I was going to do. I had to figure out how to deal with the situation instead of escaping from it.

He walked over to me, never knowing how terrified I was, and pointed to the shower. I went into the bathroom and took the longest shower of my life. It was the first hot shower I had ever taken. I was used to scooping tepid water from a barrel with a bowl. I would have liked to enjoy the warm water; but I couldn't; I had other things on my mind.

After about 20 minutes, Hans knocked on the door. I had locked it. I am sure that he said something about my coming out, but I wasn't ready, not yet! In Thai, I told him to wait. Shortly, I left the safety of the locked bathroom door to enter the bedroom. I was once again, fully-clothed.

He then said something about a towel, but I wasn't going to wear one like him. He was speaking English, and he didn't appear to be concerned as to whether or not I could understand him. I just gave him a smile accompanied by a blank stare. Then he motioned to me to remove my clothes.

I was extremely nervous and I was beginning to have trouble breathing. He walked over to me, took my hand, and walked me to the bed. He started to remove my shirt. I felt humiliated sitting beside a Farang without my shirt. In shame, I used my hands to cover myself. He thought this was funny. I couldn't understand why he selected me and paid so much money, when there were many girls, far prettier, more developed, and certainly sexier.

He now motioned to me to remove my pants. I wanted to run out of the room and never see another Farang again. He started to carefully unbutton my pants; I was too frightened to move. I have chosen not to remember anything after that.

After he was done, I went to the bathroom and threw up. We returned to the GoGo and I collected my money. I earned it, all of it! I was now of value to my family. I had made up for my father's death. My mother would be elated upon receiving this money. She could never have imagined that I could earn so much in Bangkok. She would now be able to hold her head high in the village; she would have money to show off to her friends and neighbors. That terrible little girl, the one whom they had taunted with cruel names, was now someone her mother could be proud of. But, that same little girl could never be proud of herself again. While my mother would be able to boast of the possessions that she could now acquire, I would never be the same. The loss of her daughter's honor and dignity would never be her concern. Each and every day following that life-changing event, day-in and day-out, I fought off the sickening feeling that forever clouded my mind, saddened my heart, and stole my spirit. In the beginning, I had no idea that the next seven years would be like this.

In less than an hour, I had earned more than I could have earned in 12 months of mopping floors and cleaning ashtrays, while continuing to live in poverty. Some clients have told me that people in Thailand are poor because they are lazy. At the age when they were playing little league, going to football games, or having wet dreams over their favorite cheerleaders, I was sleeping with GoGo customers to help support my family—for which I paid the ultimate price, the loss of myself.

"Women are pawns in times of need"
                                                        Thai proverb

Thai Women's Obligations

We have served an important function as the chief and often the only income earners for our poor rural families. I served my function earlier and more capably than most. More importantly, we are the individuals responsible for the financial support of our parents when they become old. We must follow strict rules regarding our behavior, as well as assuming most of the family and household responsibilities, while forfeiting our own independence. Rural poverty and limited educational and economic opportunities leave few options, other than the sex industry, for daughters to assume the support of their families. Not only are we obligated to care for our parents, we are obligated to show our gratitude to them. The commercial sex industry, whether undertaken with foreigners or Thais, has become a fact of life for many girls from Isaan.

Upon returning to the GoGo, my co-workers congratulated me and told me that sleeping with tourists was not a "Big deal." There were many 14-year old girls selling their virginity to tourists, and thousands more to locals at a fraction of the cost. Everyone at the bar felt that the money I had earned, just an hour earlier, was worth celebrating. They had been doing it for years, made a nice living, and accumulated savings from the tourists. Working at the GoGos had helped to pay for their families' purchases of new homes in their provinces or to repair their run-down houses. It also bought motorbikes for their brothers, silk custom-made clothes for their parents, and lots of food and drink for parties—which they never attended. It also bought gold and clothes for themselves. There were no other options available to girls like us. My friends said that nothing goes wrong and there wasn't anything to worry about. The opportunity to make so much money, so quickly, was too alluring. *They couldn't refuse, and neither could I!*

I was exceptionally young and very frightened when I started to go with men. My friends whom I considered my Bangkok family were very "helpful." They would interpret and set the price for me to sleep with a man. They even introduced me to some of their steady clients who liked younger girls. They looked after me because I was so young. I also learned that I was far from the first 14-year-old to sell her virginity to a tourist.

At the age of 14, I was very small; I still am. I was too young--*and looked even younger,* to work in the open-air bars and GoGos as a bar girl or dancer. This made it difficult for me to meet potential clients for sex. Instead, I began to go to Thermae Bar as a freelancer to seek out male customers. Sometimes, I just waited at home by the phone for a call from many of the men whom I had already met. For most GoGo dancers, their job is only a pretense to meet men. They earn Bt 3,750/month ($150) just for dancing and a minimum Bt 12,500/month ($500), sometimes much more, for

36

going off with the bar's customers. In order for me to make money in the sex trade, my friends gave my phone number to men who specifically requested very young girls.

During my 14th year, I had grown just enough to get into the discos and meet men on my own. I had become an entrepreneur. *All of the money that I earned belonged to me—to me alone!* At least, I wouldn't lose the cash paid to me--to a middleman. The only person with whom I would have to share my earnings was my mother. She would consume my income to *"Make face"* in our village. In time, I would learn that this was only the beginning.

My Three Years in Bangkok

Humility: State of being Humble

This is how Thai girls are supposed to behave.

- Not proud, haughty, arrogant, or assertive (of one's own dignity)
- Expressing a spirit of deference or submission
- Powerless, dependent, fearful

We are by nature a submissive people, and we never seem to have ideas of our own. We worship rich people and the glamour, power, and limelight that come with their wealth. No suffering is too great if it leads to money and "Makes face" for the family.

Age 14

In America, girls dream about being on stage and having everyone applaud their talent and their beauty. Many of them want to be famous rock singers and celebrated actresses. The closest that Isaan girls ever get to that dream is appearing in a bikini--or out of one, dancing provocatively on stage, waiting for some man to buy us a drink, pay the bar-fine, and take us home for sex. Girls from different countries have different dreams. This was never our dream as children, but it has become our reality. This is about the most we can hope for coming from Isaan.

All of us who work in the GoGos, bars, and discos are sisters, mothers, daughters, and sometimes even wives. My sisters in the province were initially very grateful for every baht that I sent to them so that they could go to school, have good food to eat, and attractive clothes to wear. My brother's only concern for my welfare was that I stay healthy, so that I could continue to send money to my mother from which he would directly benefit. Over time, Sai's concern for me decreased but it was always greater than Ying's.

The girls with whom I worked came from backgrounds similar to mine. They supported their mothers and fathers, sisters and brothers, children, and many other family members. In the provinces, there is no separation between the immediate family and the extended family. The extended family is the immediate family. Everyone even remotely attached to a family of a "Working girl" profits from her efforts—from her sacrifice. The size of the extended family increases when money begins to appear. There is generally someone younger in every family who is appreciative of the efforts made to support the entire family that now includes everyone within "shouting distance." We also support family members often made invalid due to the lack of medicine or vaccines not available in our community or due to vehicular or occupational accidents. All too often, vaccines are *sold* by the regional government's medical administrator, rather than distributed freely to the people in the community.

Dancing at the Discos

I greeted sex-tourists with demur eyes and a slow, sweet smile in one of the major sex capitals of the world--the colorful and cosmopolitan city of Bangkok. My years as a teen were far from the experience of most 14-year old girls who live their lives in a civilized society, a society where poverty is not a way of life. While teen-age girls in America or Europe might be listening and dancing to the rhythm of the latest rock band, going to slumber parties where no one sleeps, everyone devours pizza piled high with pepperoni sausage and mozzarella cheese, and giggles as they reach for the last of the spicy chicken wings, I reached for fat, unshaven, dirty, old men who reeked of sweat, cigarettes, and alcohol--to earn enough to keep my mother in gold and my sisters in school. My mother, realizing how much money I could earn, chose to wear blinders as to its source and her demands for more money became incessant. I learned that it was now my duty, not only to financially compensate for my father's death, but it had also become my responsibility to support my mother, my sisters, and the entire family. While other teen-age girls were viewing a recent Mel Gibson or Julia Roberts' release, swooning over Ben Affleck, eating buttery popcorn, and shopping for the latest fads, I was committing lewd sexual acts only viewed in XXX-rated films. I was only 14-years old; I was alone; and I was desperate.

At an age that is considered one of innocence in the West and certainly in other parts of the world, I was on my own. I was unskilled and uneducated. I knew no other way to earn money except to sell my body. I not only had to care for myself, but I was expected to send money home. I was embarrassed and ashamed; I felt dirty—dirtier than the repulsive men with whom I slept. With every *"Kak"* (customer*)*, I despised myself even more as I inflicted yet one more wound upon my soul. Although I didn't realize it at first, I had begun to hate myself. If I had ever placed any value on myself as a human being, that value was destroyed before I had ever learned that it even existed. Before my self-esteem had the opportunity to take root, to grow, and to flourish, it was buried as feelings of worthlessness in the deepest recesses of my soul. I was a whore! Even though I was barely into my teens, I understood heartache and revulsion; and I was overwhelmed by those feelings. I couldn't bathe away the dirt that I felt filled my every pore.

Posing at Peppermint Disco

Age 15

Chapter 3

Isaan Family Values: A Contradiction in Terms

Family Demands

My life was little different from that of other young girls in the Thai sex-tourism industry. Once we travel to the "Big City" or tourist resorts, our families make never-ending demands for money. My mother drained my bank account daily. Her calls to me were never to ask about my welfare. Instead, they were calls insisting that I send more money. She wanted a new sofa, table, TV, or refrigerator. She gave my brother everything that she could afford-- purchased through my earnings. In Thailand, it isn't uncommon for 14-year old daughters to prostitute themselves so that their brothers can have VCRs and motorbikes. When she gave my brother the VCR that I had bought for her, she expected a replacement. My mother demanded a noodle cart in order to open a "rolling restaurant." After a brief attempt at being an entrepreneur, she decided that it took too much effort. She had no idea what effort was. I sold myself to 10 old men, at $40 each, to buy that noodle cart—with which she so casually dispensed.

My mother threw generous parties for her friends, and for people she didn't even know, with the money I had earned by performing the most degrading and humiliating sexual acts. I gave my mother all of the gold that my clients gave to me; it was expected of a "Good daughter." I would have never considered doing anything less. Giving parties and wearing gold gave my mother *"Face." "Making face"* is not only more highly-valued than a daughter's honor and dignity; it is more highly-valued than her life. We, the less-fortunate women of Thailand, particularly the daughters of Isaan, have been brainwashed by our culture into dishonoring ourselves for the sake of our families. We have never learned the meaning of self-esteem, nor what it means to value

42

ourselves. In this 21st century, our women are still living by the 14th century Thai maxim that states *"Women are buffalos; Men are human."* In other words, our only value is in our labor—we are worthy of nothing more. It would take many more years and many bad relationships for me to fully-comprehend--and more importantly to accept the truth, that my only value to my mother was in the money I sent home.

Isaan "family values" as reflected in the rural provinces are hypocritical. Girls are not valuable enough to educate; yet, we are expected to become the primary income earners responsible for the basic needs and welfare of our families. If we earn good money, regardless of the method, we have overridden the stigma of its source which in my case was child prostitution. Unfortunately, this remains the case for millions of young women throughout Southeast Asia. Although our earnings can offset our humiliation--for the time being, our emotional suffering will eventually cause us to physically and psychologically disintegrate. Our minds fragment while our bodies deteriorate. We develop serious health problems at a young age because of the unhealthy lifestyle to which we have subjected ourselves. I have never met one woman who has fully-recovered from her past as a participant in the "Sex-for-sale" trade.

According to the Theravada Buddhism, the religion of Thailand, boys can earn merit simply by living in a temple for three months and becoming monks. This is their only family obligation. On the other hand, a daughter earns recognition by taking care of her parents. This is not a recipe for a happy family, nor as Thailand has proven--a prosperous one. Isaan families do not look after their women, but men are welcome to live off of women's earnings without disgrace. If she earns enough money, in other words, helps her family to earn a lot of *"Face,"* she can be reborn as a man in the next life.

43

"I hope not only to be reborn as a man,
but a Western man at that!"

~~~~~~~~~~~~~~~~~~~~~~~~~~~~~~~~~~~~~

Men are Gold; Women are Cloth
"Men look like gold;
When gold drops in mud, we can clean it.
Women look like white clothes;
When they drop in mud,
We can never clean them to be white again."
Khmer Proverb

From the time Isaan daughters are very young, they are told the following story. *"A family owed money to a dirty and repulsive beggar. In lieu of repaying the debt, the parents sent their daughter to live with the beggar and share his bed until the debt was paid."* The "moral" of this story: A dutiful daughter must do anything for her parents.

After hearing this story, young daughters are often, and knowingly, sent to slave in factories and brothels throughout the country; or to Bangkok, Pattaya, Chiang Mai, Phuket, or Koh Samui to join in the sex-tourism trade. The daughters of Isaan have a responsibility to the family that sons never have. Sons frequently lie around the house with their parents; they drink and are unproductive. They live off the proceeds of their sister's prostitution. This behavior is not only tolerable, but also acceptable throughout the poorer regions of Thailand--although never openly discussed.

When I return to my village and live in a home that reflects that large sums of money have been forthcoming, no one ever asks how my family got so much money; my unspoken "employment" is

44

not an issue. In essence, I have bought *"Face."* If on the other hand, I were not to have sent very much money home, I would be a whore! It is not what I am, nor what I do, but how much MONEY I bring home that determines my status. *Money buys everything in Thailand, even the "love" of one's family.*

Some Thai girls, after saving enough money from working with tourists, return to their villages and marry. Unfortunately, after the marriage which the groom often sees as an opportunity to access large sums of money, divorce soon follows after he has availed himself of her savings. He may even suggest that his wife return to the bars to work again. On the other hand, after working the sex-tourist areas, many girls may never see Thai men again; they have learned to look at men as a source of funds rather than a consumer of them.

Thailand is not the same from North to South, nor from East to West. The entire Northeast (Isaan) region produces roughly 80% of the girls working in the sex-tourist industry. The majority have only four years of primary education while only 25% reached the 7th grade. Some have no formal education. In the local flesh-trade, statistics reflect that 40% of the girls enter voluntarily while the remaining 60% are forced, coerced, or tricked into it. [1]

There are some girls working at the bars and dance clubs who have come from Bangkok, Central, Northern, or Southern Thailand; but by and large, the language of the bars is Isaan, spoken by girls from the Northeast. Even some of the girls who do not speak the Isaan dialect as their first language, learn some of it in order to understand what is being said by all of the other girls.

I always told my clients that my mother didn't know how I earned so much money. They looked at me in amusement. I reminded them that Thailand is the "Land of Make Believe." My clients asked, *"How does a young girl, one not much older than a child with little education, go to Bangkok and start sending home Bt 30,000/month ($1,250)? Your mother must know! It is your culture that denies the truth!"* They said that my Isaan society was *"Culturally disabled."* They were right. Isaan is a culturally-disabled society where *"Making face"* is more valuable than one's daughters, and it is that society, my society, which led to the development of my views then and to my betrayal of those views seven years later.

My clients told me that my mother was just a vampire sucking out my life so she could throw parties and *"Make face"* with her friends. They said that American mothers would starve before they ate food bought from their daughters prostituting themselves. I told them, *"I have only one Mother and I love her."* It is simply an issue of *"Face."* My mother could not show her knowledge of my source of income; I could not, nor can I yet, acknowledge my disdain for her value of *"Face"* and consumer goods which far surpasses the value she places on me. Yet, I love my mother and I always will. *I must as I am a daughter of Isaan.*

Upholding the facade that no one in the village is aware of their young daughter's activities in Bangkok and Pattaya, in order to send a lot of money home, is an accepted behavior. It is a reflection of the value of women in Thai society--and especially those women of Isaan. Isaan culture is an exercise in *misogyny--"the hatred of women."* It begins at their birth and lives with them throughout their lifetime.

Thailand is a perfect example of a society that cannot develop when only half of its population is valued. The lower the value of women in a society, the more impoverished is that society. Afghanistan is an even better example where women are held at a lower value than in any other country in the world. It is also one of the poorest countries in the world. The status of women, the development of a society, and its "Standard-of-living," progress hand-in-hand. When women are valued, they are free to share in and contribute to the development of their society.

The people of Thailand, Southeast Asia, and numerous other cultures lead lives that are about *"Making face."* It determines how we behave, what we hope to achieve, and how we perceive and respond to reality. We invest in *"Face"* rather than in a better "Standard-of-living," the value of people, or a more developed society. The many children of Southeast Asia--often four to seven to a family, send money home to support their parents. Japanese men used to tell my friend Nan, *"In Japan, money flows from parent to child,"* (although the issue of *"Face"* is still vital in Japan). In Thailand, it flows in the opposite direction." The U.S. and Europe are no different than Japan in this respect. This is one of the many reasons that the West and Japan are wealthy, while Thailand--especially Isaan, is poor.

In the underdeveloped world, children become self-sufficient at about the age of 12. For obvious reasons, their earning capacity registers at the lowest rung of the wage ladder. Children in the U.S. and Europe might not become independent until they are 18, 22, or older. But, their level of self-sufficiency is very high. I became self-sufficient at the age of 13 when I arrived in Bangkok. I was a sex-tourist's fantasy and every Isaan mother's dream--a daughter who could supply lots of money to help her mother *"Make face"* in the village.

Becoming a freelancer in Bangkok was never my plan as a child. There are tens of thousands of girls like me in my country and millions more who are far less fortunate in surrounding countries—all born into abject poverty. We know of no other way to earn a living that would lift us from the bleak, hopeless, and

47

humiliating life that lies ahead. *The humiliation our families suffer from poverty is far worse than the humiliation that we must endure from selling our bodies.* The socio-economic system of Isaan provides no other way to earn *"Face."* Without the opportunity for an education, we view this unfortunate choice as our only way out and far better than living our lives forever in despair.

Chapter 4

Village Life

***Understanding Thailand is not an easy task for an outsider.
In the following chapters,
I will begin to expose the hypocrisy of my country
by sharing intimate details
deliberately hidden from foreign eyes.***

To Work -- or Not to Work

Poor villagers from the province work hard when there is work to be found, if they are not fortunate enough to have a daughter working in the flesh-trade. This statement best describes my father—an extremely hardworking and dedicated family man. They may also choose not to work even if it is available. This statement describes my grandfather. Often, there is at least one female in every family who knows intuitively from an early age that she is the chosen one. She is responsible for raising her family's life from hopeless poverty while the rest of the family lives from her earnings. I have deliberately chosen the pronoun *"She"* not only because I was that *"Chosen one"* in my family, but to anyone slightly-versed in Isaan culture, it is traditionally the oldest daughter who bears that responsibility. She attempts to rescue her family from itself. In truth, in most cases, she has done no more than provided for their basic survival while young men are freed from any burden of supporting their family. This reality can and does continue throughout the life of most rural Thais.

In the province, a husband is often seen dashing off on his old motorbike for a spin around the marketplace, or the village proper, while his long-suffering wife literally "minds the store," as well as her children; her feelings of helplessness and despair clearly reflected in her sunken face. Men of all ages are often seen watching television and toddlers, in that order, while their wives and young daughters hawk merchandise or sell noodles. My father was the rare exception.

Living is cheap in the countryside. Ten baht (25¢) will purchase an hour at the Internet/Computer Game Shop—an activity in which only very few teenagers can afford to participate; for Bt 20 (50¢), one can purchase a delicious adult-size meal including soup, or 20-bite-size Thai desserts—enough to serve 10. For Bt 30 (75¢), a man can see his favorite barber, or for Bt 100 ($2.50), he can visit a local brothel to meet girls from other regions of the country. For Bt 40 ($1.00), a woman can avail herself of a combined manicure/pedicure. A lady's haircut or an hour-long healing Thai massage will cost Bt 50 ($1.25), and one can seek out a true natural-healer at Bt 100 ($2.50) whose massage will leave the fortunate client feeling as if s/he has found Nirvana. As poor as these peasants are, women frequently manage to scavenge the funds necessary to visit their favorite beauty shop on a regular basis; others do so only on special occasions. *Poverty will never diminish a woman's desire to be beautiful.*

Gambling

Villagers, as a society, also play hard—spending their last baht on the lottery or on whisky, often purchased for as little as Bt 60 ($1.50/liter). They love to drink, and they do, as frequently as possible. As for gambling, it is "Very big business" throughout Thailand although illegal--with the exception of the state lottery. Even so, underground lotteries and casinos proliferate in the cities as well as the countryside. Police are paid bribes to keep these operations running if they do not already have a percentage of the business to start with. In the provinces, it is a way of life. The *"Underground lottery"* is the most popular form of gambling. It offers a "glimmer of hope" to the poor and is affordable at as little as one or two baht (2.5 to 5¢) per bet—bets this small are not possible in the state sponsored lotto where the lowest bet taken is Bt 45 ($1.10). There is little to lose and much to gain if one wins. Only the underground Stock Exchange Lottery can render the winner 83-to-1 odds. For example, if one bets Bt 6 and wins, the payoff is Bt 500; if one wagers Bt 1,000, the payoff is Bt 83,000.

"Funeral gambling" is also a popular pastime as players travel nightly from one funeral to another. They rarely know the deceased when they enter the house where the monks have just prayed over the body. Ten percent of those participating are professional gamblers and this is their only means of earning a living. In this way, they are no different than those of us who trade our bodies. We are all uneducated and unskilled. Although our wagers differ, our stakes are high. Professional gamblers lay down their bets; we lay down our bodies. While gambling is viewed as no more than an exciting diversion to most of the world; it is the only livelihood available to many illiterate and impoverished villagers. Trading sexual favors for hard cash, an illegal and immoral activity in much of the world, is also the only livelihood available to young females born into rural poverty in Thailand--a livelihood that can lead to an appearance of financial security.

Cockfighting is another game in which the poor of the countryside take their chances. Gambling has always been the most popular form of recreation in the provinces; it alleviates boredom and unhappiness. *"Are you happy?"* is a question one often hears throughout the day.

Every religious celebration, wedding, funeral, or baby's first birthday is an open invitation to everyone to gather, drink, and dance until they can no longer stand. Villagers never miss an opportunity to dance, and men are as graceful as the women are enchanting. They also take every opportunity to participate in festive parades where pick-up trucks serve as chariots and the

51

young and beautiful, decked out in humble versions of classical Thai costumes, ride paper-mache horses mounted on tractor-trailers.

Isaan Parade

Province parades it's prettiest

Character

People of the province are as rough on the outside as they are tough and resilient on the inside. Men use outdoor urinals located at the rear of petrol stations and women can be seen using their teeth to pull the tabs off of beer cans. Nearly everyone, male or female, spits whenever and wherever they choose including from second-floor windows or on the ground while dining in an open-air restaurant. In the provinces, it is difficult to find an indoor restaurant except in a large city.

An example of resilience can be seen in the story of a 32-year old woman who was recently hospitalized and lay in a coma for two days—the result of taking the latest diet drug—her future unknown. On the third day of her illness, she awakened from her coma and returned to work as a beautician. While she lay ill, her husband, not knowing whether or not she would live or die, enjoyed a Songkhran party *(Thai New Year's celebration)* and the biggest festivity of the year. All of this is quite typical behavior for those who are born into and remain in the provinces, in the knowledge that this futile life is all they will ever know. A fact that remains unchanged throughout all of the impoverished villages of the Northeast is the feeling of hopelessness, a feeling no different now than it was more than 20 years ago--when Boontah was born.

Liquor is consumed as frequently as water and is a way of life for nearly all villagers; it dulls their pain and helps them forget the hopelessness of their condition—one into which they were born and one in which they had no part in creating. Wild celebrations filled with bizarre, often sexually-explicit costumes worn only by males, ironically combined with a belief in Buddhist concepts, make their lives bearable. It is through drinking, gambling, celebrating, and praying to Buddha that the suffering people of the Isaan region continue to perpetuate a face of optimism in spite of great poverty and injustice.

The mindset of the villagers could only be called "Backwoods." It is not uncommon for women over 40, an age considered old in the village, to walk down the street and fan or wipe their faces with their shirts by lifting them over their bras. They often can be seen in their homes wearing only a bra with a pair of slacks or a sarong while many generations of males are present. This is also common attire while gossiping with neighbors in their front yards. On an extremely hot day, older women can be seen sans their shirts while hawking their wares in the marketplace.

Yet, these same women would never consider revealing cleavage or any part of their leg above their ankle or mid-calf. The contrasts between what is acceptable and what is not may appear contradictory to the outsider, but to the people of Isaan, their beliefs are simple. To appear in the marketplace in a bra and sarong is simply a matter of practicality. It is too hot for a buxomly-elder woman to wear a shirt; since she is not seen as a sexual being, her lack of a shirt is acceptable. Their beliefs support their survival. Any situation that disturbs their fragile existence or their ability to continue--is perceived as a threat and is eliminated.

Crime, Greed, and Superstition

The bizarre and very real tales of one remote village can be lifted from one and dropped into another with amazing ease. In the spring of 2003, a married policeman brutally murdered his very wealthy lover of 18 years shortly after he terminated their relationship. She didn't want their arrangement to end. His wife, on the other hand, had given him a new automobile to end the affair, although she and her children had profited substantially throughout the nearly two-decade love affair. He thought he had made the murder appear to look like that of a robber who had entered the home through a hole in the roof. All gold, jewelry, and money were taken. There was nothing of value left for the casual looter.

When the crime was investigated, the police innocently learned from his young daughter that he had not been at home during the time of the murder. He left his home shortly before the murder was committed and didn't return for several hours. Along with many other items of evidence, his fellow officers knew that he had committed this horrific crime as did everyone who knew them. *There are no secrets in a village.* The police chose not to pursue the case—not an unexpected decision when crimes have been committed by a policeman, friend, relative, business associate, politician, or the wealthy. It makes no difference whether or not a crime occurs in a tiny village or in the mighty metropolis of Bangkok--the rich, the powerful, and the well-connected go free.

Weeks earlier, in this very same village, another policeman murdered his wife when she taunted him with talk of former lovers. The *only* crime of which he was found guilty—"jealous rage." The murder was called an *accidental* "Crime of passion." He returned to work in a matter of days after her body was dug up from under their house where he had buried it. The dead woman's aunt pleaded that he be allowed to continue to work as there would be no one to pay support to her to care for the couple's three children. His *only* punishment: he believes the spirit of his dead wife haunts the house in which she was murdered and he refuses to return. *We Thais are exceedingly superstitious.*

The verdicts handed down in each of the above cases
are only two of a myriad of cases
that accurately reflect the low value of women in my country.
Women are murdered and their killers go free!

Suicide and Superstition

During this same spring, a farmer (the father of three small boys) worked his land with the help of the few even poorer peasants he could afford to employ. He lost his land following the suicide of a 25-year old alcoholic farmhand. His body was found by a young couple seeking privacy for their amorous affections. He had hung himself from the rafters of the small grass-covered hut provided for farm workers. This farmer lived in the province where the fees for education were less expensive in order to educate his two school-age boys. His wife worked in Bangkok and cared for their two-year old toddler. No sooner had the tragic death of this young farmhand reached the ears of the farm workers than they fled the land. This poor farmer, who was now even poorer, watched as his farm was swallowed up by the voracious jungle that surrounded it. No one would come near his land—another example of how superstition can perpetuate the already downward cycle of the impoverished. These few examples represent to the rest of the world that we are even more backward than the term "Third-world" would suggest.

Police and Extortion

Every community has a few wealthy residents who have generally made their money illegally—by taking graft from others who are also operating illegally or by stealing from the poor. *In a village, the rare exception is rarer yet.* Police manage to create a second income by simple asking for it. Each and every day, bribes enter their discreetly closed fists of which they retain only a small amount. Most of the money is passed on to their superiors who give the younger officers a quota that they must meet by the end of every day. Generally, the Police Chief in each village lives far better than one who earns an equivalent salary and is not connected to the police department. The Police Chief most always resides in one of the nicest homes in the community and drives an expensive automobile. Of this, there is no secret.

On the provincial highways, a highway patrolman will randomly pull cars to the side of the road, tell the driver that he was speeding 50-to-100 meters back (there is no radar here), and will place his closed fist inside the window of the car. The unfortunate driver has two options: the first and by far the easiest is to pay the officer a bribe--generally Bt 100. The second is to surrender one's driver's license, go directly to the courthouse, pay Bt 400, and return to the accusing officer for one's license. One can lose hours from his day, a full day from his work, or much longer in completing the latter process. Most choose to tuck Bt 100 into the greedy fist resting inside the car window. The driver also risks incurring the anger of the arresting officer by refusing to tuck baht into his hungry hand. Although this junior officer is doing only what he has been ordered to do, and he has a quota he must meet, this is also the very reason he joined the police force. It is the perfect opportunity to increase his salary five-fold every month. This scenario is replicated thousands of times every day throughout Thailand--from its pastoral provinces, to its bawdy beaches, to bustling Bangkok.

"Catch the Rats"

By and large, the villages of Northeastern Thailand are filled with poor, often "Landless," people who eke out a living anyway they can, depending on the growing season. In Isaan, from November to February, the laborers toil very hard in the fields harvesting rice. Those who own land hire sharecroppers to do this backbreaking chore. The yield is split 50/50. The landless use their share to feed their family and to sell at the marketplace in order to purchase the basic necessities of life.

Rice-harvesting season is also the same time of year for catching rats because they are busy eating and getting fat on our new rice crop. In order to feed meat to their children, the rural poor forage gardens and forests for rats and snakes; they also fish for food. They collect all the rats that they can find. Rats normally weigh between 10 and 18 ounces. Rat meat is especially good during this time of the year. If enough rats are found, they can be sold during a walk through the village by hollering, *"Ow noo baugh?"* "Do you want rats?" This is similar to hearing the chime of the ice cream truck in the West. One can choose not to sell their extra rats. Instead, we score points by giving them to friends and neighbors.

Rats are skinned and barbequed with their tails to a golden yellow. As Isaan people can generally only afford the purchase of meat once a week, rats are a tasty substitute. On a lucky day, if you find an underground nest of pink baby rats, hairless with eyes unopened, they are put onto a skewer and grilled. Cambodia,

Vietnam, and Laos also serve rats from the rice paddies; these rats are distinct from street rats which feed on garbage. Rat is lean and tastes like pork. Recent outbreaks of a deadly "Bird flu" in Thailand, Vietnam, and China that killed 31 chicken handlers have made many Asian cooks reluctant to touch raw poultry, further increasing the popularity of rat dishes across the region--at least for the time being.

In the Northeast, grilled insects, water bugs, crickets, grasshoppers, and locust that taste like bits of charcoaled hamburger are also popular and inexpensive forms of meat. These tasty morsels are easily available in kiosks in the large shopping malls as well as in mobile carts found along the streets all over Thailand. We also eat frogs and lizards (tuk-gah) that taste like squid; these are very inexpensive to buy or free if found in the rice paddies and gardens. My family didn't eat dogs or cats, but some families do. When a buffalo was killed, the meat was dried in the sun because there was no electricity for refrigeration.

"Yum, Yum"…"Sap elee der"

Mouth-watering morsels, Isaan style snacks

In June and July, the first two months of our rainy season, frogs are out in force. Their mating call *"Ope, ope, ope"* is music to our ears. In three weeks, we will be able to scoop up thousands of tadpoles in an afternoon; gut them, add salt, chilies, and basil, place 200 to 300 in a banana leaf, fold it over, and roast over hot coals. Tadpoles are easy to find and easy to catch. In June, July, and August; fish mate and baby fish spawn. This is also the season when mushrooms grow. In March and April, when it is dry, fish are easy to catch because there is so little water; they must congregate in small ponds.

Income and Its Disposal Thereof

The average wage in a village is Bt 83 ($2.08) per day, (9 to 12+ hours daily/7 days a week), or Bt 2,500 ($62.50) per month, laboring under a scathing sun. Maids, and others less fortunate, earn even less: Bt 50 ($1.25) per day, (8 to 12 hours daily/7 days per week), or Bt 1,500 ($37.50) per month. *(This is the very reason that young male or female students will accompany a teacher, Thai or Farang, for a sexual encounter. The teacher may pay the student the equivalent of half the monthly salary of the student's parents–a salary earned through backbreaking labor).* A shopkeeper often doesn't earn much more than Bt 4,000 to 8,000 ($100 to $200) every month. A young, highly-talented, and computer-skilled high school teacher capable of teaching music, art, photography, and aerobics, earns Bt 6,000 ($150) monthly while a career teacher with 20 years experience can earn up to Bt 20,000 ($500) a month.

Those very few who have achieved some level of wealth may order custom-made clothing from a village tailor--a two-piece suit that would cost a poor farmer, tuk-tuk driver, a wood gatherer, or gardener—as much as s/he would earn in three or four months of very hard labor. This grand display of wealth will be deposited into a washing machine and will never again see the wrinkle-free steam or sharply-pressed crease of an iron. Although the affluent may purchase expensive goods, they have no knowledge of their care, nor are they interested in their preservation. The sole intention of their purchase is to *"Make face."*

Chapter 5

Education: Boys Only, Girls Need Not Apply

I was born female into this village of primarily poor, uneducated, Thai hillbilly folk. As with most poor girls, I was not allowed to attend school after the age of 12--or 6th grade. There was only enough money available for my brother's education. "Education for boys only" has been the general policy in Thailand since the beginning of our civilization. This chauvinistic policy places girls at the immediate disadvantage of finding "meaningful" employment. It also increases the likelihood of girls seeking a way out of their desperate poverty by turning to prostitution. The decision I made many years ago is made every day, of every week, by thousands of girls—mostly from third-world countries— particularly those countries of Southeast Asia.

In the city, the inequality in educational opportunities results in illiteracy rates of 17% for girls and 6% for boys. In the provinces, there has always been a shortage of government schools and teachers; Buddhist monks have attempted to compensate for this shortage by providing a system of education--for boys only. Girls are barred from religious schools, often the only type of education for the impoverished. As a result, the illiteracy rate for females is even higher. Young girls, like me, often leave home unskilled and uneducated, with no provision for earning a living, except one--our young and supple bodies. Our short-lived innocence is for sale to the nearest bidder.

The national dropout rate in 2003 for students between the 6th and 12th grades was 52%. In the provinces, it was over 80%. Students went to work or sat at home because their parents couldn't afford the tuition and fees for uniforms, shoes, teacher subsidies, and transportation. Boys worked in the fields and sweatshops.

Girls worked in the fields harvesting rice, Thai potatoes, and sugar cane, or took the buffalos to graze.

Another option for young girls might also be going to Bangkok to work with an older sister who is caring for children and working as a maid. They may also labor in *illegal* sweatshops. Until recently, government-regulated factories could not hire employees without a government I.D. card--obtained when a youngster reached the age of 15. But many companies did hire, in order to pay far below market wages. The legal-age of factory employment has since been raised to 18. Although this law appears to have been intended as protection for the young and uneducated, the consequences of not being *legally* allowed to work until the age of 18 severely limits a young girl's opportunities--to those options that remain mostly illicit. *The business establishment wins because deprived young people accept illegal and horrible working conditions in order to have a job, any job.*

There are paths other than those cited above. One common avenue leads to the brothel where young women generally sell themselves to locals. Another leads to Bangkok, Pattaya, Phuket, Koh Samui, and similar destinations--to meet and sleep with sex-tourists. This was the path I took—unwittingly, when I was *only 13.*

At this point in the life of a young girl, barely into her teens, it is not uncommon for her to begin to wear lipstick and go to an outdoor movie with her girlfriends. When the traveling movie truck comes to the village, it announces its arrival over a loudspeaker. Movies are shown in a football field; a giant piece of fabric is used in lieu of a movie screen and young people bring their own pillow usually made of straw. If a girl has been fortunate enough to remain in school beyond the 6th grade, it may be at this point that she will drop out. It is often here where young girls and boys meet one another and quite often marry because the girl has become pregnant. These village young people, some not yet teens, are very naïve and have no knowledge of contraception. If she has been fortunate enough not to become pregnant, but the couple has been seen sneaking around, whether or not they have become sexually-active, the girls' parents will generally demand a Brideprice of Bt 20,000 to 30,000. If the boy wants to continue to see the girl, he must comply. Marriage may or may not follow. The girl may begin bearing children in her early teens.

While I was in elementary school, state-subsidized schools were supposed to be free until the sixth grade, they were not. Ten years later, they are still not. "Under the table money," "Tea money," donations, or parent association memberships are still often mandatory for parents in order to secure places for their children in public schools.[1] Other imaginative ways that the government schools have of extorting money from parents for their children's education are fees for hiring teachers; the cost of cards to use the school's canteen facilities (not for the food itself); electricity charges (to cover the use of air-conditioners); cleaning and grounds-maintenance charges; an application fee to study computing, and an occasional gift to the teacher that ensures that the student passes regardless of their grades; this list is far from complete.[2]

In the city, some schools charge Bt 4,000 ($100) annually plus additional surcharges—all of which amount to more than a month's wages for most poor Thais.[3] Following the sixth grade, these *illegal* fees increase so dramatically that education becomes prohibitive to millions of families—particularly in the provinces. In the state-run schools that do not make *illegal* financial demands upon the parents, the mandatory cost of uniforms, notebooks, books, and pencils still make educating one's children frequently an impossible task for the country's poor. Without these essentials, children cannot attend class. *I was one of the 80% denied an education because I was poor.*

City supports pawnshop as parents spend on new school term

Photo courtesy of PattayaMail

Thai mother borrows money from a pawn shop to pay for her child's education.

In May of 2004, it was found that "... more than half of all parents of school-age children in Greater Bangkok (were) struggling to find the money to cover the costs of the upcoming school year..." They were borrowing from unlicensed money lenders at interest rates as high as 20% per month.[4] This dilemma can best be exemplified by Orn-uma, a parent who had the courage to take her story to the newspaper. She was forced to buy her 12-year old daughter a place in a provincial government school at Bt 30,000 ($750). She used up her savings and borrowed the remainder. The principal refused to accept less and he refused to give this unfortunate mother a receipt. *Our 1997 Constitution guarantees 12 years of free education but this law has yet to be enforced.*

The prejudice against educating the less-fortunate has been long-standing. That prejudice is legitimized by governmental enforcement of often impossible requirements that intentionally keep ethnic minorities and other poor children from reaping the benefits of an education. Hmong (hill tribe) children are only allowed to attend one school; as a result, that school is extremely overcrowded. Parents of these children must be issued household registration permitting them to leave restricted areas. Even if a minority child is academically successful and speaks fluent Thai, without legal citizenship, s/he is forbidden an education certificate and is not allowed to pursue higher education. If a certificate is the goal, the student must begin again in non-formal education in order to get a Prathom 6 high school certificate. Without proper papers, one has no future. *In Thailand, if one is poor, s/he also has no Human Rights.*[5]

A course in Human Rights was scheduled to be included in the curriculum (from kindergarten through college) beginning in the fall of 2003. The contradiction between Human Rights and the lack thereof, presently existing in my country, will surely present a dilemma for instructors, many of whom feel that their students no longer respect them since their right "to cane" in the classroom has been abolished.[6]

Until recently, haircuts have also been a mandatory cost of educating one's children with "Chin length bobs" for girls and "Bowl cuts" for boys. This was a national law until May of 2003; it was also a cost that most parents considered a hardship and few could manage. One teacher demanded that his boy students seek Bt 40 monthly haircuts at a hair salon he owned.[7] Clippers and scissors have also been tools of punishment. A teacher has always had the right to make the arbitrary decision that a student's hair was longer than allowed. A piece of hair randomly cut from a child's head that forced him/her to seek a haircut has been common practice throughout the history of Thailand's "modern educational system." Humiliation and a *"Loss of face"* were the result of the teacher's cruel hand. There is a great deal of room for Human Rights instruction in our educational system beginning with many of our teachers.

It is a sad and undeniable fact of life that "Denying education to the poor keeps a stable of easily exploitable, uneducated workers for the rich--assembling their electronics, sewing their clothes, and picking their fruit." As many as 200,000 children in Thailand are presently denied an education because they are not citizens[8] even though they may be of Thai heritage. Their papers have been arbitrarily rejected or lost. Without the possibility of an education, poor Thai children are destined to a life of poverty. I was destined to such a life as was my mother and nearly everyone else in my village—forever. *I refused to fulfill the hopeless fate into which I was born.*

My Sisters' Education

My sisters, as most young Thai children, wanted to go to school. I knew that I would find a way to see that they would. Finishing 9th grade is a mark of achievement in Thailand. If one finishes 9th grade, one can get a decent job in a 7-11 convenience store or in a lower-level hotel earning $100-$120/month with one day off each week. This is much better than working on a construction site or in a sweat shop that pays much less, is dangerous, and only provides two days off per month. If a child has received an education through the 9th grade, s/he will also have learned to read and write a little English, although most likely unable to speak.

I have to admit that my interest in meeting sex-tourists and ex-pats – my clients, was not for the sole and altruistic purpose of my sister's education; there was far more. Having money in Thailand is like having a famous son or daughter; a trophy wife; a luxury car; or in the case of a child--having the most high-tech scooter or newest computer game. In Thailand "One is how much money s/he has and nothing more!" This is true unless you're a monk, and it is not unusual for a monk to siphon small sums or large ones from their congregations. In 2003, a well-known monk from the south of Thailand was murdered. Upon investigation of his death, it was discovered that he had deposited Bt 119,000,000 ($2,975,000) in 11 bank accounts under several names, owned property, and a fleet of luxury cars.[9]

Thai Values Suffocate Education

"Thai Values" lead Thai people into the same "Follow the herd" mentality that both our grandparents and their grandparents lived. It is one of the many reasons we haven't financially or socially progressed. Our values are the consequence of Confucian teachings that emphasize authority and deference to it: "Stay in your place." The men who run Asia perpetuate the Confucian philosophy that keeps the wealthy in power while keeping the rest of us poor and powerless.

The belief in an attitude of deference originates in one's culture, not in one's genes. In Thailand and throughout Southeast Asia, we, as a people, continue to bow down to established social, political, and economic traditions; deference to authority is taught in our schools and demanded by our Prime Minister, Thaksin Shinawatra, even to the point of ordering foreigners to say nothing negative about the Thai government and suing members of the media who do, thereby providing evidence to the statement of his critics that "...he seeks to crush all those who would oppose him." Our deference has helped to create and keep the masses in a state of poverty.

I have met many Asian people who look no different than I do, but act just like any other Farang. These people have grown up in the U.S. and Europe. From an Asian small-village point of view --all Asian-looking people should act Asian; and all Farang should believe, think, and act like Farang. My travels have taught me that this is not true. People who possess Asian genes can behave as Farang do, but generally it is only those Asians who have had the opportunity to be raised in the West. On the other hand, Farang can act as if they were Asian, viewing women with as little disregard as do Thai men--with no concern or respect for the woman as an individual. This is particularly true of Farang male sex-tourists.

Ruling Class

The Ruling Class has been called a "Culture of power." Power has been placed in the hands of elected Ministers of Parliament (MP's) and Senators who are the "Powers that be." It is members of this body who decide what is best for them personally. These decisions are then followed with directives that state what is best for Thai society whether or not the public agrees. The government and its officials ignore the common people and use power and martial law to silence any who disagree with them. The wealthy and powerful are immune from prosecution. The rest of the population has no civil rights--except on the rare occasion.

68

In the U.S. and Europe, Farang can challenge their government and big business on any action at any time; in Asia, this is frowned upon. In fact, speaking out against the government is violently suppressed. In Malaysia: "The duck that quacks gets shot." In Japan: "The nail that sticks out gets hammered down." In Thailand, the police are openly hostile to the desires of the people, if at any time those desires differ from that of the ruling members of society--and they do, most of the time.

Thai people do not question their government's policies, especially as those policies are delivered by those with the most power. We bow to the elite or the politician in a show of respect brought about from fear. Asians have a reputation for not "Letting go" of their past. In contrast, Americans are taught to think for themselves and to "Move on." Sometimes this means rebelling against authority. They have a great deal to say in the manner in which their government operates.

Westerners and Asians who have emigrated to the West have the opportunity to create wealth that we Thais do not—at least not legally. Our system perpetuates poor laborers rather than creating new wealthy consumers. Thailand exports food, clothing, and manufactured goods to the West; the West exports its money, tourists, and technologies.

I found it necessary to seek wealth my way—in the only way I knew because I was not a part of the Thai middle-or upper-class. The Thai elite are very often related to one another and their businesses are interconnected. They work together in order to keep their power intact. The few accumulate the mass of my country's wealth because the masses live in unspeakable poverty—*a poverty into which I was born and which I rejected when I was only 13.*

Chapter 6

Exquisite Beauty, Rustic Charm, Unimaginable Corruption:
The Unabridged Truth about Thailand

In order to understand why I pursued the life that I did,
one needs to understand more about the society
into which I was born.
It was not only my family, my village, and my province
that held me and all females to be of no value—
it was, and remains, my government, my country,
and ultimately my culture that hold all women
to be not only inferior--but expendable!

Many will be surprised to learn that my country, "Amazing Thailand," where ornate costumes of brilliantly-colored Thai silk sewn with golden threads grace the svelte bodies of poised classical dancers; where perfectly exquisite fresh fruit is delicately carved into beautiful exotic flowers; and where a hungry tourist will find some of the most mouth-watering delights on the face of the planet --spiced with ginger, garlic, basil, lemongrass, and chili; that this "Land of Smiles," this country into which I was born, is also a country of corruption equaled by few on the planet.

Village Marketplace

The long tentacles of the Thai Mafia reach deep down into the bowels of the village poor. Villagers always have a desperate need for money even for the most basic necessities of life: To repair a leaky roof, purchase medicine, better quality health care than the government-sponsored 30 Bt program,* _or to enroll a child in school._ They often require immediate cash for the most basic necessity of all--food for their families. The truth be told, they can also be desperate for money to pay off gambling debts, without which they risk suffering the vengeance of the moneylender—

70

vengeance that comes with the speed of a bullet.

---

*Bt 30 Health Program

A newly initiated health care program whereby a Thai national can seek out medical care at the clinic or hospital in his province by paying only Bt 30 (75¢). The government will subsidize the remainder of the doctor or hospital fees. If one becomes ill outside his/her province and goes to the nearest medical facility for assistance, the total medical costs remain the responsibility of the patient alone; the Bt 30 program is of no value except in one's own province.

Unfortunately, doctors are fleeing hospitals providing this populist form of health care—950 in the first nine months of the program and over 2,000 doctors in its first four years. A total of 77%, (795) "new" MDs resigned from state-run hospitals in 2003. Prior to the implementation of this new scheme, usually, about 200 physicians left the state's health care system each year. In June of 2005, seven out of every 10 doctors working at state hospitals had made the decision to leave or were considering it. Only three doctors of every 10 had not considered resigning. A surgeon at a private hospital makes about Bt 20,000 for one surgery, equal to the entire monthly salary earned by his counterpart at a state hospital.

The Bt30 plan brought 20,000,000 previously uninsured individuals into the health scheme. Doctors presently see 100 patients daily and often have to work until Midnight assisting with forensics, in addition to placing themselves "On call" for years at a time. When they resign, they are often not allowed to leave and they are not told the reason for the refusal.   Thailand Forum, 6/15/05

A village market is a hub of music and activity beginning at 2:30 A.M. when cars, trucks, and motorbikes begin to roll-in and unload their cargo. Succulent fruit and vegetables picked fresh the day before from their small farms, fish caught the night before along the local rivers, pigs recently slaughtered or still alive, chickens ready for the grill, cheap plastic goods, aluminum shelves, and hand-woven straw baskets fill the tables under the shabby and dilapidated nylon awning that offers little protection during the rainy season. Often as early as 5:00 A.M., contemporary Thai melodies begin to play from the speakers while farmers and vendors prepare for their customers. As Thais are notoriously superstitious, vendors traditionally wave the cash they receive from their first sale of the day over their goods to bring them "Good luck."

Every village has its resident blind person or two who slowly click their way throughout the marketplace--each with cane and begging cup in hand. Well-worn grandmothers with teeth stained black by decades of chewing betel-nuts; backs bent at 90 degrees; and skin wrinkled from a lifetime of exposure to a sweltering sun; sleep on large, splinter-laden wooden tables whose original rich teakwood beauty has faded to gray, and its enduring strength has been weakened by generations of torrential summer rains. Two-year old girls are seen carrying packages as they toddle alongside their grandparents, four-year old girls are folding towels, and 10-year olds girls are seen pushing wheelbarrows long after the sun has fallen below the horizon. On the other hand, boys of the same age can always be found at play.

A market vendor's day begins long before the sun rises and ends long after the sun has set, seven days a week, each and every day of the year. A day or weekend off, paid summer holidays, medical insurance, or employee benefits are non-existent here. Nightly, when the vendors have sold their last catfish or pig's leg, rambuttan or mangosteen, pumpkin custard or kilo of rice, sticky rice basket or aluminum rack—the moneylenders come calling. *"In the blink of an eye,"* the poor shopkeeper or hawker is Bt 2,000 richer—enough to pay for medicine, food, or school fees for his children--at a price he can ill afford. The Bt 2,000 is a loan for 24-days. It is repaid nightly at Bt 100--5% of the loan. The poor shopkeeper or hawker will repay a total of 2,400 baht--a whopping 20% interest in a short 24 days. Every night the moneylenders return, armed with revolvers, to collect their pound of flesh. These small time thugs are often heard to viciously threaten the poor shopkeeper who pleads that sales were poor that day, *"Do you want me to separate your body from your spirit?"* They can be seen tapping the hapless debtor on his back as he slowly rides away on his motorbike, children well in-tow. Few villagers seldom rise above this desperate cycle of poverty into which they were born-- reason enough for a lifetime of drinking and gambling for which the rural downtrodden are known.

Isaan Marketplace

Vendors seek shade from a sweltering sun beneath a torn awning.

Grandmotherly butcher catches a long, lazy nap

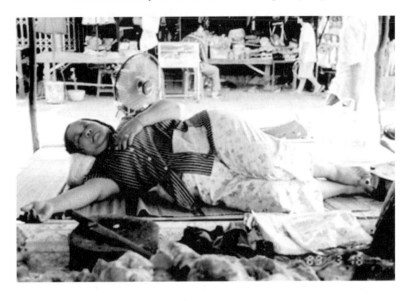

... in the heat of the day.

Crime and Passion

For one of influence whether residing in a rustic village or modern Bangkok, even murder goes unpunished. In August of 2003, a 45-year old respected academic and lecturer at the National Institute for Development Administration was given a "deferred" jail term after beating his wife to death with a golf club while in a jealous rage. His original three-year jail term was reduced to only 50 hours of community service. His anger had been provoked one evening when his wife arrived late to pick him up from the university. He suspected that she had become friendly with another man. The three judges stated that this "grateful man and good husband" was not an evil man, but he acted out of jealousy. The prosecution was barred from appealing the verdict except with their permission or that of a lower court.[1] His personal and professional status excused the murder of his wife while the value of his wife, the mother of his two sons, was not even a matter for consideration.

74

"Social Values Need To Be Re-examined"

"This is the big problem with Thai society.
No matter how bad, no matter how corrupt,
no matter how many people you kill,
If you have power and money, you can still get respect."

Author: Siva
The Nation, May 18, 2004
On the death of Thanom Kittikachorn,
'Democracy's bitterest foe,' 1911-2004

Crime and the Powerless

While another murderer is set free due his influence and affluence, the powerless continue to pay the price for their crimes. 1) A leader of the Bo Nok power plant protest movement was jailed for one year for throwing the mobile phone belonging to the company's major executive into the sea following a confrontation. The court refused to suspend his sentence. 2) A small-time hoodlum convicted of killing a popular mayor was sentenced to death while the wealthy politician, charged with being the mastermind of this murder, was set free. He claimed he would commit suicide if he were convicted. He wasn't.

In 2003, Thailand began its assault on "Dark Influence," essentially a "War on drugs." Small-time drug-dealers were murdered by our police department while the major players went free. Their names often known only to those murdered. Well over 2,000 men, women, and children lost their lives to government-paid assassins. Many of those who died were innocent.

It is probably safe to say that everyday of the year, one reads of documented misdeeds carried out by our police force,[1] Ministers of Parliament, or others who have been placed in powerful positions by those very same MP's. Most often, rather than being forced to resign; these corrupt officials are transferred or

75

"promoted" to an "inactive post" where they continue to receive salary, often greater than that received in their prior positions. Only now, these servants of the people serve no actual function until retirement, and in fact, they have been rewarded for their crimes.

The deep-seated corruption in my country begins at the very top of the political ladder and reaches down into the hopeless abyss with which my country's poor have been doomed. In Thailand, there is a strong wind against the poor; it is like a tornado and it is filled with corruption within our legal system and our public policy. Those who have power can break every rule and never be prosecuted. Our legal system serves only the rich. *I was born into this abyss, but I would not be doomed.*

Thailand: Sex Capital of the World

Prostitution: A Popular Pastime for Thai Men

There will always be an abundance of customers, both Thai and foreign, to purchase the services of Thailand's prostitutes with dangerous consequences. Thai men view frequenting prostitutes as a normal part of life--no different than enjoying their morning coffee. This is one of the reasons why the prevalence of prostitution remains high.[1] Thai women believe that having their husbands visit prostitutes is the lesser evil to their spouses keeping a "Mia noi" or "Minor wife" who is entitled to free separate housing, support, and other benefits as an extra-marital concubine[2]--all of which would seriously jeopardize the first wife's "Standard-of-living" and that of her children.

Thailand's Sexist Double-Standard

Although Thai men are notorious womanizers, Thai women are not allowed to sue their wandering husbands for adultery unless they can prove that a spouse acknowledged his new partner as his wife. Yet, a straying husband may sue his wife for committing adultery and is not subject to a "Burden of proof." Thailand's husbands are also safe from prosecution of spousal rape. While rape is illegal in Thailand, rape of one's wife is not. It is considered only a sexual violation. As in so very many areas of my culture, marriage and family laws discriminate against women.

There is a general decline of moral standards among Thai men, especially among the wealthy who consider sex as the ultimate form of entertainment with "Ladies of pleasure." As a result, there are very few streets in Bangkok that do not have sex dens. Many Thai males pay for sex throughout much of their lives even if they are married or have a steady girlfriend.

- *81% of Thai men use prostitutes.*[3]
- *6,000,000 Thai men use prostitutes each week.*[4]
- *100,000 Thai men bed 26,000 HIV-infected prostitutes every night.*[5]
- *Only 5% of the men using prostitutes are foreigners*
- *400,000 to 600,000 HIV carriers live in Thailand or one percent of the population.*[6]
- *97% of military conscripts have visited prostitutes.*[7]

Strippers perform on army base

Soldiers snap furiously as a stripper dances in a scene from a video taken during an annual farewell party for conscripts at Phokun Phamuang camp, Phetchabun province.

Similar erotic performances are commonplace as part of the entertainment at conscripts' annual farewell parties. But, in the past no evidence of the shows had been leaked because cameras were banned. Security was lax at this event when this video was filmed.

Senior Government Officials Have Reasons to Fear

Paranoia was created when a Member of Parliament told reporters a beautiful prostitute in his northern province of Chiang Rai died of AIDS; before her death, she submitted to the Chiang Rai Public Health office a list of 21 senior government officials who had used her services—*she was only a part-time prostitute who served only senior officials.*[8]

Human Trafficking:
The Thailand Connection

"...the third largest source of profits
for international organized crime,
behind only drugs and guns."
Madeline K. Albright,
Secretary of State,
Clinton Administration

My life has been far from a fairy tale,
but it has been better than that of hundreds of other girls
from my village, and much better than that of tens of thousands
of girls from similar poverty-stricken villages in bordering
countries, whose lives often ended far too soon,
as they served as nothing more than sex slaves
for the men of my country, Thailand.

Eighty percent of the prostitutes in Thailand come from the Northeast, the place of my birth. They come from my village and similar villages that abound throughout Thailand, Southeast Asia, and pervade the entire third-world. Tragically, far too many of these children and very young women are caught up in human trafficking—the most horrific of crimes against humanity. It is essential and certainly appropriate to address this issue here—even if ever-so-briefly. I can only hope that I do so without doing a disservice to its millions of victims. Trafficking is an unspeakable crime that shows no mercy and I could have so easily become one of its victims. I was one of the lucky ones! I was saved from the living nightmare of being sold into sexual slavery while still in my village, and I managed to avoid the sex traffickers after traveling to Bangkok when still quite young. I was extremely fortunate!!

Smuggling and trade in human beings
generate an estimated tens of billions of dollars in profits
annually to criminal organizations worldwide.

Bureau of Int'l Information Programs,
U.S. Department of State
July 2004

Sexual Slavery

"I was never sold, only sold out!"

From every poor province and every shantytown in
Southeast Asia come the very young who become the victims of
sexual and job slavery—a crime against humanity that is still very
much alive and well in this new millennium. The latest statistics
reveal that 27,000,000 young girls and boys, young women and men,
are held in bondage worldwide (forced prostitution or labor), with
up to 1,000,000 children held in sexual slavery and prostitution in
Asia.[1]

My country of Thailand is often at the heart of this ruthless
and brutal crime. Human Rights Watch and numerous other NGOs
recognize Thailand as *the* major transit country for traffickers;[2] this
means that my country both sends and receives its victims. Young
females and children, from all over the third-world, are the most
vulnerable to being sold or lured into prostitution, although young
males are also exploited. My province of Ubon is one of many
where international human rights' groups, along with official and
unofficial Thai social workers, step-in--in an effort to save these
victims from a fate "Worse than death."

- 200,000 prostitutes service the industry in Thailand—*excluding* foreign prostitutes.[3] Most NGOs seem to agree that 25% to 30% are under the age of 18.

- 700,000 to 1,000,000 prostitutes--including 200,000 Thai prostitutes working abroad appear more frequently among the documentation.[4] Statistics vary widely and are difficult to accurately assess due to the underground nature of the industry.

- 200,000 children were trafficked from neighboring countries into Thailand for prostitution, construction, and sweatshops.[5]

Slavery, indentured servitude, and forced labor are all major crimes against humanity whose perpetrators reap fortunes (Bt 40 billion a year) [6] in Thailand alone, at the expense of the poor and powerless, all too often costing trafficking victims their lives. Although police involvement remains largely undocumented in Thailand, it is a fact well-known to its victims and to those who attempt to rescue these young girls. Police are guilty of trafficking, accepting bribes, owning brothels, raping, and even murdering their victims. Due to the bribes paid to the police and immigration officials, trafficking is extremely successful and highly lucrative. All of this makes it extraordinarily difficult, if not impossible, to end this brutal crime.

Neither the Thai police, Thai border officials, nor any of the foreign border officials at the many immigration points of exit and entry surrounding my country, have ever been convicted of trafficking the poor and unsuspecting immigrants who are illegally brought into Thailand.

When traffickers buy girls who are uncooperative, the young victims are repeatedly beaten, raped, and starved until they comply; they are threatened with death or the death of their families until their debts are paid off. Many girls have lost their lives in this "Seasoning" process." Although this is a ritual few girls escape, intended for the sole purpose of stripping away their power and breaking down their self-esteem, agents and brothel owners prefer to go to the hill tribes for young girls who have little or no knowledge of the sex industry. Brothel owners and their customers want girls who are uneducated and easily manipulated.[7]

Human trafficking has been a tragedy of immense proportions for hundreds of years, yet, its victim's stories do not come to light frequently enough. It is only when a crime so horrific sees the light of day as in the case of Puongtong Simaplee, a 27-year old Thai female who was taken and sold into prostitution at the age of 12, that we are reminded that kidnapping or selling of young females is still very much alive and prospering, not only in third-world nations—*but in industrialized nations as well*—in this 21st century. These girls most often come from the poorest provinces in their respective countries. Puongtong's story reached the front page of newspapers worldwide; her case was the exception. The horrors of beatings, torture, and starvation are endured daily by girls entrapped in brothels and in other forms of slavery; their stories are often only discovered by those involved in the job of rescuing them—and not always then. Often these young girls cannot bear to speak of the terror to which they were subjected, even following their rescue.

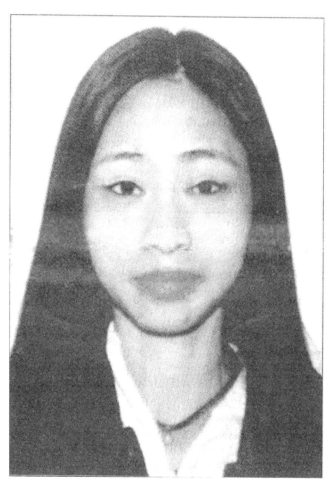

Puongtong Simaplee

Puongtong's short and tragic life is but one of the four million women and children worldwide who have been reduced to chattel. She is important because her story represents that of millions of trafficked young women who have survived this horrifying nightmare and of many who didn't.
Her story could have been their story--or mine.

Puongtong choked to death on her own vomit while being held at the Villawood Immigration Detention Center in Sydney, Australia, in 2001, where she spent the last three days of her life. She weighed only 31 kilos, was suffering from heroin withdrawal, and had been vomiting for over 65 hours into the same small bucket where she kept her toiletries. She received no medical care. This is not yet a civilized world when these tragedies are allowed not only to occur, but to continue. She had been enslaved for 15 years. Following the release of her story two years after her death, her parents claimed that she was never taken nor sold. This is a common response among parents of prostitutes, and more common among those whose children have died so tragically. Admitting to having a daughter who has died as a prostitute would cause her parents to *"Lose face," her failure as a prostitute being greater humiliation than the tragedy of her death.*

Even if Puongtong's story that she was "taken" is proven one day to be false, there are thousands of other young women from Thailand and all of Southeast Asia who will share their stories of being forced to work as sex slaves and held as prisoners in "Safe houses" in Australia and elsewhere around the world. Young women have told of servicing thousands of men to pay off their Bt 810,000 to Bt 1.35 million ($20,250 to $33,750) debt contracts. If they refused, they were raped, beaten, and forced onto drugs as was Puongtong, according to her testimony, before her death.[8]

Two years following Puongtong's death, it was estimated that the trafficking industry in Australia was worth about $150,000,000 a year, up from $50,000,000 just five years earlier and involving 1,500 women. Yet, the Australian government stated that sexual slavery was not a problem. In fact, by 2003, no one had ever been arrested or prosecuted under Australia's anti-sex slavery laws.

When immigration officials raid brothels, they do not want to hear the women's stories; these victims are taken to the detention center to await deportation. One courageous young woman gave details to the federal police after helping some girls to escape, but the police stated that they would "not be taking any action." Instead, they prepared her for deportation. With witnesses deported, there can be no prosecutions.[9]

Thai Families Exploit Their Children

It is incomprehensible to most of the world that parents could sell their children. Yet in Thailand, it is not uncommon among the Isaan or hill tribe poor—although now illegal. There are those who look sympathetically upon third-world countries and believe that abject poverty is the *only* reason that families would sell their children into a life of sexual slavery. Sometimes, this is true; girls are sacrificed in order that the rest of the family can eat.[10] Yet, this is not always the case. If it were, countries that have become industrialized over recent decades like Thailand would have seen a decrease in the number of girls entering the sex trade. Instead, it strongly appears that greed--the family's desire for consumer goods is at the core of the sale of many young girls. Ever since the early 70's, the number of girls leaving the North and Northeast to work in the sex industry has been increasing. *My mother certainly never objected to my choice of a career; in fact, she encouraged any activity of mine as long as I continued to send her money and lots of it!*

"Thai women are just another kind of crop"
Thai Official

Some families honestly believe that trading one's body in the form of sexual acts for cash is easy money. They do not view sending a daughter into the trade as a sacrifice. If the girl is held in a brothel, a male relative may show up to collect her earnings—

after she has paid off her traffickers. If she is "fortunate enough" to be a free-lancer, her family awaits her phone call that indicates that money has been deposited into its bank account. *My mother eagerly awaited my every call.*

So very many girls like me are making the choice to enter the industry so that they can improve their families' homes, buy motorbikes for their brothers, gold for their mothers, and the latest consumer fads for their parents. These purchases are made for the sole purpose of *"Making face."* Initially, I wanted to compensate for the death of my father. Secondly, I wanted to improve my family's standing in the community which included my sisters receiving an education so they would never have to lead my life. *I made that choice!* There are many villages where every family has at least one daughter in the sex trade supporting them—voluntarily or involuntarily. The number of involuntary prostitutes is extremely high—64% in girls from 16 to 19 years of age.[11]

According to Amnesty International, the age of the 4,000,000 women and children worldwide who are trafficked for prostitution is dropping to as young as 9—and sometimes younger. Children are sold, tricked, or drugged into prostitution. They have also been burned in their beds when their brothels burned down and killed by their traffickers and by policemen—sometimes one in the same person.

As for the trafficking of very young girls, there is a misconception among Asian men that children will not carry or transmit HIV/AIDS. It is for this very reason that Japanese men, insistent on disease-free girls, travel into Thai villages in the highlands. They want girls who are "guaranteed to be fresh and safe as well as cheap."[12] Now, it has become more often the practice that young Thai women are trafficked to Japan. Many Asian men— particularly Chinese "…believe that having sex with very young girls will improve their virility, cure a sexually-transmitted disease, or make them more successful in business."[13]

"My only regret is that I should have asked for more."

Response from a Hill-tribe woman in Thailand
after being asked by a reporter if she had any regrets
about selling her 14-year old daughter into prostitution—
for the grand sum of $12.

Ripe for Trafficking

Girls from the Northeast or the hill tribes of Thailand come from families who are financially desperate. Hill tribe girls are also racially-discriminated against and denied Thai citizenship, an education, and the freedom to *legally* leave their city. They are young and *"Ripe for trafficking."* Agents for brothels travel into the mountains of the hill tribes, or into the lowlands of the Northeast, seeking out available children whose desperately poor parents are willing to sell them for a few baht. Upon promising to give jobs to the children in Bangkok or other big cities, they are taken from their families; and often, they are never seen again. Girls as young as 11 are locked inside brothels[14] and girls of 12 and 13, if they have not already been sold, are pledged to the sex industry in return for a deposit given to their parents by agents. This practice is commonly referred to as

"Harvesting still green rice."

Most readers will find it even more shocking that pregnant women will pledge their *unborn* children to agents for the purpose of prostitution. Opium-addicted parents in Northern Thailand, particularly near the Myanmar border, will part with their children for money to feed their own addictions. Village headsmen will broker the sale of village children to finance their lifestyles and drug addiction while other families will sell their offspring to purchase television sets. Sadly, these are not isolated incidents.[15] Children as young as seven have been known to be sold into brothels. In the case of one seven-year old girl, when rescued at the age of 12, she was found to be HIV-Positive.[16] Other girls who have been rescued tell of being sold into brothels and being forced to have sex with four or five men a day, others claim to have serviced as many as 30 a day—*without ever being paid. These stories are all too common and pervade every corner of Thailand, particularly its poorest provinces.*

Although I was never trafficked into sexual slavery,
I was one of tens of thousands who made the personal choice
to sell my body to foreign men. I can understand deep in the
recesses of my soul, the profound pain, the deep sadness,
and the all-encompassing feelings of lifelessness
that exist within the souls of its victims—while yet, still alive.

Thais Exploit Thais

The statistics cited in this chapter are only numbers. Although meaningful, they cannot begin to reflect how traumatized these young victims are, nor how humiliated and helpless they feel. Above all, these numbers cannot convey the absolute emptiness suffered by those who are exploited. Each statistic reflects someone's life story—one that has recently taken place or is taking place right now in this new millennium where Thais and others completely devoid of any thread of humanity take advantage of the weak, the powerless, and the vulnerable, even when the victims are "their own people."

Men, women, and teen-agers are guilty of trafficking human beings—buying and selling them as if they were cattle—their only value being in the profit they bring to their captors. In

Thailand, thousands of traffickers, mafia, or less-sophisticated gangs are in operation at any one time. I strive to put a face on these numbers whenever possible and to reflect these victims as flesh and blood. Each is someone's daughter, granddaughter, sister, aunt, niece, or cousin. Each is a living, breathing human being who has been violated and denied her human rights. Each is far more than a statistic.

In Europe, Australia, Asia, Southeast Asia, especially my country of Thailand and anywhere in the world where people exist only to amass wealth *by any means—including the enslavement of the poor and helpless—one will find Thais not only among the exploited but also as the perpetrators.* If the girls are not kidnapped or sold outright by their parents, they are lured away with the promise of good paying work. They are locked up in brothels, starved, beaten, brutalized, and threatened with death or the death of their families if they attempt to run away. Once they arrive in a major tourist or brothel city of Thailand, or in a foreign country where they have gained illegal entry, they find themselves owing their traffickers outrageous sums of money that can only be paid through selling their bodies. They are forced to repay from $2,700 if they are trafficked within Thailand to as much as $110,400 if trafficked overseas. Children and young women will have to service hundreds to thousands of men, working from six months to several years, without ever receiving the cost of their services--until these illegitimate costs are repaid.

Their debts continue to grow as they are charged for room, board, personal hygiene articles, make-up and clothing—all at inflated prices. If a girl is allowed to return home for a visit, her brothel owner will withhold many thousands of dollars that she has earned, even if her debts have been repaid, in order to ensure her return. Many girls are in debt to brothel owners, one after another, for their entire lives because they are resold which forces them to repay the cost of their sale—time and again. Tragically, their young lives are often cut-short because they have contracted HIV-AIDS.

Help is Available

Fortunately, there are a number of "grassroots" organizations in Thailand whose sole-purpose is to save these children from being sold into brothels or to the nearest pedophile. *Development and Education Program for Daughters and Community Center (DEPDC)* in Mae Sai at the Thai/Burmese border, whose founder, Sompop Jantrak, was twice nominated for the Nobel Peace Prize, provides education, job training, and employment assistance. Shelter and food are also provided when the girls are too vulnerable to remain in their parents' home. If the girls are able to live at home, they are provided with the cost of tuition; books; uniforms; lunches; transportation; and equipment. Sompop's organization saves hundreds of girls every year and has saved over a thousand girls since 1989. It is because Sompop has chosen to save young, at-risk girls that he is stalked daily and threatened with death. Agents for the brothel owners, and others who have lost access to the revenue these children would have produced, continue to harass and intimidate him. Yet, with his life in constant jeopardy, he won't be deterred.

Like Sompop, 30-year old Thai, Guljohn Jeamram, has a mission to save the children—mostly those of ethnic minorities on both sides of the Thai-Myanmar border. In 1999, he created Childlife. He provides shelter for children at-risk and those who are already taking or selling drugs. [17]

Harbor House is another shelter in northern Thailand that provides room and board, education, daily living skills, vocational training, and people who care to young vulnerable girls, primarily from the hill tribe villages who are at-risk to succumbing to the sex and/or trafficking industries. Harbor House was founded in 1995 through the efforts of Thai businesswoman and writer, Lady Chumnongsri Hanchanlash. It also operates an Outreach Program that educates and informs the community of the needs and rights of children and women.

Sompop, Guljohn, and Lady Chumnongsri are not alone!! YMCA to the Rescue!!!

In 1995, the Bangkok YMCA initiated a program that has developed into a boarding school. Located outside the city of Phayao, it cares for 54 children at high-risk of sexual abuse, prostitution, or of being sold. Agents for the YMCA also go into the mountains and the lowlands seeking out the same parents as do the traffickers. But the representatives for the YMCA never offer money; instead they promise parents a safe, nurturing environment and free education for their children—*something that my government does not provide.* This program to educate those most vulnerable is at the heart of destroying this plague which pervades my country, as well as all other underdeveloped countries.

Kred Takarn

Perched on an island near the Chao Phraya river in Bangkok is Kred Takarn, a refuge for trafficked girls who have been rescued from brothels or from their abusive Thai employers. In 2002, 242 girls resided at the center; half of them were from Burma, Laos, Vietnam, and Southern China. Vocational education and classes in hairdressing, foot massage, aerobics, weaving, computing, batik, and English are available in order to teach skills so that they can legitimately support themselves. Pimps have tried to poison the girls and brothel owners have attempted to smuggle out their former workers. Some of the girls have been rescued a second time after being sent home. Their parents had returned them to similar work in Thailand. Cambodian children, as young as three, who have been found begging and selling flower garlands on the busy Bangkok streets are also cared for at the facility. [18]

Thais Exploit Burmese, Lao, Cambodians, and Chinese in Thailand

Thais not only exploit Thais; they exploit over 2,000,000 victims from nearby countries including China. In 1994, there were over 1,000,000 Burmese economic and political refugees in Thailand—50% of the total, with 20,000-30,000 Burmese females working as prostitutes, [19] 60% of them under 18. [20] A decade later, the number of Burmese had increased from 50% to 89%. Many were trafficking victims; upon returning home, they were arrested for illegal departure or for prostitution and were injected with cyanide by their government in order to stop the spread of HIV.

Foreigners Exploit Thai Girls Abroad
Japan

Just as easily as Thais exploit their own and foreigners in the slave trade, foreigners exploit Thais. Japan, Australia, and nearly every country in Europe are the receiving nations. Japan holds the reputation for being the largest importer and exporter in the Asian sex industry for the last several decades. They export 80% of the child porn available on websites. In the 1970s and 1980s, NGOs in Thailand and the Philippines began protesting Japanese sex tours to their countries which had taken place since the early 1960s. As a consequence, young women were instead trafficked to Japan for sexual services. [21]

There are more than 30,000 Thai women working as prostitutes at any one time in Japan [22] with 50 dying every year from HIV-AIDS. Most have been tricked by the Japanese Yakuza (mafia) to come to Japan under the guise of other work. These young women enter Japan illegally, their passports are confiscated, and they are forced to pay off massive travel debts. They are often moved from one brothel to another so it is impossible for them to be found. Although many are infected with HIV-AIDS, or develop it after arriving in Japan, they are not entitled to healthcare as they are most often illegal aliens. They are forced to continue to work as prostitutes until they become so sick that they are returned to Thailand to die or until their debts are paid—in which case they are picked up and deported. About 3,000 women escape brothels in Japan every year and flee to the Thai Embassy.

Landmark Compensation Case

A 38-year old Thai woman sues her Thai/Japanese traffickers in civil court for Bt 4.68 million ($118,000).

Urairat Soimee, a poor and uneducated peasant woman with a disabled husband; three small, hungry children; and no access to the outside world; was lured to Japan with the promise of a well-paying waitress job by a trusted and wealthy Thai/Japanese couple in her village. The young woman borrowed Bt 40,000 ($1,000) to pay the couple for travel expenses.

Immediately upon Urairat's arrival at Narita Airport, she was taken to a brothel in Nagoya where she was told that she would provide sexual services in order to repay the brothel owner Bt 1,840,000 ($46,000). Initially confused because she had come to Japan for a waitress job, she then became hysterical and begged to be sent home. She was told that if she didn't comply, she would be sent to a brothel on an island where she would be locked in a room to receive customers all day. If she attempted to escape, she would be thrown into the sea. Gangsters were sent to terrorize her and the mama-san's husband threatened to kill her. Urairat agreed to obey. During the months to follow, seven days a week, she was raped, tortured, and brutalized by dirty, drunk, and sadistic men, and even had the few coins she kept in her bag stolen from her. Her mama-san kept her tips and fined her Bt 66,700 ($1,668) if the customers were not satisfied. She was forced to pay for room, board, medicine, and even the required phone calls to tell the mama-san that her customer had finished, so that the next one could be sent to her room. Shortly after her arrival, she developed a painful Sexually-Transmitted Disease but was forced to continue to work.

Five months later, Urairat had repaid the original debt and asked for her release. She was told that she had been sold to another gang and owed another Bt 333,000 ($8,325). Desperate to secure her freedom, she reached another woman from her village (who had been trafficked by the same couple), who in turn contacted a Thai male friend working nearby, to rescue her friend. In the melee that followed, Urairat escaped only to learn later that her rescuer had killed the mama-san. He was sentenced to 10-years in prison.

Pleading innocent to the charge of murder, Urairat was held in solitary confinement for five years while the "Wheels of justice" moved on—ever so slowly. She was eventually given a seven-year sentence. After three months in jail, she learned that the sharp pains she had been experiencing were a result of terminal ovarian cancer that had spread to her breasts, liver, and other parts of her body. Her disease was believed to have been caused by prostitution. Japanese authorities allowed her to return home to Thailand to die.

Urairat's tragic case is extremely important in a country where human trafficking is rampant. Not only is this the first civil case brought against human traffickers, but victims who have been lured into the flesh trade do not press charges out of fear or shame of being condemned by Thai society—particularly that of their village. Urairat hopes to set a legal precedent to prosecute human traffickers in civil court as well as in criminal court. She has been given only a short time to live and is not expected to survive the trial.

Drawn from original articles by
Sanitsuda Ekachai, Bangkok Post
February 2 & 12, 2006

Europe

Thai women can also be found throughout Western Europe working as prostitutes—often having been brought there by their boyfriends or newly-acquired European husbands—who have married them for just that purpose. Sometimes this arrangement has been agreed to by the young woman and sometimes she is totally unsuspecting. Often, she has married in the belief that she has found a new life, a man who will support her, and she is now able to leave the sex-trade behind. Britain, Denmark, France, Switzerland, and the Netherlands are popular sex-tourist destinations. Every year, approximately 3,500 women from Asia and Eastern Europe are trafficked to the Netherlands to work in secret brothels or illegal escort agencies where they are often held captive and abused. [23] Some of the worst records for sexual enslavement in Europe belong to Germany and Italy.

Job Slavery
Men, Women, Children

Sometimes trafficking is not for the purpose of selling young girls into the nightmares of sexual slavery; sometimes it is for the purpose of indentured servitude where traffickers again operate without mercy. In one case, 30 Burmese women and children were imprisoned in a locked building, forced to work 16 to 18 hours a day, allowed only two meals a day, and refused their wages of Bt 1,200 to 1,500/month until they had completed a year of employment. Some workers escaped leading to the rescue of the rest. But, the employer still refused to pay their salaries and overtime. In a groundbreaking action, a trio of courageous female attorneys seeking to right this injustice took this case to the Labor Court. While all odds were against them, they convinced the court that labor laws were non-discriminatory and applied to everyone— including illegal aliens. The court found in their favor and a precedent was set. For the first time an employer was ordered to pay those he had enslaved. Five years later, those wronged still have not been fully-paid.

This court order has not stopped other employers from continuing to abuse immigrant workers who have in the past been murdered or "made to disappear" when they complained about inhumane working conditions and unpaid salaries. This brutality has intimidated and terrified others who would also seek to complain. When illegal aliens are discovered, they are deported, never to receive their wages; labor officials have always maintained that labor laws did not apply--until the above case was prosecuted.

Burmese immigrant worker

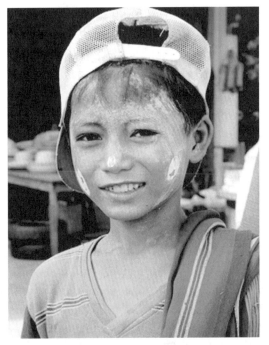

Photographer: Sanitsuda Ekachai   Photo courtesy of Bangkok Post

Immigrants are denied all basic human rights while their children are denied the right to their nationality (refused birth certificates), to an education, and to healthcare. These children are easily exploited and often forced into begging gangs.

In Southeast Asia, while most trafficking victims are forced into prostitution; and others are trafficked for bonded labor (mines, markets, factories); domestic work; and forced marriages; more recently, still others are forced to work for begging gangs in Thailand.[1] There are 15,000 street children in Thailand with more than 5,000 in Bangkok[2] --immigrants from Laos, Cambodia and Burma are at the greatest risk of being trafficked.

Two of the thousands of street children in Bangkok

Photographer: Philippe Lopez

Begging Gangs

Children who have been sold to begging gangs thriving in Thailand are forced to sell flowers or other tokens. If they don't meet their quota, they are starved, beaten, and even tortured. They often work between the hours of 10:00 PM and 6:00 AM. Lek, a 12-year old boy, was sold into slavery by his father for Bt 1,000 ($25) and told to send Bt 30,000 home for a down payment on a new car. He sold flowers on the street and had to earn Bt 1,500 a day or he was beaten and deprived of food. No one makes Bt 1,500 by only selling flowers. Thirty-one other children between the ages of 6 and 14 were prisoners of the same gang—just one of thousands that traffick children in Thailand.[3]

A son sold into slavery

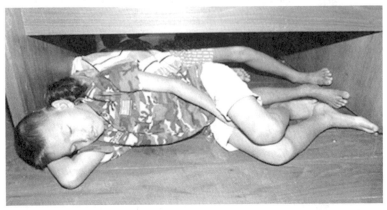

Photographer: Boonnarong Bhudhipanya   *Photo courtesy of Bangkok Post*

Twelve-year old Lek sleeps under a desk at the police station following his rescue.

Child Labor: In the Factories

It is estimated that there may be as many as 4,000,000 child workers in Thailand. NGOs put the number higher. Bangkok's Ministry of Human Resources states that 5,000,000 Thai children work—some are as young as 5-years old. A large number of these children have been sold by their parents into the largely unregulated garment factory industry.[4]

By law, children between the ages of 13 and 15 are permitted to perform "light work." They are not allowed to work between the hours of 10 P.M. and 6 A.M. This is where the law and reality part ways. In the garment, gem, leather bag, furniture, shrimp and seafood industries, children are exploited--working from 11 to 15 hours a day or more, from 8:00 A.M. to 11:00 P.M. with one break only from 30 to 60 minutes during mid-day. These children slave from 6 to 7 days each week; some are never given a single day off. They earn from $60 to $70 per month. Children in the garment industry earn 5¢ for every 100 buttons sewn--piece work that is illegal. In the gem industry, children receive *"unpaid training"* for months. After their training period, they allegedly receive Bt 30 to 40 (75¢ to $1.00) per week including lunch. In the leather bag industry, children work 13 to 15 hours a day; they are not paid for overtime; they receive two days off per month and they are paid $1.00 a day. One leather bag company employed over 200 children who were given amphetamines to keep them working exceedingly long hours.

In 1987, one shop house caught fire, killing 19 people including children. *They were trapped inside locked doors—a common practice among companies that use and abuse slave labor.* In the wood and rattan furniture industry, the situation is worse with children working 85-hour weeks for $16 per month. In the shrimp and seafood processing industry, child slaves work under horrific conditions in order to pay off loans made to their parents. Some children return with missing fingers and diseased skin.

> ### To traffick in human beings
> ### is to steal from those victims their present,
> ### their future, and ultimately their lives.

The Brutality of the Thai Wealthy: The Domestic Industry

Brought to Thailand with the promise of well-paid jobs, Burmese, Lao, and Cambodian children are beaten, starved, and tortured by their wealthy Thai employers. Many of the girls bear scars from wounds inflicted by their abusers. They have been beaten with rattan sticks and burned with hot irons. Some are allowed only one meager bowl of soup a day while slaving 16+ hours a day. A 14-year old was allowed only one hour of sleep a night and she was sometimes beaten until she blacked out. The ugly, dark irony in this case was that her employer was a traditional healer. These young girls may labor unconscionable hours for years. They are shown no mercy and far too often, they are also never paid. Rich Thai families remain that way from the sweat and blood of poor Thai peasants who have been enslaved, or who work in the fields for $60/month, or from the sweat and blood of immigrants from Burma, Laos, and Cambodia.

> *Although an anti-slavery law exists in Thailand, abusive employers of child workers have never been legally punished for enslaving other human beings.*

As in the case of Puongtong who was a sex slave for 15 years until her tragic death, Ma Suu, an 18-year old Burmese maid, is an example of "Man's inhumanity to man" in Thailand's job-slavery market. She had only been in Thailand for a year. She had paid a trafficker Bt 7,000 to locate work for her in the north of Thailand. Several months later, she paid another trafficker another Bt 7,000; he found her domestic work in Lopburi province—three hours northeast of Bangkok.

Ma Suu had been working for her new employer for only three months when she was accused of stealing; she denied the charges. Her employer ordered her to be beaten until she confessed, but she continued to deny the theft. Her assailants poured gasoline on her, set her afire, and left her in a room without treatment for three days. When she regained consciousness, she was beaten again and left for dead by the side of the road--at the order of her Thai employer. Just before she died, she was able to tell the authorities who it was who had brutalized her. When her employer was approached by the police, he denied ever knowing her. A year later, her killers and employer remained free. *Thais have no remorse.*[5]

> ### *"Why are we Thais so heartless?"*
> *Sanitsuda Ekachai writes "... the policy on immigrant labor must be changed, not only to rescue exploited workers but to rescue ourselves from heartlessness. If we care to feel that is."*[6]

Thais Enslaved by Thais Overseas

Some Thai parents will sell their children into sexual or job slavery, in Thailand or abroad, in order to buy drugs; gold; and consumer goods. Other Thais will exploit poor Thai and Southeast Asian children, and young men and women, into slavery for no other reason than financial gain—no matter how small.

> *2,491 job seekers lost Bt 115,000,000 ($2,875,000) to crooked brokers.*
> *670 job brokers are wanted on fraud charges.*[7]

Sometimes trafficking is for the *sole* purpose of extortion where traffickers again operate from heartless greed. As in Thailand, where vulnerable Thais and Southeast Asians are enslaved into sexual and job slavery—domestic or industrial, those same desperately poor victims are trafficked abroad only to be left penniless after paying job brokers enormous sums for jobs that never existed. If a job does exist, the newly-recruited may be imprisoned behind electrified wire fences where they labor 16 to 18+ hours a day. They may be paid 60 cents an hour—*or they may never be paid.* Their Thai captors threaten to harm their families and burn down their homes in Thailand if they try to escape. "A bullet is cheap..." [8] Families will pool their resources and mortgage their homes, their farms, and their land in the belief that a good job overseas awaits a son, a daughter, a niece, or a nephew—a job that would improve the quality of life for the entire family. Instead, the family will lose everything that they hold dear and the job seeker will be abandoned or held prisoner in a far away land.

Job trafficking is extremely prevalent in my country. The poorest are manipulated and controlled by anyone from anywhere promising them a better life. *It is their poverty that drives them into being easily exploited--and far too often--into my career.*

Pedophiles

***Rape and child molestation, reported and non-reported,
occur daily in Thailand; these horrendous acts
are ugly testament to Thai life, and until recently,
have remained hidden from the unknowing tourist
and are of no concern to the Thai public at-large
--with few exceptions.***

Thai children and young women are not only enslaved, raped, and held prisoner in Thailand and abroad by their own, they suffer the same tragic fate at the hands of other Asians and Westerners as did Puongtong. At the time that her horrific death was made known to the world, a similar story from Australia exposed that children, as young as 12, were being held hostage and enslaved into prostitution. Of those who managed to escape and reach the police, their stories were denied by those very people who were supposed to protect them and these young victims were deported.[1]

> ### *Criminals are Set Free while Victims are Imprisoned*
> *On November 17, 1997, Thailand enacted the Measures in Prevention and Suppression of Trafficking in Women and Children Act, allowing authorities to detain suspected trafficking victims caught in searches of public places, airports, railway and bus stations, seaports, entertainment establishment, and factories for as long as 10 days for authentication of their travel documents. The law does not permit authorities to detain suspected traffickers who are accompanying victims. Therefore, traffickers have the ability to manipulate legislation so that they are immune from prosecution and their "cargo" is detained. Their cargo will then be returned to them after the police have made a "profit" from them as well, in Thailand, Burma, Laos, and Cambodia.*

Massage Parlors

Thai police were recently found to have "turned a blind eye" for the past six years, to underage girls working in massage parlors of the wealthy Bangkok businessman, Chuwit Kamolvisit. In exchange, the police—*many who were members of the Crime Suppression Division*—had received Bt 12,000,000/month ($300,000), in addition to gold watches, other luxury items, computers, refrigerators, furniture, free massages, and women. Police chiefs and others on the police force were said to have flashed Rolex watches while one highly-placed member of law enforcement drove a Bentley. All were said to have been made possible by gifts or cash provided by this businessman known worldwide as the "King of Commercial Sex." In 2003, Chuwit's personal fortune was estimated at $250,000,000, much of this wealth made off the backs of young girls. He was indicted that same year for luring underage girls into prostitution[2] only to be acquitted the following year. The judges stated that 1) There was no proof that 15-year old prostitutes were employed in his massage parlors and 2) It was the pimps who were to blame for fooling Chuwit. Contradictory statements such as these are typical of our court system when litigating cases of "Influential persons." Any excuse is found or fabricated to allow the guilty rich to go free.

Later that same year, Chuwit ran for Governor of Bangkok, hoping to turn his "newly-found popularity" into votes. He placed third of 22 original candidates with 300,000 votes, proving that the citizens of Thailand would choose to elect a man who took pride in his self-proclaimed "Bad guy" image. He had stated that many related to him and would vote for him because he had embarrassed and exposed the highly-corrupt police department of Thailand. He was right!

Prostitution with Minors is Illegal

In Thailand, it is illegal for a man to have sex with a prostitute between the ages of 15 and 18 with resulting penalties of from 1-3 years imprisonment and/or a fine of Bt 20,000-50,000. Penalties increase to 2-6 years imprisonment and/or a fine of Bt 40,000-120,000 [3] for men who have sex with girls under the age of 15.

Four-to-20 year imprisonment and/or fines of Bt 8,000 to 40,000 are penalties that already exist in the Criminal Code even if the minor under the age of 15 has given consent. Three-to-15 year jail terms and fines of Bt 6,000 to 30,000 are handed down to procurers who have provided girls from 15 to 18 years of age. More severe jail terms of 5-to-20 years and fines of Bt 10,000 to 40,000 exist for those who provide girls under the age of 15. Penalties are increased by one-third for parents who sell their daughters into prostitution. [4]

Although the laws governing prostitution are now a part of our legal system, the actual application of these laws lies in the ease with which the police dismiss pedophiles. These laws are not enforced—and it appears that no one worries about them. It was no secret that Chuwit was guilty of this crime and of running expensive prostitution parlors consisting of 1,000 girls and young women who catered to men's sexual fantasies—all under the guise of high-class massage parlors—*yet, he was acquitted.* His crimes were punishable by prison terms of from three to 15 years with fines of from Bt 60,000 to Bt 300,000. Lax enforcement and corruption are the reasons that Chuwit and others enjoy the freedom they do in the commercial sex trade. He was found *"Not guilty."* This judicial decision reflects, once again, the power of the rich and influential in my country.

Shortly after his acquittal, and after losing in the gubernatorial race, Chuwit was elected to Parliament. His support by the electorate is glowing testament to the fact that Thais have no problem with overlooking the manner in which he built his fortune—including having underage girls in his massage parlors. *Instead, he was "Hailed as a hero" for exposing rampant police corruption—the far greater evil.*

"Coh ga ghin ya ahn,"
Old cows like young grass

Pedophiles: Who Are They?
Pedophiles travel from one country to another and build new lives; they often take legitimate jobs in schools as teachers, in orphanages and rescue missions as caretakers, or in any organization that will allow them to maintain a steady supply of children. One Australian ran a sex-tourism business from his travel agency where he trafficked underage boys; organized gay tours; and possessed and distributed pornographic material. Pedophiles come

105

from every country and every profession; they range in age from young men to the very old. They may even be married and have children of their own.

A Catholic priest who raised funds for a project for boys; an American Mormon who ran a pedophile network from Bangkok to Chiang Mai; an Australian psychologist responsible for eradicating pedophiles from the Anglican church; and an Anglican chaplain who fled Australia with the intention of seeking new children and avoiding arrest in his own country have all been guilty of this crime. A 30-year old Fin; a 60-year old Swede; a 56-year old Aussie; a 61-year old American; a 61-year old German; a 26-year old Brit, another aged 49; and a 66-year old Canadian teacher—what they all have in common is that they all know that Thailand is the nation to pursue their sexual obsession with children—of either sex. Lax laws are the incentives that bring pedophiles to Thailand. If they are arrested, they pay a small fine which doesn't dissuade them from returning to solicit other children.

A vivid example of the ease with which pedophiles continue to ply their perversion is found in that of a 43-year old Finn who was originally detained on suspicion of molesting at least 445 Thai boys, making pornographic films, photo albums, and disks. He was sentenced to 11 years in prison in Finland, for committing more than 160 acts of pedophilia since 1989—*in Thailand.* He had traveled to Thailand 26 times in 16 years and sought out mostly young Thai boys between the ages of 10 and 13. It was the Belgian authorities who alerted the Finnish police to his activities when he was mentioned in connection with a pedophilic case in Belgium. The perpetrator had kept a diary on each of his victims. *The significance of this story is that it was the Finnish Police and the Belgian authorities who finally curtailed the illegal acts of this child sexual abuser; it was not the Thai police.*

Children: For Rent or For Sale

Children are not only sold in Thailand; they are also available for rent. Drug-addicted parents are always in need of cash. They can rent to new customers time and time again whereas a "sale" is a one-time affair—at least for the parent. Once the parent makes the original sale, these children are often resold by traffickers.

From Bangkok to the Provinces:
Children are not safe anywhere in Thailand, in school, or in the hands of the police

"At least one school teacher sexually abuses one student each week...most cases involve rape..."[5] Not only have some teachers proven themselves unworthy of the trust placed in them to care for our children, many of Thailand's police (the uniformed protectors of the people) have also proven themselves unworthy. From taking cash bribes and gifts and demanding free sex from massage parlor sex workers, to demanding payments from beggars and unsuspecting motorists, to committing rape of school girls—there may be no crime from which they have shied away.

From Chiang Rai at the North to Phuket in the South

Pedophiles travel freely throughout Thailand from Chiang Rai at the Myanmar border and Chiang Mai--a short jaunt southwest of Chiang Rai, to Pattaya Beach located 95 miles south of Bangkok, to Phuket in the South. These cities are well-known among those involved in the "Child-for-sex" seeking crowd for its ready-availability of children. In Phuket, a neon-sign openly proclaims "Uncle Charlie's boys for men."[6] Chiang Mai has become one of the latest frontiers for international pedophiles exploiting Thailand's lax law enforcement, indulgent attitude to sexuality, and easy access to desperately poor children. Chiang Rai traffickers seek out parents knowing that they will part with their children for cash. Poor parents have been known to sell their babies for as little as Bt 2,000 ($50).

"When will we face up to the sex industry?"

On May 15, 2005, The Nation, one of Thailand's two major English speaking newspapers, published an article entitled "When will we face up to the sex industry?" The author cited a recent and expensive public relations campaign to promote the natural beauty and rich culture of Thailand was, in fact, a massive attempt to erase its present sordid image as one of the sex capitals of the world. The writer supported claims of numerous NGOs: 1) Foreigners come to Thailand to avail themselves of easy access to the sex industry which includes readily available children because they know that there is very little chance that they will be caught or punished. 2) There are a growing number of children being drawn into the industry because they have no other way of caring for themselves and pedophiles take advantage of this sad reality. 3) Police corruption, the apathy of ordinary citizens, and the hypocrisy of the Thai government are reasons that this industry continues to prevail. The conclusion reached was that Thailand is not willing to give up its lucrative sex industry because it is not willing to give up the vast revenue it creates for those who perpetuate it—and the children be damned!!!

HIV infection is a serious problem among northern children, over 6,000 of them have the virus...part of it results from prostitution.[7]

Sexualizing Children

Isaan Parade

Lipstick instead of Lollypops

The average age of girls entering prostitution is 16. In my country, the seemingly innocent make-up from eye shadow to lipstick, upswept hair-dos, and classical strapless Thai costumes are all worn by little girls often no more than three years of age. This is done in the name of holiday festivities, pageants, parades, weddings or other special events and does no more than sexualize little girls in the name of tradition.

Miss Sexy Body Competition

Photographer: Apichit Jinakul   *Photo courtesy of Bangkok Post*

How young is too young?

A perfect example was a contest held in 2003 that promoted *"Miss Sexy Body"* for 3-to 12-year olds, a title which was eliminated from the competition just before the curtains were raised. Nevertheless, it was a contest where scantily-clad little girls, in costumes generally found only on strip dancers, were encouraged to parade and perform in a provocative manner.

These events are an all-too-frequent occurrence in Thailand. No wonder it is so easy to exploit young girls who see that their parents, as well as other adults, encourage these activities. Children only want to please and be acknowledged; this is particularly true for young girls who are held to be of far less value to Thai society

110

than male children. It is easy to understand why Thailand, the country of my birth, is a country to which pedophiles flock. Poverty and child exploitation, like this beauty contest, create a haven where pedophiles have no reason to be concerned with their victims. These criminals are safe because until recently, the Thai government as well as the public-at-large have demonstrated *little* concern over their actions even when they are caught.

Thailand's Sexual Hypocrisy

Photographer: Somchai Laopaisarntaksin   *Photo courtesy of Bangkok Post*

Showing off the latest package designs.

A photo campaign using teen-age girls dressed in revealing leather shorts and halter tops to promote Duo Confidence condoms, flagrantly contradicts the government's unofficial "Social order" campaign for preventing sex among teen-agers. Encouraging "Safe sex," rather than the libido, might have been a more responsible choice for this brand of contraceptives.

111

In Thailand, as in the rest of the world, sex is used to market every manner of merchandise from dental hygiene to condoms. Yet, in Thailand, more than in the rest of the world, advertising is unabashedly blatant while simultaneously more seductive. *Jaspal*, an upscale clothing boutique, features in its signature ad a long, leggy Western model reclining on an acrylic chair. She wears an off-the-shoulder blouse that barely conceals the top of her hips and a pair of high-heeled sandals, her right ankle strategically placed on her left knee. An equally tall, attractive, young male model bends toward her, his right hand carefully placed high on her left thigh at the hem of her blouse. What does this photo have to do with Jaspal's merchandise? It would appear nothing, although it definitely grabs the reader's attention with sexual innuendo. It requires the *"50 % off"* copy emblazoned across the left half of the page to inform the reader of its purpose.

Sofitel Silom Bangkok also used an equally seductive photo to attract customers to *Nikai-i, The New Age Dining Experience.* While the handsome young male model reclines on a chaise lounge, his beautiful date kneels on his knees holding a Japanese horsd'oeuvre and her lips just a breath away from his. The copy reads *"...everything from food to the décor and music has been creatively blended to bring you a refreshingly new experience in dining and relaxation that invigorates all your senses."* This provocative ad evokes images of a very lovely evening, one that is intensely more intimate than an elegant dining experience.

When members of Thailand's high-society brazenly flaunt their lovers and make front page news and well-known government officials pay for the sexual services of high-priced prostitutes—what kind of example are they to the young people of my country? In December of 2003, plans were being considered to order a ban on our Ministers of Parliament keeping mistresses and visiting brothels. Outrage was expressed by the MPs--one claiming that keeping a

112

mistress was his right. Another MP claimed that if this order were enforced--only 30 of the 200 MPs in his party now sitting in parliament would remain eligible for their seats.

While Thailand's kiddie contest organizers, advertising executives, and MP's are busily expressing their sexual fantasies in living color and in public without a second thought to the consequences of their actions, the Ministry of Culture proposes a ban on 18 love songs that should be removed from the airways because they are "deemed to romanticize infidelity and sexual promiscuity." Wilasinee Phiphitkul, assistant professor from Chulalongkorn University, stated that "...if the government really wished to tackle social immorality, it should make clear what is right and wrong and those standards should be applied to all industries." For obvious reasons, that will never happen. It would seem apparent to many of us that the first industry to which those standards should apply would be the government in order to set a good example. But the MP's will never give up their "Mia nois," nor will the senior officials ever give up their high-priced prostitutes. They have already asserted their common irate refusal to such an unthinkable idea. "Morality" is not in their vocabulary—at least not when applied to themselves.

Chapter 7

The Creation of Poverty in Thailand:
The Setting for My Future

Definition of Poverty

The American definition of poverty would probably border on my definition of wealth. Asians, particularly Southeast Asians, know true poverty—the kind you see in a *"National Geographic"* magazine, a television promo or magazine ad for *UNESCO,* or *"Feed the Children."*

Struggling to survive in shantytown

Photographer: Kosol Nakachol   *Photo courtesy of Bangkok Post*

Toddlers of poor and virtually homeless families,
all abandoned by the system and living near an expressway,
are left 'home' alone by parents and grandparents who
desperately seek out recyclable waste to buy food.

In the squalor of Bangkok, elderly women, who have usually left the provinces of the Northeast to seek a better life, care for their infant and toddler grandchildren. While living under leaky roofs in shacks that near collapse, their husbands dig in trash bins for recyclable materials to resell. They often go hungry and sleep to relieve the pain. They also have no access to health care nor public services. Until recently, there have been no public services available in my country for those who are desperately needy: the aged, poor, blind, and the physically or mentally disabled. Even though a meager form of assistance has been written into law, it is still almost impossible to apply for and even more difficult to receive.

Abandoned and alone

Photographer: Somkid Chaijitvanit   *Photo courtesy of Bangkok Post*

*An elderly grandmother, forgotten first by her children,
and secondly by her government, finds a safe, lit alcove
in which to sleep on the streets of Bangkok.*

In July of 2003, there were at least 2,000 homeless on the streets of Bangkok (although other estimates reach 10,000) and another 3,000,000 residing in slums—soon to be evicted by landlords who planned to turn their property into commercial developments. The downtrodden, who mostly come from the Northeast and Central provinces, have no money and no shelter. Those who suffer the greatest indignity dig in trash bins for food for themselves and their grandchildren.

Photo courtesy of The Nation

Dogs among 500 destined for cooking pots in Vietnam lie in cages in a truck in Sakon Nakhon (Thailand's northeast). This driver was arrested.

Hotel for the Homeless—Dogs That Is

In Bangkok, plans to erect a five-story apartment building for 1,000 homeless dogs, rather than provide housing to the homeless, are typical of my government's complete insensitivity to the destitute.[1] In contrast, in the North and Northeast, stray dogs are rounded up and thrown into trucks like bags of laundry and taken to slaughter for food. Hundreds of dogs can be seen lying spread eagle and piled high—one on top of another. Some are whimpering, while those on the bottom are silent, having suffocated under the weight of those above. The downtrodden, whether dog or peasant, are sadly given equal treatment by my government. *"The homeless should be rounded up and treated like stray dogs or sent home,"* said the mayor of Bangkok in 2003[2] a statement that reflects the lack of compassion and humanity that Thai bureaucrats have for the poor and disenfranchised.

Words have different meanings in different lands. Poverty is not just a lack of money. It is a lack of every value that cultures and religions hold to be at the heart of their beliefs: honor, morality, pride, honesty, and quality relationships between people—including the relationship between a government and its citizens. Poverty is a lack of financial and material wealth, and it is also a lack of character. Most importantly, in my country, it is frequently an unfair and dishonest allotment of the nation's resources and services. In effect, it is a manufactured gross inequity between the "Haves" and the "Have nots." *Rather than improving along with Thailand's economy, this disparity between the rich and the poor becomes greater every year.*

Thailand: Second Largest Overseas Market for Mercedes Benz

Prior to the 1997 economic crisis, Thailand was the second largest overseas market for Mercedes Benz, following only the USA. The fact that a "Third-world" country with a population of only 57 million could buy more Mercedes Benz' than Japan, England, France, or Italy would be very difficult to understand unless one looked at the simple--yet massive disparity between the wealthy and the poor. The very few amass extraordinary riches because the multitudes, *the common people*, earn incomes that barely sustain themselves and their families. The rich, with the powerful as their allies, make the rules that intentionally create poverty and keep the masses poor. This oppressive scheme has been in place since the birth of my ancestors and maintains a steady supply of ready labor to the wealthy. Thailand's present Prime Minister is a telecom billionaire because he was allowed a monopoly concession by the government of General Suchinda who led a coup and shot down 50 to 100 protestors in the street more than 10 years ago. *Wealth was, is, and will continue to be concentrated in the hands of the very few.*

In the most expensive manufacturing areas of Thailand, the minimum wage paid by foreign companies is only Bt 164/day ($4.35), Bt 4,264/month ($113), for 26 days of labor. Thai companies pay less. The average wage for my people in Ubon is about Bt 100/day ($2.50), Bt 2,600/month ($65)--many earn far less. The poorly paid will never become consumers, a fact that creates more poverty as there is little need for goods and services beyond the bare necessities of life, particularly in the provinces. The poor can never reach that next rung on the ladder, lifting themselves up, generation by generation, from belonging to the "Have nots." They cannot even hope to improve the quality of their lives nor that of their children.

Monopoly: The Only Game in Town

In Thailand, there is little competition; local monopolies are not only allowed, they are encouraged. Criminal groups (including corrupt politicians and "businessmen" who benefit from policy corruption) control nearly every area of my country's infrastructure: transportation, logging, large scale farming, immigrant labor, and land acquisition—to name just a few. Pathetic beggars in the street, airport taxi drivers, motorcycle taxi drivers, and elite strip dance club/massage parlor owners are just a few of those who must pay extortion money to the police, military officers, gangsters--or a combination thereof, in order to stay in business. While thousands of timber logs (one of our greatest natural

118

resources) routinely disappear from national warehouses, the wealthy take land deeds intended for the "landless" in Phuket-- deeds provided to them by government officials. When the fraud is discovered, the investigating land official is murdered. A proposal is made to pay the wealthy for the return of those deeds and discontinue the program. My country's people lose again at the hands of the rich and powerful. My family loses again. *I lose again!*

There is no end to the graft and corruption that pervade every corner of my country—most often by those at the helm who are placed in their high positions to improve the very conditions from which they steal. The Forest Police who arrest timber poachers with six truckloads of teakwood logs are another example of corruption. The thieves and a single truckload of teak are turned over to the government as evidence. The remaining five truckloads are sold and the profits are split between the Forest Police and their chief. As a result, the Forest Police are wealthy and powerful and will gain high government positions. There is simply no way for the poor to advance in my country. This is the very reason that poor girls head to Bangkok and Pattaya to meet sex-tourists that will provide a far higher wage than we could earn any other way. We, alone, receive the financial rewards of the transaction.

What they don't tell you in the "Amazing Thailand" tourism advertisements

Thailand is an obscure country to the Western mind. Elaborate and glossy travel brochures feature exquisitely beautiful young Thai women adorned in richly-ornate and colorful costumes, standing with hands poised and toes flexed in that extraordinarily graceful manner that only Southeast Asian dancers can. Their silky, shiny, raven black hair and their naturally-tanned and perfect bodies give the appearance that they were cut from the Thai version of a Barbie mold.

These same brochures reflect the charming beauty of the countryside highlighted by quiet rivers and peaceful streams, while villagers in their broad-brimmed sun hats throw fishing nets into ponds, lakes, or the sea. In other photos, crystal-clear; turquoise blue oceans snuggle up to white sandy beaches, while emerald green coconut palms sway to the warm, sweet breath of every breeze. Television, magazine, and travel ads reflect a myriad of gold shops--walls covered in red velvet where glittering 24K gold jewelry fills every corner and bedazzles the eye. In these same eye-catching ads, tailor shops abound where one can purchase three custom-made suits with silk shirts; ties; and handkerchiefs; all for less than the price of one "Off-the rack" suit in the West. These richly-colored illustrations and photographs entice the visitor to come play in my country and to discover the greatest bargains in the world, found only in beautiful, tropical, exotic Thailand.

These brochures also reflect Thais prone before Buddha in prayer, or ochre-robed monks performing their morning prayers with alms bowls in hand. In other photos, artisans are delicately carving wood, creating silk flowers, or hand-painting paper umbrellas and gold-trimmed ceramics. Others are cooking and hawking savory noodles, beef salad, and grilled fish. In these photos, the modern day Thai is seen raising well-behaved children dressed in crisp, clean, school uniforms and riding the air-conditioned sky-train to their office jobs as in other civilized societies. Colorful postcards feature smiles on the faces of laborers in the fields. In truth, no one smiles while working in the fields, although a fair wage and a day-off would definitely give them something to smile about. This is only the beginning of the deception my country promotes to the rest of the unknowing world.

The Tourist Authority of Thailand (TAT), for obvious reasons, does not show my village in its advertisements. If they did, dusty roads and primitive living conditions would fill its pages. Our homes are dilapidated wooden structures often built on stilts with corrugated tin roofs and holes in the floors. Trash-filled vacant lots and human waste polluting the rivers where many children swim—this is the Thailand that tourists never see. *This is the Thailand from which I was banished when I was only 13.*

Neither Wealth nor Poverty exits in Nature: Both are Creations of Man
Reasons for Poverty in Thailand

There are many reasons for the poverty of my people. This poverty shapes how we live, what we do, and how we are perceived. You will never read about sex-tourists going to Switzerland nor Monaco to meet teenage girls; young women in these countries have no need to sell themselves in order to buy a noodle cart for their mothers, a VCR for their brothers, or send their sisters to school. I was lucky enough to rise out of this world of poverty. This is a world that creates desperation so great that young, pretty girls from Thailand's poor provinces feel they have no other choice than to see sex-tourists for money in Thailand's many red-light districts.

The types of poverty are many: from that of Ethiopia, Sudan, Pakistan, and other third-world countries--all the way to the poverty in rich Western countries. The poverty in Southeast Asia is not indigenous to its land. Thailand has very high-quality farmland and it produces and exports a great surplus of food. In fact, it is the largest exporter of rice in the world. There is no need for anyone in my country to go hungry, yet tens of thousands do. Bangkok is the worst offender and other major cities follow closely behind. Beggars sit along every street, on every bridge, on every staircase, and under every stairwell; their grief and despair permanently etched in their dark and wrinkled faces as they appear old beyond their years. Most of these beggars come from the villages of the Northeast because begging provides a higher income than the thankless labor of working in the rice paddies.

In America and Europe, there is an abundance of Thai agricultural products--rice, canned fruits, vegetables, and tapioca shipped in raw form. We do not have a shortage of food as in Ethiopia or Sudan due to our mostly fertile soil, good rains— sometimes too good, and "Back breaking" labor which leads many Thais to die much earlier than they would otherwise. Many of the clothes available in the Western world are manufactured in Thailand. These clothes might even have been sewn in Ubon, while others are manufactured in countries even more impoverished and with worse labor rights abuses than in Thailand. Local and international companies manufacture clothing and shoes in Thailand for only one reason: Cheap Labor! In Bangkok, Bt 164 ($4.00) per day, in Isaan --the poorest region in Thailand, wages are Bt 100 ($2.50) per day for a 10-12 hour day; there are many who earn no more than Bt 50 ($1.25) per day for 8 to 12 hours. Organizations like the Occupational Safety and Health Association (OSHA) do not exist; and in fact, even kidnapping and murder are used to keep them out.

No Labor Unions, No Benefits, No Human Rights!
Labor Unions, health insurance, and sick leave are unknown commodities in most of Thailand. Tanong Phoarn, our last union leader, disappeared more than 14 years ago. His case was never pursued by the police at the order of the military; Mr. Tanong played a key role in opposing military dictatorship and fought for the rights of workers. His fate and the names of his kidnappers are known to some. His family lodged petitions with the government in power at the time of his disappearance as well as with succeeding governments. During the past decade and a half, their appeals have received little attention.[3] He was not the only labor union leader to

122

disappear in Thailand. Cambodia's record on labor rights is similar; murder recently silenced their labor union leader. There is no question as to why there has been little union organization and virtually no increase in wages or safety, all over Southeast Asia. The lack of unions keeps corporate leaders rich and laborers poor. At the salary of $4/day, a married couple cannot afford to send their children (especially their daughters) to school. In the villages, one can only dream.

Citizens in countries that have unions, labor rights, and safety regulations earn incomes which allow them to live an adequate lifestyle—allowing them to buy products from those who do not have these protections. Throughout all of Southeast Asia, government spokesmen and corporate heads who work together, hand-in-hand, state that their homelands are not wealthy enough to afford unions; labor rights; freedom of the press; freedom of speech; and true democracy. In other words, human rights are too expensive. *But, it is these rights that create wealth. Human rights are free! In Thailand, the government has taken them away.*

It is a simple matter of economics; many parents don't earn enough money to pay the small school tuition or purchase uniforms and supplies that would enable them to send their children to school. Therefore, their children are deprived of an education. If labor rights were enforced, parents would have enough money to support their households and educate their children. These rights do not exist because the wealthy in my country have the power to keep these rights from becoming law. There should be no question that public schools should be totally free. No child should ever be denied an education due to a lack of family funds.

The downtrodden of my country, in their desire to get increased wages and rights, are often suppressed by the Thai military. The military, police, and criminal groups terrorize people to remind them of who is in charge. This is common knowledge among Thailand's citizens. This is the truth of modern Thailand that is governed by a parliamentary system where the present Prime Minister believes in maintaining total control rather than in decentralizing power. According to his opposition, *"Only I shall be right"* is his mantra, and Thailand's citizens are treated like tenants in their own country while being told to refrain from criticizing the government. [4]

Results of Asian Poverty
"Asian Economic Miracle?" It's Hardly Miraculous!

As I was growing up, I looked around Ubon and saw barren land with miles and miles of poor quality farm land. I couldn't see its beauty but only the land that required me to work from sunrise to sunset in addition to going to school--until I was no longer allowed to attend. There was some money in the province that mostly belonged to crooked government officials and local criminal bosses. As I had no family connections to any of that money, I was destined to contribute to their wealth rather than to my own. The poor citizens of Ubon were the ones from whom these well-dressed and well-protected thieves of status made their money. They certainly had no interest in any of us making any money of our own. As a result, they structured the government; laws; and all of the businesses in the province; so that we were unable to move up from our destitute status. For this reason, there are hundreds of thousands of girls, at this very moment, selling themselves for an income greater than they can earn working in the rice paddies. Their only other recourse is to remain poor—forever!!! *The choice they made, or the one that was forced upon them, was the same one that I felt forced to make many years ago. It was and remains a direct result of Asian poverty!*

Chapter 8

Tourism vs. Sex Tourism

Tourism

People love to visit Thailand. We have approximately 10,000,000 visitors each year. Hotels provide their own vans at the airports to quickly whisk the happy holiday-seeker off to a comfortable hotel room, well-armed with all the information necessary to have an exciting foreign holiday. My country is exceptionally tourist-friendly with everything conveniently arranged to provide the visitor with a stress-free holiday. Thailand has most of its signs in English--even in the smaller cities. Air-conditioned tour buses run every day to every exciting and historical destination any wide-eyed and eager visitor might want to see. A recent addition to public transportation in Bangkok is the sky train that has made traveling in and around Bangkok fun, fast, and efficient. It is also very easy for the first-time traveler to Thailand, with a Lonely Planet Guide in-hand, to traverse my country from Mae Sai in the North, to Phuket in the South--located in the Andaman Sea, across the peninsula to Koh Samui in the Gulf of Thailand, and throughout the countryside.

Many tourists come to Thailand because very little cash goes a very long way. There is a lot of competition between airlines for the tourist's business, so international airfares are inexpensive, as is domestic transportation once the visitor arrives. For example, a tourist from California could spend $300 on a round-trip flight to Hawaii; $150/night for a hotel; and at least another $150/day on food; transportation; and entertainment. Or, one could spend $600 on the flight to Thailand; $30-$60/night on an equivalent hotel; and $50/day would buy everything that $150/day would buy in Hawaii INCLUDING a beautiful young girl--like me! There is no reason for an American male tourist to go anywhere else. Many male

125

Asian travelers agree. They come from Japan, Korea, Hong Kong, Singapore, and Taiwan. They have as much money as any Farang; and they all can have a wonderful holiday without having to count Dollars, Yen or Won.

Sex Tourism

Three of Thailand's most popular Tourist Information Magazines are *"Look," "Touristways," and "Thailand"* available FREE absolutely everywhere, hotels; travel agencies; restaurants; news racks; shopping centers; movie theaters; and shops selling all matter of merchandise from ice cream to upscale jewelry. These *freebies* are nearly impossible to miss.   These three magazines always feature the beauty of my country on its cover: a traditional Thai flower bouquet of lotus and benjamah; the Loi Krathong Festival; the impressive and breathtaking Temple of Dawn; Wat Pho's golden, ornate warrior gods, an elephant trek in Chiang Mai, or any other exotic cultural attraction that will leave the tourist excitedly anticipating his/her holiday, knowing full-well that s/he has chosen the perfect location in which to spend a well-earned vacation.

In *Touristways,* turn the cover and the eager reader will find the first 10 pages filled with glossy ads for custom tailors with prices not-to-be-believed. *One should trust their instincts!* The middle section of this magazine consists of 21 pages in black and white—16 pages provide "nutshell" explanations of my country's most famous tourist attractions, a hotel guide, Airline and Embassy phone numbers, a map of Thailand, and 25 massage services making women available for prostitution: *"Kittens Massage and Escort Service," Sexy Dool Massage and Escort Service," "Hot Special Girls," and "Number 1 Models"* to name just a few. Four more pages within these 25 are advertisements for escort services. The remainder of this mini-tourist guide is filled with glossy and colorful ads for even more massage and escort services with

126

beautiful girls in lacy lingerie revealing lots of cleavage while many are posed to reveal a great deal more. Other advertisers ignore the need to obscure the intent of their services and promote themselves for what they are — *"...We have the hottest girls in town who can give you the sweetest pleasure in your life," "Body to Body massage," "Special Masturbate Show," "Specialist in Fetish and Fantasies," "Hot big men," "Submissive ladies and lesbians,"* and *"All staff have weekly health check."* Half of this guide to Thailand tourist's attractions is selling sex.

"Look's" guide also receives approximately 50% of its advertising revenue from the sex-trade. *"Thailand"* provides about one-third of its advertising space to these same services with a few, small, less-obtrusive ads throughout the magazine. Thailand's not very well kept-secret is out and absolutely everyone is invited to participate in the festivities. *The sex-trade is one of the major sources of foreign revenue in Thailand.*

The one major product that Thailand offers, that Hawaii does not, is pretty girls who will stay with the tourists all night for the cost of an average dinner in the U.S. Young and attractive prostitutes in Hawaii will cost the tourist $400/night. This is why tourists, Farang and Asian alike, come to Thailand instead where a beautiful young woman will cost the fun-seeker only $25.

The Tourism Authority of Thailand (TAT) paints a picture of tourists who arrive to sunbathe on our beautiful beaches and explore our exotic temples. The truth is that many of our beaches are far from their pristine beauty of 30 years ago. One must generally travel to the south of Thailand, far from the popular tourist area of Pattaya to find one. But, few tourists come to Pattaya for its beaches. Few also come to Thailand specifically to visit our many temples, as exquisite as they might be. Ask most male travelers what they think of when they think of Thailand; the answer

127

will most often be available, young, and sexy women. This is the reason that the majority of tourists will always be men.

Sexual access to women has always been a part of Thai culture. Thai and Burmese rulers exchanged young women as gifts for centuries. Females have always played a role in housekeeping, food production, and child rearing; all the while being little more than property. It is just one of the many tragic exploitations existing in my society. The transition from servicing Thai men to catering to foreign men occurred during the 1960s when U.S. military personnel came to Pattaya Beach on R&R from Vietnam. Pattaya's image of a sleepy fishing village quickly changed to one of being infamous for its beautiful women—women who were willing to provide sexual favors for very few baht. Servicing Americans became a lucrative profession.

Thailand would still have tourists if there were no young women available. But without all of the men coming to Thailand for this very reason, airports; hotels; shops; restaurants; and bars would not earn enough revenue to remain profitable. The truth is that the "Very heart" of Thailand's tourist economy would be seriously damaged. *Another very unfortunate truth is that young women like me are grateful for the opportunity to earn money without working in a sweatshop--even if it means servicing men.*

Many of us who work with foreigners are entrepreneurs and independent contractors while girls in the brothels are not. We set the price; we receive all of the profit. No union assistance is required. A poor seamstress in a sweatshop earns 1/10 the amount paid to her employer for an object over which she has labored. Girls who come to Pattaya and Bangkok to meet tourists cut out the middle-man. Government and businesses have set themselves up as "Middle-men" between poor workers and the tourist or overseas shopper in order to "Take the majority" of the profit. We, in the sex-tourism trade, earn far more money on our own while also keeping the profit that is rightly ours because of our direct relationship to the Western buyer. The Thai government and its businessmen beg the World Trade Organization (WTO) for free access to the Western markets in order to access wealthy buyers. Bar girls expect no more and no less! It is that simple. *We are doing the equivalent of exporting our services to a higher wage earner simply by bringing the buyer to Thailand.*

Sex-Tourists' Views

Customers walk around Patpong, Nana Plaza, Soi Cowboy, and Pattaya Beach with "pockets full of money." Some brazenly flash their money and credit cards in a futile effort to add value to their feelings of inadequacy. My clients have told me that they see a bunch of *"Little brown-skinned whores,"* or *"$25 sex machines,"* who are willing and eager to perform almost any humiliating and degrading sexual act to get at their money. It would never occur to them that these same girls have children, are trying to feed their families, or that they are also human. Although these customers view us as trash, they still feel the need to "Pump up" their egos with cash and "Show off" for us--the "Ladies-of-the-night." Their lack of self-esteem and worthlessness is beyond explanation. Those of us in the sex-trade often sleep with men for money out of our own feelings of inadequacy, believing that we have no other skills. Therefore, we know inadequate behavior when we see it. Some customers actually require psychiatric hospitalization. On the rare occasion, others are pleasant and take a genuine interest in our welfare.

There were times when I went with men in whom I had absolutely no interest at all. One time, one man was especially nasty and told me I was *"A waste of rice."* In his eyes, I was so lowly that I did not deserve to receive the minimal cost of rice at Bt 5 (12¢ per serving). He and many other men often referred to us as

"LBFMs" or *"Little Brown F***ing Machines."* We are from a society and a region of a country that is so poor that we leave our rural slums to sleep with their drunken and disgusting bodies that no Western woman would ever entertain. They project their feelings of humiliation and rejection onto the easiest and most vulnerable target—those of us who are desperate for their ready cash and will tolerate their abuse for a few baht. They call us *"Liars and thieves"* when we convince them to send us money for family obligations. We endure all of this to send our sisters to school, pay off family debts, and try desperately to get out of the financial abyss into which we were born. The tourist who occasionally travels to Thailand for sex is different, but for the most part, the men who regularly travel to Southeast Asia for sex have as many emotional problems as we have financial ones--coming from our impoverished villages.

Bar Girls' Views

The truth is that money is what bar girls see and not the man. Our biggest complaint is the poor perception our clients have of us. They may be briefly attracted to us, or that attraction can last over a period of time, but regardless of how much money they might pay us or how long they stay with us--even years, they still have no respect for us. We are their sex-machines, sex toys, or concubines. The painful realization is that because they pay for us, we are a commodity. Earning a living as a prostitute does not automatically surgically separate us from our feelings. We want to be treated as equal human beings. No Thai or Isaan man, nor any male member of our families, sees us as equals. We appreciate how Farang men pay us, and *some* demonstrate concern for our welfare, but few view us as equals; and there are *some who view us as less than human.*

It is because our customers do not see us as people that they cannot understand that we are unwilling victims in the cultural and

130

economic system of our country. Farang tourists spend more in just one day while on vacation than most Thai women earn in a month--waiting tables, sewing clothes, or as hotel receptionists. Few jobs in my country pay a salary of even $200/month without a college degree, an accomplishment that few in Isaan could ever attain. *(A newly-graduated M.D. who accepts an offer of employment with the Thai government will earn from $200-$350 a month).*

Some of us spend our money on mobile phones, gold, and alcohol, but many of us send nearly all our money home to supplement our family's meager incomes. Some of us do a little of both. Most of the farming families of Isaan live in abysmal poverty. They borrow from moneylenders at an interest of 20 % month or much more, and then they slowly but surely get behind in their payments. This is one reason that young girls are motivated to move to Pattaya and Bangkok for work. Their families often borrow this money in order to get over a bad harvest, pay for fertilizer, men's consumer goods--including motorbikes and alcohol, or to play the government lottery.

Thais will borrow to gamble when they believe that they know the winning lottery numbers--money that must be repaid with huge interest. Why would they believe that? Often, it is because their dreams symbolized the winning numbers. We Thais believe that if we dream about fish, we must bet the number 8; about frogs, the number 9; about Buddha, the numbers 8 and/or 9. To dream of a baby indicates that we should bet the number 1; a lady—the number 4; a man—the numbers 5 and/or 6; and shrimp, the number 9. If we dream about human feces--this is a sure sign that we are going to lose. But, in our dreams if we touch and/or play with the feces, we are going to win. We also bet numbers given to us by a monk--prior to his receiving a token gesture of appreciation.

Why I Went With Men: The Economics of Prostitution

Prostitution: The act of performing paid sexual acts.

Attractive young girls leave their poor villages out of desperation and in search of better lives in the city, only to become hopelessly caught up in the business of prostitution. Not every girl leaves her village to do what I did. Some girls work six days a week in hotels and restaurants serving tourists and locals alike, or in sweatshops making the clothes and shoes that are worn in the West. Those girls are exploited just the same. They work under slave-like conditions for greedy, inhumane bosses *who are most often Thai,* receiving only a few dollars a day. Many girls from my province go to the cities for as little as a $20 up-front payment and the promise of $80/month. All too often, that money never materializes, or the Thai employer takes many false deductions in order to keep these girls enslaved. These young women often work all day and all night. At the end of the month, they receive very little of their earnings, or they may even be in debt to the owner because their room and board have been deducted from their salaries. I learned early on that I needed to work with foreigners, so that the fate that befell these girls did not befall me. I always "Sold" directly to the Western buyer and took home all of the profit. *Yet, many girls from my province continue to live in a state of perpetual servitude with never a chance of escape!*

My Options

If I hadn't become a prostitute, my option in Ubon would have been working as a day laborer for $2.50-$3.00 for 10-12 hours per day. This is the reason that a can of sweet Thai pineapple in America is so cheap. It costs less to produce; therefore, it cost less to the consumer. Over time, more work has become available in factories and on golf courses in the tourist areas; the latter is a relatively newer business that primarily serves the Japanese where girls can earn about $5/day plus tips. Due to this substandard wage, many female caddies often sell themselves after a round of golf. At

4' 8" and 75 pounds, I was obviously far too small to carry a golf bag. Female golf caddies are not the only employees *"For rent"* after their workday is through.

Prostitutes who cater to sex-tourists average from $400 to $700 per month. The attractive and more determined girls can earn more than $2,000/month, as I often did. Many also end up with houses paid for by customers; funds to send their children or siblings to school; and to purchase cars, motorbikes, and mobile phones. Girls from the brothels never ever end up with a pay-off like that. Sex-tourism has had the influence of making prostitution an increasingly likely choice for poor girls of Thailand. Although sex-tourists are a small number of Thailand's sex industry's total clientele; tourists pay four to 10 times more than do local men who frequent the brothels. Western men also view girls differently, even those men who come to my country as sex-tourists. These men have influenced an increasing number of girls to enter the sex-trade by offering a better hourly, daily, or nightly rate than was previously available. Also, the prospects of a long-term relationship or marriage, and money for one's children or younger siblings to attend school are a strong attraction.

In the seven years I participated in the sex-trade industry, men spoke to me at length about everything and nothing. I would sit quietly and listen intently as if they were the wisest men I had ever met. All the while, I was steaming inside--waiting for them to finish and *Pay Me!* Yet, as long as they were willing to pay me to listen, I was willing to nod my head, keep my eyes wide open, and my ears closed tight while telling them that I understood. My petite size, my feigned attentiveness, and my youth would endear them to me, and they became increasingly generous. In fact, Farang would pay me just to listen to their ideas and impressions about other Farang men coming to Thailand. *"I used their information to take them for all that I could."* One man actually wrote me a letter when

133

I was 17. I think his feelings were a reflection of the guilt he felt about being with a girl of my age, rather than the very low cost of our encounter. I also believe that he hoped that pouring out his feelings would relieve his guilt or even get me to reduce my price.... *"In his dreams!"*

We, the young women of Isaan, make a "choice," our choices being limited to bad or worse because of our poverty to partake in the sex trade rather than:

1. Earn a few dollars for a 10-to 12-hour workday, 6 to 7 days a week in companies like the Kader Toy factory, a Board of Investment (BOI) approved project, where 188 people were burned to death and 468 were injured due to locked exits.

Kader Toy Fire Memorial

Photographer: Chanat Katanyu   *Photo courtesy of Bangkok Post*

A little girl honors her mother who died in the fire

Toy factory fire victims remembered

Hundreds of labour rights activists and bereaved relatives of the victims of the country's worst industrial fire at the Kadar Industrial toy factory gathered yesterday at the site in Nakhon Pathom to remember the tragedy. Today is the 11th anniversary of the blaze that killed 188 workers, most of them young women from impoverished rural families, and injured nearly 500 others, many seriously and permanently, on May 10, 1993.

The gathering laid wreaths and flowers, erected a temporary memorial and held a parade in honour of those who died. They also called for the establishment of an institution for safety protection in the workplace and a budget and permission to build a permanent memorial at the site. Their attempts to build a memorial have so far been obstructed by the landowner.

Chaliew Liangraksa blamed negligence on the part of the factory's owner for the death of her daughter Wantana. "How can we bear the burden of raising Wantana's young son on the Bt 4,000 per year compensation paid by the factory?" she said.

The Nation, 05/10/04

---

2. Work in the fields 10 hours/day and fight off malaria or other health problems for $60/month.

3. Wash floors in a hotel for $80/month or be a waitress 10 hours/day with two days off each month for $120.

These are the reasons so many girls leave their villages for Bangkok, Pattaya, Koh Samui, Phuket and other tourist resorts. We make the choice to meet and sleep with tourists rather than participate as laborers in Thailand's rapidly industrializing, yet still agricultural and sweatshop-based economy.

Tui

My friend Tui (a non-bar girl) recently got a good job at a good hospital in Pattaya City, one of the top resorts in the country. The job pays about $140/month, considered a good salary. She needed to provide a security deposit of $110. Farangs are not required to provide security deposits to their employers in their countries, nor in Thailand; but Thais are. One evening, she forgot to turn the air conditioner off in her office; the next day, she was penalized $22. That was 15% of her monthly salary. The electricity used could hardly have been more than $3. Recently, her uncle died, and she needed to return home to her village for only three days. She was fined $33 or 23% of her monthly salary. This is standard policy in a good Thai company. One can only imagine what it's like in a disreputable one. This is why I decided to go my own way. I didn't want to work for a Thai businessman, nor have a middleman come between the Western buyer of my services and me.

An attractive and uneducated 20-year old girl can earn $180/month base salary dancing at a GoGo bar. Add this amount to tips from drinks, bar-fines (which her admirers pay to take her out), and direct payments for sex, and she may very well earn $700, or a lot more; GoGo girls earn more than bar girls. My attractive friends and I rarely earned under $1,200/month. Thip made as much as $2,400 on one weekend from one man. This same man also sent her $1,000 the following month. He met her in a shopping mall and asked her to dinner. He never knew she was a prostitute, but simply gave her money as a prelude to marriage. *We learned never to underestimate the generosity of a man who has just spent the weekend with a sweet, young, and pretty girl—20, 30, or 40 years his junior.*

136

Thip

In 1997, Thip, one of the prettiest of all my friends, went to work in Japan. She made about $3,000/month. Her life in Japan had been going very well until one day, while eating in a Thai restaurant, Immigration authorities began questioning her. Thip had overstayed her three-month Student Visa by 21 months. Following two weeks in jail, she and other Thai women were forced to pack their bags for Thailand.

Upon their arrival in Thailand, they were met by Thai authorities who took away their passports and escorted all of them to a location where they would train to become seamstresses, beauticians, or pursue other vocations. Any of these professions could have earned $120/month. So, she did what any bright, freelancing bar girl would do, she returned to Pattaya where she could earn $40/day. Thai sex-workers can return to their villages with an unblemished image as long as they have saved money or contributed to the welfare of their families, in effect, "Made face." This is of primary importance in Thai society. There was no embarrassment in returning to her village after being caught as a prostitute in Japan because she had been sending a lot of money home every month. I once told her that she was so lucky to be born beautiful. She replied, "Great, so I can make a lot of money as a prostitute!!!!"

Suputa

"I am not a bar girl. I am hungry and I have no money. That is why I go with a man." At age 20, Suputa was all of 4' 11" and 77 lbs. soaking wet. She came from Surin, near the Cambodian border. Her mother-tongue was Suay, a dialect of Thai, with strong similarities to Khmer (Cambodian). She started working at a clothing factory when she was 12-years old. She worked 12 hours/day, 6 days/week, for about $80/month. Although it was illegal for the company to employ her at this age, as long as her mother was working there, she was welcomed with open arms.

After several years of slave-like labor, producing clothes for foreign markets, she came to Pattaya Beach to work at the 19th Hole Super Club--a Sports Bar. Although her job was that of a waitress, earning her a monthly income of Bt 4,000/month ($95) and Bt 2,000-3,000 ($48-72) in tips, she would on occasion meet some of the customers after work for another Bt 1,000 ($25). It was not a difficult choice: working as a seamstress for $80/month definitely ranked below that of a "waitress-escort" for an exceedingly higher income. "Face" gained by the additional income far surpassed "Face" lost by being a part-time "Escort."

She once told me that when she was 10, there was no food in her house. Her mother told her to go over to her grandmother's house to see if there was anything to eat. When Suputa arrived, all 30 pounds of her, she asked her grandmother if she could have something to eat. Her grandmother responded, "OK, but don't eat too much." That is the kind of poverty that exists in Isaan, an area that covers one-third of Thailand. That poverty results in the desperation that leads so many girls to the brothels and sex-tourists resorts of Thailand. Not even my family was that poor.

Some Thai girls grow up waiting until they are old enough to go to Bangkok, Pattaya, or Phuket, so that they can earn the kind of money that would not be attainable any other way--with as little education as the government has made available to them. I never considered the sex-trade when I was in Ubon, but to others it is simply a waiting game. Even with an education, many young Thai girls still turn to the oldest profession to support their families and gain *"Face"* in their villages.

Money: The National Pursuit!!!

We would all like to have more money. Everyone in Thailand wants more money. But in Thailand, money is the national pursuit. Besides helping my sister to complete school, I wanted to improve the "Standard-of-living" for my family and the condition of our home in Ubon. *In Thailand, one either has money and lives a comfortable life—a life that comes from the toil, sweat, and anguish of the poor--or one is "The Poor."* In Thailand, to *"Make face,"* one must have money, and the more money one has the more respect one receives. I wanted my family to *receive respect*, rather than to have to *show respect* and to *bow down* to those of wealth.

The only way for me to earn any "real money" in Thailand was to sell my body in the age-old exchange of *"Sex for money."* Thailand has a huge tourism industry, and a lot of it is based upon men coming to my country to meet girls like me. Generally, these men are older, sometimes much older. In rural Thailand, sex is usually reserved until after marriage. I didn't know what to think about the possibility of sleeping with tourists for money; it had certainly never been an option that I had considered while still in Isaan. After moving to Bangkok, I noticed that so many of the girls in the bars and GoGos had no trouble *"going with men,"* and those girls had a lot of money and a lot of gold. They could send home tens of thousands of baht (Bt 10,000 = $400) every month, wear nice clothes, and speak English well. I wanted to have what they had, and be what they were. *I wanted to have "Face" for my family. Most of all, I wanted my mother to welcome me home.*

Who is Responsible?

In order to solve the overwhelming problems of prostitution in Thailand, the Philippines, Cambodia, and elsewhere, the situations which create prostitution must be addressed rather than prostitution itself. Sex-tourism, in contrast to providing sex to locals, is the only way that upwards of 30,000 girls and women in Thailand alone, have of increasing their "Standard-of-living." This does not include the hundreds of thousands of girls involved with locals. The girls are not to blame, nor are the tourists, anymore than one would blame every Western buyer of clothing made in the sweatshops, or every consumer of food picked in the fields of Southeast Asia. Neither the worker nor the consumer is to blame for the exploitation that exists. The blame falls on the shoulders of the government and the business elite which control it. They alone are responsible!

Chapter 9

Working Bangkok

A Day in the Life of a 14-year old "Working Girl"

One of the several jobs I held during my first two years in Bangkok was as a cashier at The Food Center, a restaurant that featured both Thai and Farang food, located at Soi 5/Sukumvit. While living on Soi 93/Sukhumvit, I would wake up at 1:00 P.M., shower, dress, and ride the fan bus #26 or #2 for Bt 2-1/2. The ride to work took about 30 minutes. After several hours of work, the staff would eat shortly before 7:00 P.M. when the dinner crowd arrived. Although the food selection for employees was rather limited, it was free.

When I finished accepting cash from the customers at 11:00 P.M., I would check the bills until 11:30 P.M. Then I split the tips among the counter staff; we usually received about Bt 20 to 40 each. This was the end of my shift. I went into the bathroom and changed into my sexy clothes--purchased with the sole intention of attracting the eager male sex-tourist. I told everyone at work that I was going to a party. I went to work looking like a poster child for *UNICEF* and I left looking absolutely adorable—and highly desirable.

I walked four blocks to Thermae Bar on Sukhumvit Soi 13. Frequently, I would find a client during my short walk to Thermae. I normally received between Bt 700 and 1,000 ($28-$40) for a short-time. A beautiful 14-year-old, walking near the red-light district toward the most infamous bar in Southeast Asia, had no problem meeting the kind of men who visited Thailand just looking for girls like her. I was seeking them out just as they were seeking me. It took little effort on my part to leave them spellbound. After all, I was pretty, petite, and precocious. They generously emptied

141

their pockets while I provided them with fun and fulfilled their every sexual fantasy with an exotic Lolita.

While working at The Food Center, there were two waitresses, a cashier, a cook, and two other counter girls. One early morning, at about 3:00 A.M., the cook saw me on the street with a Farang. The next day, he told everyone at the restaurant causing me to *"Lose Face."* I was very embarrassed and extremely angry; I had to quit. Although prostitution is frequently a "Career of choice" in the tourist areas of Bangkok because there are no other practical options for earning "Good money" and it is not considered a "Big deal," no one at work knew that I had adopted this alternate source of income. I had been promoting the facade of a *"Straight girl"* and my "Cover had been blown."

Personal Relationships:
Jorg from Germany

It was at The Food Center that I met Jorg who picked roses for a living. I stayed with him for a few months after quitting my job. He was kind enough to support me and send me to school. *This was more than my government or my mother had ever offered to do for me.*

Robert from England

Almost simultaneously with meeting Jorg, I met Robert; he was 30-years old and very attractive. He gave me Bt 1,000 the first night and also promised to give me Bt 300 per day to be his girlfriend. I accepted his offer while still managing to make a lot of money on the side--including Jorg's support. I was certainly not going to turn down Robert's guaranteed salary of Bt 9,000/month ($360) while keeping in mind the unlimited financial possibilities available at and around Thermae.

Relaxing in my room

Age 15

Juggling Relationships
Robert vs. Jorg: Double Dipping equals Double Trouble

As fate would have it, Robert and Jorg both lived at the Sai Ban Pen Apartments near the Malaysia Hotel. Robert lived on the 4th floor while Jorg lived on the 2nd floor. Whenever I told Robert that I was leaving his room to go home, I requested my Bt 300. Then I went down to see Jorg on the 2nd floor. After I told Jorg that I was going home, I really did go home. One day, while they were both at Thermae, they struck-up a conversation. Needless to say, they discovered that I was seeing them both—to my great misfortune. This ill-timed piece of information led to a big fight in the bar.

Always the center of attention

Jorg was a good man and wanted me to come to Germany with him where he would take care of me. The German Embassy told him that because I was only 15, I was too young to be granted a Visa. Instead, I asked him to send me Bt 6,000-8,000 per month to take care of me and pay for school while he was away. He agreed and flew home to Germany shortly thereafter. I didn't go to school very long, but failed to mention that to him; I had no intention of jeopardizing my income. He had also seen photos of my sisters. Whenever a man saw that I was taking care of my sisters, he always wanted to help, especially when he saw how cute they were.

Sai and Ying at a waterfall near our village

Steve from the United States

After Jorg left, I met Steve, a really nice American who was working as a teacher in Chiang Mai. He told me that I was lovely; a description I often heard. He also said that he didn't have any money, but still asked me to go home with him. I responded, *"You have no money?!"* He said that he would look in his room when we arrived at his apartment. Upon reaching his hotel room, he said that I looked too young. I said that I was 17. He didn't believe me. I had the receptionist at his apartment read my ID for him; she lied for me. I was only 15. It was there that we showered, kissed, hugged, and slept together.

He had to return to Chiang Mai immediately and I promised to come up and see him. He took the train which is how most Farang travel. I traveled to Chiang Mai by bus which is how most Thais travel. It was a 12-hour journey and Steve met me at the bus station. We spent a few weeks in Chiang Mai. I had never really traveled throughout much of Thailand before and it was nice to see more of my country. Sadly, I also knew that there would be no big money in a relationship with him. He could never support my family, so I made the decision to return to Bangkok.

Once again, my wishes for a healthy, "normal" relationship were dashed by my need to financially care for my family. *In order to do this, I had to unburden the nearest available male of his immediate assets—immediately!!!*

Juggling Relationships
My Mother's "Face" or My Happiness

The two relationships that a bar girl must learn to juggle are those between her family and her clients. On the rare occasion that I met a really nice young man, and I thought that I might like to stay with him long-term, I had to think about the response that my mother would have to my human desire for real affection. No man would be willing to replace my earnings from the GoGos in order for me to stay with him on a long-term basis. My mother would expect me to continue to send home the same amount of money, day after day, "rain or shine," regardless of whom I was with.

It made no difference to her whether I was in a happy relationship or working as a prostitute. Worthwhile young men are looking for girlfriends, not bar girls with parasitic mothers. I could not stay with a nice man because my mother would pester me endlessly for the income that she had become accustomed to receiving. She was only concerned that I continue to feed her insatiable hunger for money and material goods that earned her "Face."

Common Characteristics of Bar girls and GoGo girls

1. We are Isaan; we are not ethnically Thai. Our heritage is Laotian. The difference is that we have darker skin and broader faces than ethnic Thais. We are country people from the poorest region of Thailand.

2. We are not treated equal to Thais.

3. We have a 3rd, 4th, or maybe a 6th grade education. We are not qualified for anything but the lowest-paid employment—or Prostitution.

4. We are from families that are not only poor economically, but many are also dysfunctional and even devoid of conscience. It is not uncommon that many girls have been molested by uncles or step-fathers.

After we have made the major decision to stop seeing men for money on a daily basis, few employers will hire us to work in the tourists areas of Bangkok or Pattaya. They think, and rightly so,

147

that we will not be content with the hard work and wages that they offer for very long. They know that if a tourist wants to see us for a few days, we will "jump ship" because he will pay us the equivalent of one-month's salary, plus also shower us with gifts. A few years ago, a tourist-area Bangkok restaurateur wrote, *"I cannot keep a good waitress employed for longer than a few months. Some tourist or ex-pat will make her a better offer, one with which no restaurant can compete."*

Common Characteristics of Sex-Tourists

Sex-tourists frequenting the GoGos, discos, and bars of Southeast Asia are here for sex and companionship. I assume that they are not getting enough of either at home. I don't know for sure why they solicit prostitutes, but I will provide a few observations based on my years of experience.

1. They are not the most attractive men on the face of the planet. They look nothing like the men we see in American movies or on TV. The occasional handsome guy is often so "full-of-himself" that he believes he doesn't have to pay. *No one is that good-looking!* That is why we often avoid the younger, more attractive men.

2. Older guys also pay more. They always have and they always will! They are also more respectful and have a lower tendency to get drunk and "go ballistic."

3. Many of these men come to Thailand because their wives have left them; they do not communicate with their families; or they cannot find a girlfriend back home. Sometimes they are here for company or "Companionship" which may not even be sexual (although it usually is) that they can't find in their own countries. Thai people, even the poorest of us from Isaan, do not have the same social problems that these men do. If they ever really

knew or understood the problems of poverty that we face, they might be able to reconcile their own problems in the U.S., Europe, or Australia. Many of their problems are of their own creation. *Ours are not!*

4. Some of our clients treat us like their girlfriends; others treat us like their wives; and others treat us like trash. It is an issue of respect. The service we render is in accordance with the behavior rendered toward us.

In the GoGos, there are men who continually touch or grab that part of our anatomy that is closest to them. It has never occurred to these "Barbarians" that we are human beings with feelings. In fact, I don't think that it has occurred to very many people around the world that prostitutes are living, breathing human beings. *"They are only hookers, do what you want,"* is often heard. As far as most men are concerned, we are only sex objects; we are here for their amusement and sexual gratification, and nothing more. We are *"Free for the groping"* as long as we are in the bar.

I have often thought that I would like to take pictures of these men and send those photos back to their wives, mothers, daughters, or employers. I have often, secretly, taken immeasurable delight in the fantasy that I, alone, had been responsible for these crude, rude, immature, and insensitive boors being fired from their jobs. We do become very angry—even outraged! We use our bodies to earn a living; we are not *"Free for the taking."*

Payment determines the difference between our feeling degraded a little or a lot. Payment compensates us for touching and for sex. Believe it or not, *"Copping a feel"* without payment leaves us feeling violated. Most girls do not mind being "pawed" as long as tips for drinks or money is exchanged for the groping. This is considered fair exchange. Those who grab for free are viewed as disrespectful. When the girl receives money for the action, it becomes acceptable. *Although it may be a surprise to the reader, GoGo girls have their standards too!*

Bar girl and GoGo Girl Etiquette

Some of the men, who my friends and I have met, have asked us to stay with them for a few weeks, a few months, or longer. If other clients want to see a different girl every day, that is their choice. We don't mind if they make this decision. On the other hand, it is not acceptable for a man to ask one girl to go home after sleeping with her co-worker the night before. This is considered extremely rude and very disrespectful. The rule is that if a tourist is not happy with one girl or another, he should try a different GoGo. Two girls will inevitably fight because the first one will *"Lose face"* over not being taken again. The second girl is also "taking" an income that might have otherwise gone to the first one. As much as the *mama-san* wants to receive the bar-fine, she would rather not have problems created by girls fighting over the same man's money.

Cultural Courtesy

Maybe in the U.S. it is acceptable for people to touch each other on the heads, but in Thailand it is not. Although many of the girls get used to it, and will accept it if we believe that it will lead to the payment of a bar-fine, we would really rather not have sex-tourists touch the top of our heads as soon as they meet us. It is a Buddhist precept; we do not expect tourists to understand it, but we do expect them to abide by it. It is the first or second rule mentioned in every Thai travel book.

My Friend Nan

While working in Patpong, I met a pretty girl my age named Nan. The first time I saw her was at Crown Disco. We were both 14, and we were both there to meet tourists. As we were the same age, spoke the same dialect, and were both seeking to rise

150

above our poverty, we quickly became friends. In Patpong, we were little stars; young, beautiful, and reasonably well-to-do. This was an incredibly different life from that of a rural village. It is what attracted so many young girls, and it is the reason we stayed.

Nan was my best friend for a long time. She came from Mukdahan, an Isaan city on the Mekong River, at the Laotian border. The population is rather small, and there is little there in the way of business or tourism. Her village, as mine, held no prospects for a better life. So like me, and thousands of other young women, she came to Bangkok to improve her life.

Nan started seeing men when she was *only 13*. Like me, she never had a childhood; she was also from a poor home and had no other way to take care of herself. She also received no support from her family. She was one of the few to start out even earlier than I did. We both danced at the discos and made very good money. We shared a room together and had "Comfortable" lives considering we were freelancers in Bangkok and saw tourists for a living. We always had plenty of money to do whatever we wanted to do, go where we wanted to go, eat what we wanted to eat, and buy whatever we wanted to buy. We had the money necessary to buy *"Face"* in this "Land of Make Believe."

Nan and me at Peppermint Disco, "Knockouts" at only 15.

Seeing us at the door, sex-tourists stopped "in their tracks."

Nan couldn't speak English very well, but her looks more than made up for it. She was six inches taller and more slender than I was. She had longer limbs, larger breasts, lighter hair and skin, and more subtle features. On the other hand, I was pretty, petite, and I could speak some English. I learned to speak English quickly because the more English I could speak, the more money I could earn. To be brutally honest, it helped me to separate my clients from their money. *Fortunately, I was a quick learner.*

Nan used to make a lot of money from Farang or Asian men who she would meet on the street, or at places they would frequent while they searched for underage girls. She would take that money--a lot to a 14-year old in Thailand, and head off to the Thai discos; she would buy drinks for young, attractive Thai men while pretending to be from an upper–middle class family. This was her escape from reality. This was the opposite of my behavior; I would never consider doing anything for a Thai man. I didn't care what they thought of me, and I had no interest in helping them nor in gaining their approval. I didn't like Thai men. I made sure that as much of my money as possible went to my family, and I made very sure that neither of my sisters would ever have to follow in my footsteps. Nan, on the other hand, had only herself to look out for; she had left her family at the age of 13, and she had not been in touch with them since.

I always went with Farang men while she sometimes went with Asian men from Japan and Hong Kong. It was not due to her lack of English skills--Farang do not take us to talk. As she had lighter skin, Asian men were attracted to her and really wanted her. She also preferred how Asian men treated her. In contrast, I much preferred how Farang treated me. In fact, I would never even consider going off with an Asian man, even if they did pay more. I had my preferences and she had hers.

153

Nan and I made more money than most of the girls. It was for reasons other than the fact that we were young and attractive. Most Farang tourists are here simply to find sex that they could not otherwise find in their own country--especially with girls as young and attractive as we were. Although, it is also true that some men were into more unusual activities. They enjoyed sex with two girls instead of one. That was where Nan and I came in. We would often initiate the idea of threesomes whenever a man had an interest in only one of us. Most men just wanted one girl, but some of them could be convinced that a threesome would be a sexual fantasy fulfilled and the highlight of their holiday. They would pay a premium for this service. If the going price for a night was Bt 1,000 ($40.00), then together Nan and I could usually get Bt 4,000 ($160.00). We would earn double the money for one-half of the work.

When Nan and I would go home with one guy, she always wanted to spend lots of time with him while I was *"Strictly business."* Nan wanted to make friends; I wanted to make money. She was very friendly and feigned a lot of interest in their affairs, although she didn't know what they were talking about. This would really irritate me; I wasn't interested in anything more than the next dollar, and every minute spent with one man was another minute taken away from locating another paying client. I was always in a hurry and tried to make the guy happy enough to pay us ASAP so that we could get back to the disco and meet another customer.

Abortion

I was 15-years old and I had been seeing a British man for a few months. He treated me very well, and I was so happy to be with him that I became his live-in girlfriend. He was a lot older than me, but younger than most of the men whom I had seen in Patpong. The time finally came for him to return home and while I was very sad, I also hoped that this just might also be my "ticket" out of Thailand. I was silently filled with anticipation, desperately wishing to believe that he would ask me to go home with him.

He was one of the first Farang with whom I really wanted to stay. Like so many girls in Patpong, I hoped beyond hope that a Western man would take me with him—far away from Thailand. This is the dream that fills the heart and soul of nearly every bar girl—that one day she will find a man who truly loves her and will take her away to a better life, taking financial responsibility for her and her family--forever. Finding a boyfriend is only the first step; getting him to ask you to stop working at the bar and offering to supplement your family's finances is the second. Getting married in Thailand or getting a Fiancé Visa to his country is the third. I was standing on the first step of that ladder and deep, deep in my 15-year old fantasy world, I was incredibly happy.

One day, he told me that he had to return to his country--alone. I was heart-broken. Not only had I fallen in love with him, but my secret dreams of moving to Europe, living a prosperous new life, and leaving the sex industry for good were shattered. Immediately following his return to England, I returned to work; staying at the discos until 2:00 A.M. and going to Thermae Bar until sun up, or until I could get a customer. I would have much preferred to go to England, even with its cold, damp, and drizzly weather.

In love and only 15

A little more than a month following his departure, I missed my period. Initially, I didn't think much about it. When I missed the second month, I realized that I was pregnant; I couldn't believe it. I didn't want to be a mother; I was only 15-years old. But, if I were going to have a baby, I was happy to have his baby. There were so many possibilities: We could marry and live in England; I could get a Visa with our baby; or he could send me money and I could care for our baby here. Or, he could come to Thailand and stay for a month, twice each year, a common scenario among many men from the West who have Thai wives and children. Regardless of our final decision, I knew that I would have him, and that he would have me--forever. I was at peace. Although I was not ready to have a baby, I was ready to do whatever I had to in order to have and keep this man, and to improve the future of my family.

My rude awakening came while speaking with him on the phone. I told him of all of the possibilities available to us. He responded with one that had never occurred to me. He stated that he would send money for an abortion. I was surprised, frightened, and terribly hurt. I said *"I am carrying a baby, not a dog."* I cried that we could not kill it like a farm animal. He expressed no interest in me, nor the baby--my baby, his baby, our baby! He wanted no future responsibility for our child. He would do no more than send money for the abortion. He wanted no longer to be my boyfriend, and he never wanted to be my husband. My dreams for my baby, of marriage, and for the future of my family in Ubon had all disappeared into the blackness of this single devastating phone call.

I could not continue to work and send money home if I had this baby. Reluctantly and tearfully, I accepted the money and I had the abortion. The emotional pain and loss that I suffered brought grief that could not be easily dismissed. Rather than realizing my dream of marriage and a comfortable life in Europe, I was going to a hospital to sacrifice the life of my unborn baby in order to continue to support my family. This would not be the time that I would be so fortunate to leave behind the poverty and degradation that I knew only too well. I would return to my life as a free-lancer. I was in despair, yet I had no time to indulge my emotions.

From earliest childhood, poor Thai women are filled with the notion that we are "Girls" until we have a baby. It is only with this act of childbirth that Thai society views us as having become "Women." In other words, we must first become a "Mother" in order to earn the title of "Woman." We are never valued as individuals. Once we have children, we have little time, energy, or money, to pursue life's other educational or employment opportunities. Society will rank us by our performance as mothers and/or by our relationships with the men in our lives—our fathers, brothers, or husbands. Poor Thai women are never valued as productive human beings—as individuals in our own right, even though we are financially responsible for our families.

"Too many women...
From too many countries...
Speak the same language...
Of Silence."

A letter entitled *"The Female Squad Has Shown the World It Will Not Be Silenced,"* written to the Bangkok Post on August 8, 2004, cited the above verse written by a teen-aged East Indian female. The author noted that as a Thai male growing up in Thailand, he "witnessed a lot of women being treated like submissive slaves and sex-objects by too many men." His letter was in response to Thai female weightlifting competitor, Yaowapa Boorapolchai, winning an Olympic gold medal. *"This has proved to everyone that women are now speaking with their true voices. I hope that all of you are proud to call yourself 'a woman,' because you have earned it so...."*

Thai women from my poor socio-economic sector of society want to have children to provide for their future support when they can no longer provide for themselves. Thailand is primarily an agricultural nation. Poor Thai people generally work outdoors. They are subjected to scorching heat, dusty air, and contaminated river water. They work from dawn until long after dusk, and as a result they are often physically depleted by age 50. A woman of 50 will often look 10 to 20 years older than she really is. They need their children to financially care for them when they can no longer be the providers. Children are not only a Social Security system, but for their mothers, they are much more. Thai men have a reputation for being on the far side of monogamous. They wander when their wives are young, and they often wander permanently when their wives have aged. Asian women, poor Thai women in particular, have children in order to have someone love and care for them after their husbands no longer do.

Bangkok John

I had been working for two years in Bangkok; from cleaning up after customers in the Cockatoo Club, and cashiering at The Food Center, to cultivating customers of my own, when I met an American named John. He was employed by a large U.S. company with a branch in Bangkok, and he earned a lot of money. He had a great place to live, a fine car, a big screen TV, a mobile phone before everyone else did, and all the comforts. He showed a lot more interest in me than any one ever had before. It didn't take long for me to learn in what direction those interests would lead.

John had so much money that he could buy just about anything that he wanted, particularly in a poor country like Thailand. He enjoyed his money and spent lavishly. He dined well and never waited for anything. He simply pulled out his wallet and paid for whatever he wanted—on a moment's notice. Although money *"Talks"* in the rest of the word, it *"Screams"* in Thailand! He knew many restaurant and bar owners and a lot of other rich Americans living in Bangkok. One would have thought that he owned this exciting city as he strutted his way from one late night spot to another. He stayed out late and enjoyed everything Bangkok had to offer--including very young girls like me. John had a preference for us. He had other prurient desires as well. I was neither the first, nor the only 15-year-old he would meet. He knew where girls my age worked and he scoured the city looking for us. He was not the only man who liked young girls, but he was the one who was the most attracted to me.

I started to see John pretty regularly—at least once each week—sometimes more often. He was a little different and a little rougher than most men. I always thought there was something peculiar about him, but I was not sure what it was. We had been seeing one other for a little while when I learned what he was really looking for. John had highly-unusual desires. It was not only that he enjoyed young girls, but that he enjoyed S&M (Sado-Masochistic) sex with them as well. I had never been with a man who wanted S&M. A man taking pleasure in slapping me was beyond my understanding. How could this make him feel good? What benefit could he possibly receive from inflicting pain and bruises upon my tiny body? I thought that I was someone to whom he was sexually-attracted, someone from whom he wanted to receive sexual pleasure. How could he intentionally cause me this pain? I wondered where he learned of this perversion. *What would his family think if they only knew?*

My English did not have to be very advanced for me to understand how much money John was offering to pay me to be the object of his perversion. He didn't have to speak Thai to understand that I agreed. He did not just pay well; he paid exceedingly well! In fact, he was the best-paying steady customer that I had ever had. He paid double that of most men. I learned to live with his bizarre personality, perverted behaviors, cruel infliction of pain, and his blatant disrespect. I hated the time I spent with him, and I hated myself even more. Yet, I made the decision to endure this insanity for the payoff--for the *"Big Money."*

In Thailand, money is everything. Money is so important that Thais, rich or poor, will do almost anything for it. Not only had I started to sleep with men at the age of 14, but a year later I was involved in S&M--for an extra $20, $30, or $40. Every extra dollar counted. While American and European 9th graders were discovering the opposite sex--I was allowing the opposite sex to brutalize me—for the grand sum of $60 or $80. I was willing to sacrifice my body and soul to put my sisters through junior high school, to improve my family's shed of a home, to be allowed to return to my family, and most importantly, to be loved and accepted.

John had been married many years earlier and had a teen-age daughter in the U.S. I had the opportunity to meet her on the occasions she came to Thailand. What I learned about her was interesting, and what I learned about John was even more interesting. She was a tall, slender, and pretty 13-year-old. She had all of the characteristics that I wished I had--long legs, blonde hair, fair skin, and blue eyes. I thought that she must have looked like John's wife. On her visits, I cooked great food or bought "Take-out" for all of us; I made every effort to be an older sister to her. Although she tolerated me, she was unfriendly, and she was definitely unhappy that I was around. After her first visit, I realized how very much she disliked me, and I tried to limit my time at the house whenever she was there.

I learned that John had not been much of a father while he was married—and certainly not after he left. He thought money would be a satisfactory substitute for his absence. Like many foreign men who live in Thailand, he was greatly mistaken. John was protective of his daughter—far more protective than most parents. He was obsessed with her whereabouts and imposed many restrictions on the kind of friends she had. He lived in fear that she would date boys--a normal teen-age activity that was forbidden to her. If he learned that she defied this rule, he would "Go through the roof." His biggest fear was that someday she would meet a man--a man just like him!

Bangkok John took me to Singapore a couple of times when he had business there. He was about 50; I was 16. When we went through Passport Control in Bangkok, the Immigration official told me that I was too young to enter Singapore as I was not yet 18. But, he also had no legal way of restricting my leave. I continued through Immigration and to the departure area. The flight was uneventful, but it was exciting to be on an airplane going to see a new country. In Singapore, Immigration asked me a few questions then allowed me to enter. John quietly stood a distance away.

In Singapore, I stayed in a fine hotel while John went to work everyday for his U.S. firm. We traveled first-class at the company's expense and enjoyed the best food and drink the hotel had to offer--and room service as well. John told me to stay in the hotel all day. He worried that I might look around and find someone much younger and much more worthwhile than him. He also worried that I could possibly be picked up by the police for being so young and out alone during the middle of the day. In Singapore, all 16-year olds are still in school-- unlike Thailand, where many children above the age of 12 are already working. My height and appearance would have immediately drawn the attention of the police or a truant officer.

John took me to see many tourist attractions and bought me my first mobile phone. I was thrilled with my new toy! I kept it for a few weeks until I decided that I had even more interest in the money it would bring. We dined out at several Thai restaurants because I had no interest in Chinese or Western food. He also introduced me to the MRT (subway and sky-train). It was very quiet, very fast, and I was thrilled to ride it for the very first time. Bangkok's own sky train had been under construction for years and was finally completed in 1999—three years after its scheduled opening and millions of dollars over budget. This was typical of the manner in which my country did business.

During my three years in Bangkok, I had become a seasoned professional while still rather young. I was sought out by former customers and sought after by new ones. I was beautiful and it took little for me to attract the most discriminating set of eyes. I was comfortable with my new profession and I knew my way around.

Already a professional

…and only 15

A Day in the Life of a "Working Girl," Now 16

I would get up around 3:00 P.M., shower, and dress. I would stop at one of the many paint shops (beauty salons) to have my hair done and my make-up applied. This would cost about Bt 50/$2. I would grab a bite to eat at one of the noodle stalls in Patpong prior to arriving at Crown Disco, or any other similar venue, at 8:00 P.M. I would dance all night, or until I met a man who liked me. That could happen at 9:00 P.M., 11:00 P.M., 2:00 A.M., or not at all.

If a man wanted me, we would go back to his hotel for sex. After sex, I would collect my Bt 1,000 ($40) and return to my small room; or I might choose to get something to eat at one of the many sidewalk food stalls that are opened all night. In the past hour, I had just earned as much as a dishwasher makes in two weeks. Finally, it would be time to sleep. After marketing my charms all night, I needed sleep and a lot of it.

If the evening were slow and I hadn't met anyone that night, my friends and I would go over to Thermae Bar. We would share a cab or a tuk-tuk (a three-wheeled open-air taxi) to get there; Thermae was always full of men. Many of the tourists went there in order to avoid paying a bar-fine. I would often meet a man because as was one of the youngest and smallest girls, I stood out from the crowd. From the bar, we would return to his hotel for sex. I would collect my Bt 1,000 ($40), and maybe pick up something to eat on my way home at 4:00 A.M.

On the rare occasion that no one picked me up from Thermae, I would go home around sun-up and then sleep until 5:00 P.M. I would return to the same schedule seven days a week, 52 weeks a year. I might stop by the doctor's office and pay Bt 200 Bt ($8) to get a health stamp certifying that I didn't have a sexually-transmittable disease (STD). This was useful to show customers

Who's cute?

that I was disease-free. I wasn't checked for an STD—that cost $12. There were doctors willing to sell us a health stamp for $8.

Why I Left Bangkok

The Bangkok police decided to start enforcing the laws against underage "Working-girls" frequenting the discos. This placed Nan and me in an unfortunate situation as we were only 16. Now, we were not only unemployed, we were also unemployable in Bangkok. But, we had an idea. We decided to take a bus to the beach resort of Pattaya City (the city of open-air bars and GoGos) where the police DID NOT enforce the "Under-18" laws (in exchange for regularly-paid bribes). "Jimmy the Switch" helped us move from Bangkok to Pattaya. Upon our arrival, he saw that we had a place to stay and food to eat. This beach city was a welcome change from the heat, traffic, and pollution of Bangkok.

In Bangkok, and throughout the rest of Thailand, the police owned their own brothels full of 14, 15, and 16-year-old girls who were there for Thai men and ethnic Chinese tourists. But, when it came to the foreign media exposing the girls who were under 18 in Patpong and Nana Plaza, the government did not want *"Mud on its face."* It chose to enforce the "18-and-over" rule in those areas, for the purpose of appeasing the foreign media and putting on an *"Honorable face."* Or, at least they made it appear so. In truth, they closed the doors to their brothels and reopened as massage parlors, karaoke bars, and restaurants—while others went underground. None of the underage girls, myself included, thanked the foreign media for exposing a situation which terminated our employment. *Although the foreign press managed to change the location of our employment, they could not change our job descriptions!*

It is critical to young girls everywhere that the foreign press has expressed vital interest in this issue of underage prostitution. Exposing the grave reasons poor young Thai girls seek this tragic way out of poverty is vital to the world at-large in order to stop those who would take advantage of their desperate situation. Far too frequently, girls are sold by their parents, wittingly or unwittingly, into the sex-trade—an inhumane situation that occurs all over Southeast Asia. When not sold, they are often tricked into the trade which can be the beginning to a young life savagely cut short. On the other hand, making the choice to "Freelance" is a contradiction in terms. The choice is between choosing the Sex-trade and providing for one's family or allowing them to continue to exist in abject poverty. Elder daughters of Isaan are not allowed that choice. *Our culture has made it for us.*

Chapter 10

Pattaya: A Sex-tourist's Paradise

"Pattaya, a unique "Sin City," with an originality all its own, has a multi-billion dollar, multi-national sex industry with links to drug trafficking, money laundering and an expanding regional cross-border traffic in women."[1]

Building sandcastles, Age 16

"Jimmy the Switch"

"Jimmy the Switch" or "Jimmy the Twist" lived in Bangkok. I met him through "Bangkok John." Sick men tend to have sick friends. He was the most sexually-perverted man I had ever met. He initiated nasty behaviors during foreplay that normal, healthy men would never even consider.

"Jimmy the Switch" earned his name because he went both ways. He equally enjoyed attractive young Thai boys and Thai girls. He was also called "Jimmy the Switch" because he liked to hit his victims with a stick or a switch. His other nickname was "Jimmy the Twist" because he was a twisted and sadistic man. As with Bangkok John, he not only liked S&M, he relished it. I didn't like being hit with a switch; it hurt a lot. But, I put up with it for the sake of money. I couldn't think of any other way that I could earn as much.

Jimmy's behaviors were beyond bizarre. Under the guise of teaching young girls sophisticated sexual techniques, he would gradually lead them into increasingly more degrading acts: urinating on them; forcing them to say, *"I'm a piece of shit;"* beating them; and destroying their self-image and their self-esteem. He hurt them physically and he broke them psychologically. Although he told them he was doing this to increase their sexual pleasure, the truth was that he was punishing them for being women. He was incapable of responding to the desire they incited within him. He couldn't maintain an erection for very long and he had a bad back that impaired what little sex he could perform. He punished women for his inadequacies. He took pride in saying that he was a pervert. I think that he was being much too generous. *The fact is that he was Evil—pure and simple!* Never did he exhibit any compassion for the girls he hurt. They were objects for "Sexual experimentation" and torture—and nothing more.

170

I was one of those objects. Jimmy would beat on my breasts and urinate on me. He would start out by urinating on my crotch while I was sitting on the toilet; gradually move up to urinating on my breasts, and finally urinating on my face. As much as I hated it, I allowed him to do whatever he wanted to because deep down inside, I had no self-respect. His sick behavior became even sicker as I continued to offer myself up to be beaten, battered, and defiled—all for the sake of money. It was only with money that my nightmares of my sisters replacing me in this *Living nightmare"*--would never come true. I was in Pattaya to make money, and I would do whatever I had to for as long as I could stand it.

Why would I, or anyone, put up with physical, emotional, and sexual abuse to this extreme? The simple answer is nearly $600/month for an hour or so, every day. This gave me my nights free to work in a GoGo, or to look for men elsewhere. Our agreement was that I could work my "regular job" and also have an extra $600. For girls in my position, this was considered a very good arrangement. An option would have been to find a man so "taken" by me that he would send me that kind of money from overseas while he waited to return to Thailand.

Jimmy paid me the usual monthly stipend of about Bt 15,000 ($600). He also kept a daily record of every single baht he ever gave me: Bt 5 for a bag of potato chips, Bt 10 for a bowl of noodle soup, every single baht was recorded. At the end of the month, he would show me the accounts, and I would often receive only one-half of the agreed upon amount instead of Bt 15,000. I never thought about this during the month when I was being subjected to such unspeakable humiliation. Jimmy also liked to play pimp. He would call around to see who wanted to purchase my services that day. He claimed that he did this so that I would not have to personally suffer rejection. The truth is that he liked to impose himself between other men and me.

On one occasion, a client had a portrait of me painted from a photograph. He had it framed and he was going to give it to me for my birthday. He made the mistake of showing it to Jimmy who came directly to me to tell me all about it, stealing the other man's joy of seeing my surprise. Jimmy was twisted, devious, and evil!

On another occasion, he asked me to come over to see him. Upon my arrival, I discovered that he had a 16-year old Thai boy with him. He wanted me to watch the two of them together. Since I was being paid for watching, I agreed. They played around for a little while, and then Jimmy motioned to me to perform oral sex on the Thai boy. I snapped back *"You do it! I never touch Thai men!"* He decided to change his mind rather than risk losing me.

When my brother and sister had a serious motorcycle accident, Jimmy called all of my clients on my behalf, soliciting donations for the hospital fees. Another client of mine was ahead on his payments to me at the time because I had borrowed from him, but he still gave me Bt 16,000. Jimmy gave me nothing, pleading poverty as usual whenever I needed anything above and beyond the large sums of money that I was already sending home to my mother. Everyone who donated instructed me to take the money home and pay the hospital in-person. I didn't listen and I deposited all of it into the bank. Of course, my mother withdrew it immediately. Later, I learned that she never paid the hospital bill. She kept it all—every single baht!

My brother's accident demonstrates just a few of the myriad of problems in Thailand. We have a lot of collisions on motorbikes and it is usually young men who are responsible for them. My brother caused this accident; my sister Ying sustained serious injuries to her leg; their medical bills totaled Bt 16,000—the

172

equivalent of my income from sleeping with 16 old men. The motorbike was destroyed; a bike which I had paid for by sleeping with 30 old men. My sister was injured; my mother pocketed the money; my brother bore no responsibility; and I paid for all of it.

Working Pattaya Beach

After living with Jimmy while freelancing for a couple of months, it was time that Nan and I found jobs. Pattaya had about 200 bars and another 40 GoGos. As we were young and pretty, it wasn't going to be difficult for us to find work. Shortly after our arrival, Jimmy asked me to marry him. When I declined, I decided it would be better if Nan and I found our own place to live.

Pattaya was, and remains, a great place for attractive girls to meet tourists. There were lots and lots of them, spelled "CUSTOMERS," and the cost of everything was less than in Bangkok. The weather was a major improvement from the heat and humidity of Thailand's capital city, and the cool, ocean breeze blew the beads of perspiration from our neon-lit faces. There was also less traffic and less pollution than in the big city of Bangkok. This was a dream city to work my trade. That is probably why it maintains bar girl employment in the neighborhood of 10,000 at all times. There isn't another city in the world that can compete with Pattaya for the number of prostitutes available for sex-tourists. The more girls there were, the more tourists they would attract. I never had to worry about my competition. I was pretty, charming, clever, and my English skills had become quite good.

When Nan and I first arrived in Pattaya Beach, we ran around the city checking out potential customers by watching to see who noticed us. We did this for a while until we met a few men whom we began seeing regularly. *There was no shortage of clients for lovely 16-year olds!* We met many men who lived in Pattaya and who were happy to see us a couple of afternoons each and every

173

week. We had lots of time on our hands and lots of money in our pockets. It was a financially rewarding life for two poor girls from Isaan. This was so much better than being in Bangkok. One of the best things about this city was that it was full of native Isaan speakers. The shops were full of Isaan girls and the food stalls were full of Isaan people. I could speak Isaan virtually everywhere I went. It was great. We should have come down here earlier.

Tony

I met an Englishman named Tony while staying at Marine Place on Soi Buakhow. One day, my phone rang and a lady named Lo was calling from England. *"Oh sorry,"* she said, *"Can I speak to Tony."* I said *"There is no Tony here, only Nan and Lon."* She responded, *"Oh! Isn't this room 304?"* I said, *"No, you have the wrong room."* She hung up the phone. Always thinking about new ways to increase my income, I wondered if Tony couldn't be my next customer. I called room 304 and asked for Tony. When he answered and said that he was Tony from England, I acted so surprised. I acquired a new client and a lifelong friend.

Tony treated me very well. He took me to English pubs on Soi 8 and a holiday in Phuket. We traveled to animal parks, Samet Island, Nong Nooch Village, and the Crocodile Farm. We also saw live shows and flew on airplanes. I was beginning to like flying. Sometimes, he even took Nan. Tony had fallen in love with me. *I had become so charming and desirable that a very nice man wanted to marry me. I was only 16.*

My happiest moments with my friends

Dumbo

Smokey

Tony...then again, who's the real tiger?

George

Jorg returns to Thailand

A year after I first met Jorg in Bangkok, he came to Pattaya to search for me—to no avail. I had told him that I had found a new school in Pattaya—one which he believed he was paying for. He returned again, this time he found my apartment at Marine Place. I wasn't at home but at Larn Island with Tony. Jorg slid an envelope under my door. When I returned, I opened the envelope, saw the money, and never read his letter. I had no interest in his letter. *His money or anyone's money was all I cared about*! When Tony came in the door, he asked about the envelope. I told him that it was from my mother. He didn't know that my mother was illiterate.

Later that evening, Jorg called. I told Tony to see his friends that night. That gave me the opportunity to renew my relationship with Jorg, or at least that part that brought money my way. Jorg came at 8:00 P.M. He spoke Thai, so he stayed chatting away for two hours. He asked me to marry him even though he was angry after learning that I had quit school. I avoided answering his question. I suggested that he return home and that I would meet him at his apartment later.

I showed up very late that night, making him wait and wait. When I arrived, I told him that I had AIDS. He didn't believe me. So I told him, *"Okay, let's have sex and then we can go to the doctor."* Through tears, he swore at me endlessly. In a way, I had always enjoyed being able to make men angry and hurt them. It was my way of getting even for all of the pain that they had caused me. After he finished his outburst, he left for Bangkok. He called me everyday after that.

On the other hand, Tony was worth Bt 1,000 to Bt 1,500 per day, plus lots of shopping, food, presents, and fun. *In essence, he bought me happiness*. So, I chose to hold onto him. I didn't really care about Jorg, Germany, marriage, or school--only about the money I was receiving from Tony. Tony decided to become my long-term boyfriend, although he eventually returned to England for three months. From England, he sent me Bt 10,000 every month. That is a very good boyfriend in my eyes. I became very lonely without Tony around, so I used some of the money to buy a dog to soothe my loneliness. I named him "Lucky."

Lucky and me

Cedrik

Following Tony's departure, Nan and I started our new careers at Pretty Girl GoGo. I had not been there long when I had a fight with the 35-year old *mama-san* whose jealousy stemmed from the great money I earned through bar-fines, tips, and lady-drink commissions. Although she appreciated the money I generated for the bar, she definitely didn't like my personally earning so much money and getting so much attention while she earned so little. Following the fight, I quit and Nan left with me. We found work at Sexy GoGo, which is where I met the first man I was to marry, a 25-year old Swiss named Cedrik. He was only eight years older than me and the youngest man I had ever stayed with.

Cedrik and I met on his very first trip to Thailand. Once he saw me at Sexy GoGo, he was smitten. I went home with him every night from the first evening we met. We would spend the day together, along with his friend and his friend's Thai girlfriend. He spoke French and knew only a little English, so it was difficult to communicate. Sometimes his friend would serve as translator; other times, he would just nod his head as if he understood me. I was surprised that a Swiss man couldn't speak English, having had all the advantages of a good education in a rich European country. I thought that if I, a poor and uneducated young Thai girl could learn, so could he. This was not to be the case.

Cedrik was a computer specialist. He knew nothing about girls, nor the ways of the world. He especially knew nothing about the ways of the girls in *my* world. He was a "Mama's boy" and new to Thailand. He was every bar girl's dream; he had lots of money and the desire to show it off. Bar girls who have been working the tourist scene for a while, generally have the ability to quickly help these naïve and unworldly young men empty their pockets. Cedrik really wanted to impress me. We ate at expensive restaurants and stayed at nice hotels. This was in contrast to his normal life in

Switzerland where he lived at home with his mother. His father had died years before, and he and his mother had only each other. He knew nothing of the world, but he was about to learn. He was soon to take a "Two-week Intensive" in life, and I would serve as his teacher.

I always loved meeting men who were new to Thailand. A phrase frequently heard among bar girls is *"I love the man come to Thailand the first time."* I appeared sweet, cuddly, and charming, qualities that left them totally unprepared for how cunning and full-of-guile I really was. My fragile looks and my innocent smile were quite deceiving. Men like Cedrik were easy prey.

He paid the bar-fine at my GoGo for two weeks, the entire length of his Pattaya holiday. I soon learned that he was extremely possessive and wanted sex all of the time. I don't think that he had ever been sexually-active before coming to Pattaya, so the opportunity to spend time with a petite and pretty girl was the highlight of his life. By the time he left, he wanted to marry me. As far as I was concerned, our time together was rather uneventful and relatively uninspiring. My interest in him was hardly reciprocal. In fact, I never developed any attachment to him at all. But, he was in heaven. It was the beginning of a romance, a fantasy fulfilled--or so he thought.

Although sex tourists who come to Thailand have generally experienced women, their bedroom antics are rather juvenile as is their knowledge of the opposite sex. Others are unable to meet women in their own countries because they are physically unattractive, emotionally immature, or socially and/or developmentally delayed. All of this is to say that they simply do not have the ability to relate to women, nor communicate with them.

181

A computer to Cedrik; $700 to me!

    I told Cedrik that I would like to learn to use a computer. Farang men always like Thai girls to express an interest in gaining more skills and education. They think that we want to lift ourselves from a life of prostitution. They especially enjoy it when we show an interest in the same fields of endeavor that they pursue. I convinced Cedrik that I would learn to use his laptop computer if he would leave it with me. There was no question but that he would readily agree. Following his departure, I realized that I didn't have a clue as to what to do with it—with a single exception. *I could sell it!* I received about $700 for the sale. It cost him twice that amount. I had convinced him to leave this valuable piece of high-tech equipment with me for my unspoken purpose of selling it. I had developed exceptional skills of persuasion.

During the last few days of Cedrik's trip, we stayed at a nice hotel in Bangkok where my mother came to meet us. She was overwhelmed with its luxury; she had seen little outside our village other than the outskirts of Bangkok. She and I walked past the receptionist's desk toward the elevators. When no one stopped us, or asked us where we were going, she asked why. I told her it was because Cedrik always tipped very well and that also made me a VIP.

My mom and I entered the elevator and went up to our room on the third floor. When we exited the elevator, she looked down at the floor and said, *"Look, someone stole my shoes!"* I asked my mother where she had taken them off. As Thai people remove their shoes when they enter rooms, my mother had mistaken the elevator for a room. She said, *"I put them right there,"* pointing to a place right in front of the elevator. I told her that we had gone up a few floors and that her shoes were right where she had left them, in front of the elevator, on the ground floor. We returned and picked up her shoes; she was relieved. It was her first trip in an elevator.

While my mother rested, Cedrik and I had a "talk." The one thing that I was able to communicate to Cedrik was my need for funds. I convinced him to send me Bt 25,000 ($625) every month following his arrival home. That was about the only thing I liked about Cedrik. He believed that I would be true to him and wait for his return. He had been in Thailand two weeks, but he was as inexperienced and naïve when he left as when he arrived. Although he had just received an intensive course of instruction in "A Bargirl's Rules to the Game of Life," he failed—most miserably. My mother returned home, delighted that he had failed, and secure in the knowledge that I had met my obligations. *Her income would continue unabated.*

Nan Shifts Direction Down Another Self-Destructive Path

A little over a year after Nan and I moved to Pattaya, she began seeing a Yabah (amphetamines) dealer and was no longer seeing tourists; we were no longer in the same field of employment. I wanted no part of her life while she had a drug-dealing Thai boyfriend, so we had very little contact.

At this point in time, it has been years since Nan and I first met. Currently, she changes her name and phone number every month and moves around from one friend's home to another. She has been living like this for a couple of years--ever since she was released from prison for selling drugs. I have seen her only once in many months although she has told me, time and time again, that she would visit me. She borrows clothes from one person, and then leaves them at the next person's home where she borrows clothes once again. It is a good thing that we are all tiny and can share our wardrobes. The same can be said for her use of mobile telephones. I have never received a call from her from the same number for more than a week. She has developed a lifestyle that is constantly *"On the run."* Selling her 13-year old body for sex followed by a period of drug-addiction, has contributed to the making of a sad, even tormented, yet still quite beautiful young woman who is running away from herself, but who can never run far enough, nor will she ever be free.

184

Sai Moves to Pattaya Beach

About 18 months after my arrival in Pattaya, and after Nan and I had gone our separate ways, my mother sent Sai to stay with me. Sai had been left on our family's doorstep by her mom (my mother's sister) when she was only an infant. She was raised as Ying's twin because they were born within months of one another. Now that she was 13, she was causing my mother a lot of trouble. Sai had learned at the age of 10 that she was not our natural sister. She felt that she had been "dumped" by her mother and she became inconsolable. She was now the same age that I was when I was sent away. I have always wondered if my mother thought that by sending Sai to live with me in Pattaya, the money sent home to her would be increased.

On the other hand, I could understand my sister's desire to leave Ubon. She saw how much money I had, how well I spoke English, and all of the goods I could send home. She wanted to experience "The good life," too. But, she was unaware of exactly what I did to earn so much money, or the price I paid.

The main attraction

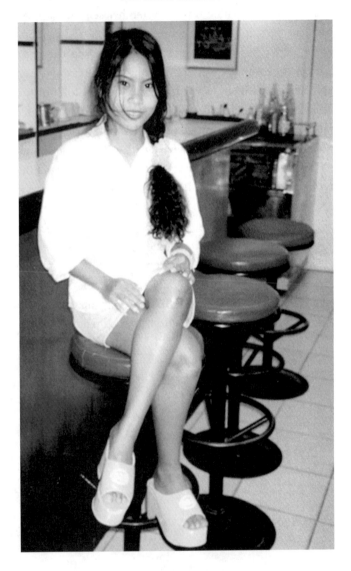

Age 17

Once Sai arrived in Pattaya, I immediately enrolled her in middle school. Taking care of her was a lot of work. I was only 17 at the time and usually stayed out until the early hours of the morning. I would arrive home to our apartment between 2:00 and 4:00 A.M., get a few hours of sleep, and then wake her up at 7:00 A.M. to go to school. I would always see that she had Bt 100 for the bus, food, and school supplies. She was better off than nearly all of the other girls in school. Even in a bad month, I earned Bt 40,000 to 50,000 ($1,000 to $1,250). We had everything we needed. In terms of my finances, I had created a very rewarding career.

One day, Sai came home crying. She asked me if I had sex with tourists in order to bring home all of the money that I did. I told her the truth. I slept with tourists; and it was necessary in order for us to pay the rent, buy food, and pay for her and Ying's education so that they could eventually get good jobs. What had occurred to bring on Sai's tears? She had been talking to another girl who said the reason I came home so late and had so much money was because I was a prostitute. I know that this girl intentionally hurt and humiliated Sai because Sai had more spending money than she did. Sai vehemently denied her statement although she didn't know exactly how I ended up with so much money. She threw herself on our apartment floor, crying her heart out. She screamed that she didn't need to go to school and that she would get a job. She begged me to stop. My mother never would have made that same request. *Sai loved me so much more than my mother ever did.*

Sai Shows Signs of Delinquency

Two days prior to Cedrik's return to Switzerland, I called Sai in Pattaya to see how she was. She had been living with me for a while by now. It was an expensive call by my standards at Bt 10/minute (25¢). Bar girls use every opportunity to take advantage of the men they see. My young and generous client would pay for

187

this call made from his hotel room. My sister wasn't at home. It was 8:00 P.M., and she knew that she had to go to school the next morning. I was angry with her; I was her surrogate mother in Pattaya, not just her older sister. A half-hour later, I tried again, and again there was no answer. I was angrier now, and I was worried. I tried again at 10:00 P.M. I called every 10 or 20 minutes without an answer. I became frightened; she was barely 15. I couldn't imagine what had happened to her. I was afraid to imagine what had happened to her! I had always feared that she would start seeing men for money, just like me!

I was in Bangkok, and she was in Pattaya—two hours away. I didn't know where in Pattaya she could be. I also didn't know what to do. I couldn't talk to Cedrik because he couldn't speak English. He couldn't understand why I was crying. I could only think of one option; I called someone who always managed to be there for me; I called Dave, and I cried. He had been teaching English in Bangkok and had been my friend for a couple of years. He loaned me money when I had sent too much home, or when I spent too much, or whenever I simply needed it. I was desperate to talk to someone.

It was now 1:00 A.M. I knew that there was really nothing that he could do, but at least he would listen, and he would understand my deepest fear. I called in spite of my worry over awakening him. I also worried that he might not answer. Who would call him at this hour knowing that he needed to go to work in the morning? I would! He finally answered the phone. I was afraid that he would be angry with me. I was wrong. He was happy to hear from me, even at that hour and even under those circumstances. I told him that my sister had not returned home yet, and I was terrified that she had been in a motorbike accident; or something even worse, that she had gone to Walking Street to find a Farang. There was no legitimate reason for her not to be home at that hour.

She was much too young to be out so late.

Through my tears, I explained the situation to Dave the best I could. He was consoling while telling me that he didn't know how he could help. I knew in my heart that there was really nothing that he could do, but I needed someone with whom I could talk. I wanted him to listen and allay some of my fears. We talked about 10 minutes, and I began to calm down.

Shortly thereafter, I called my sister once again; this time she was home. She had never heard me scream as loud and as long. I was angry and I had been very, very frightened. From this moment on, she knew that she was going to follow my rules all of the time or she would return to the village. She was really afraid that I would send her back to our mother. She would have to leave the tourist mecca of Pattaya City, and the beach playground she had come to love. With my threats firmly implanted, she promised to be home by 8:00 P.M. on every school day from that day forward. After I learned that my sister was safe, and after experiencing the range of emotions from fear, to rage, to relief, I could go to sleep. There would be no sex for Cedrik tonight. I was exhausted!

I had been trying to raise Sai for a long time. She was in 8th grade and needed only one more year to finish 9th grade. This was an achievement for a girl coming from my part of the country. A 9th grade education would enable her to get a better job than I could ever have found. I was not going to risk her losing that opportunity. I had suffered too much and too long. We had come too far to stop now. She was going to straighten up, not ship out!

Cedrik Proposes

Cedrik asked me to marry him before returning home. Of course, I accepted. To one in my profession, "Marriage" provides a work contract with a good monthly salary and an upfront bonus, regardless of productivity throughout the contract, and a European Visa as well! Cedrik flew home with a smile on his face and the belief that I would be true to him. He promised that he would send me Bt 25,000/month ($625) so that I would not have to work. I assured him that I loved him and would be faithful. I told him everything he wanted to hear. I told him that I would never work in a GoGo again. Fortunately for me, he believed everything I said.

He had asked me to marry him after knowing me for only two weeks. Any thinking person would know that his whispers of affection never originated in his heart, but instead were borne from his loins in the heat of passion. He had been swept up in the overwhelming and all-consuming sensation of lust—for the very first time. Whatever he was feeling, it was most definitely not love. He tried to control the way I dressed and choose the food I ate; he didn't like the smell of Thai or Isaan food—my food. He always wanted sex whether I was interested or not. He treated me as if I were his employee rather than his girlfriend. I tolerated him so that I could leave Thailand for a better life in Switzerland, for my first trip to Europe, and for all of the money that would flow from him, through me, to my family.

Once he returned home, as a result of his generosity, I was receiving a steady income. But, I could no longer work at Sexy GoGo where his friends might see me. Instead, I became a freelancer, meeting tourists at discos and in shopping centers-- making even more money. I made about Bt 50,000–60,000 ($1,250-$1,500) every month.

I was now living with another man who gave me Bt 30,000 ($750)/month while I was also working. During that first month after Cedrik's return to Switzerland and for several months thereafter, I made Bt 77,000/month--equal to about $1,925.

To further put Bt 77,000 ($1,925) into perspective, the per-capita GNP of Thailand of nearly Bt 150,000 ($3,750) is not spread evenly among the population. In January of 2002, only 19% of the population earned over $350 a month ($4,200/year), according to a major credit card company. More significantly, to look at these figures from the opposite perspective, 81% of Thailand's struggling society earned less than $350/month and many of them earned much less--somewhere in the neighborhood of $800/year. In the poorest provinces, it was even less than $600/annually. We do not have a middle-class like in the West. We have a handful of millionaires and billionaires who run our country, and who do everything possible to keep the rest of us exceedingly poor. This is what leads girls like me to see tourists for "Big Money."

Tony vs. Cedrik

Tony returned and bought me another dog named "Gigi." Although Cedrik had been sending me money every month, I really thought that Tony would be the best man for me. So, I took him to Ubon to meet my mother. But because Tony was 52-years old, my family didn't like him. While staying in Ubon, Tony bought me another dog which I named "Dummy." He had hoped that this would endear my family to him. *Little did he know that money was the only thing that endeared my family to anyone.* We eventually left Dummy with my mother and headed back to Pattaya.

My family preferred Cedrik to Tony because he spent more money on them, and he was much younger. So, they wanted me to stop seeing Tony in order to marry Cedrik, hoping for a *Big Money* marriage pay-off. But, they were still quite happy to receive money from both men while those men were overseas. When I told Tony that I was planning on going to Switzerland to meet Cedrik, he was heartbroken, and he left the apartment. In time, he found another girlfriend to soothe his aching heart.

Heartbreaker

Age 17

Working at a new GoGo:
Dancing Again

After freelancing for a while, I decided to get a job again. This meant dancing at a GoGo bar, but far away from Sexy GoGo. I was a very good dancer and had bronze skin—the kind of skin for which Western women spend a fortune in sun-tanning parlors or many weekends at the beach, and the kind of skin Farang men love. Getting customers to buy me drinks and pay bar-fines was easy, so the GoGos were always happy to hire me. The next GoGo for which I worked was Baby GoGo. It was the nicest in Pattaya. I was hired "on the spot," for a salary of about Bt 6,000/month ($240). This was the salary paid for dancing alone. There was also additional money for getting men to buy me drinks, pay for "short times" in the rooms upstairs, and the bar-fine to take me home.

My Approximate Monthly Earnings

Salary		Bt 6,000	$ 150
Lady's Drinks	Bt 30	Bt 2,100	$ 52
Short Time Bar-fine (my share)	Bt 200	Bt 3,000	$ 75
Short Time tip	Bt 1,000	Bt 15,000	$ 375
All Night Bar-fine (my share)	Bt 150	Bt 2,700	$ 67
All Night tip	Bt 1,000	Bt 18,000	$ 450
Subtotal		**Bt 46,800**	**$ 1,169**
Cedrik sending money	$625	Bt 25,000	$ 625
TOTAL MONTHLY INCOME		**Bt 71,800**	**$ 1,794**

Compare this amount to what any other girl, working in any other profession, with my education--or lack thereof, would earn in Pattaya City, a tourist resort where the wages are well-above those in the rest of the country outside of Bangkok:

Maid	Bt 3,000	$ 75
Waitress + Tips	Bt 5,000	$ 125
Unskilled Seamstress	Bt 3,000	$ 75

Age 17

The girls of Bangkok and Pattaya, including myself, make large amounts of money from tourists by simply telling them any one of a number of wild tales. These men continued to believe us time and time again. They had never had someone like us "love"

194

and "care" for them before. They had also never had anyone like us lie to them endlessly, to get every dollar, pound, mark, or franc that we possibly could.

Examples of our lies:

1.	My mother is sick and needs Bt 5,000 for the hospital
2.	My sister needs Bt 5,000 for school. (Bt 5,000 would actually pay for one full-year of public school and a lot more).
3.	My sister is sick and needs medication, I need Bt 2,000. The public hospital will take weeks to give her medicine, so she needs to go to a private hospital.
4.	The buffalo died. I need Bt 10,000.
5.	The roof in my home in Ubon leaks. I need Bt 3,000.
6.	Bad rains have led to a bad rice harvest. I need Bt 10,000. (Tourists don't know the seasons).
7.	The refrigerator stopped working. I need Bt 4,000.
8	I need more money to send to my mother for Chinese New Year, Thai New Year, Isaan New Year, Buddhist New Year, or any other "New Year" I could invent.
9.	My cousin is having a baby. I need Bt 2,000 to send to her for good luck from Buddha.
10.	It's my birthday or that of a member of the family; of course, I always needed to send money or gold as a present. I always had another birthday, and so did everyone in my family.

Farang would just hand me the money without batting an eyelash. They wanted to improve my life because they felt very sorry for me. This is why I did what I did, and why it would be difficult to quit being a bar girl. I really enjoyed lying to men and getting everything out of them that I possibly could. My family had also become accustomed to this kind of income.

For many years, I never saved very much, but I saved my sisters. I had to make sure that they would not end up like me, and that they would never have to see men like Bangkok John and Jimmy the Switch. This was one reason that I always sent money to my mother, as fast and as much as I could. I wanted to make sure that the two of them stayed in school. We all lived on my income. My family and I enjoyed what it could buy in a poor country. We didn't want to go back to the old way of life--a life that possessed no material goods, foretold only bleakness ahead, and remained financially destitute. I can't imagine that anyone would. *There is no life without "Face!"*

> **If there had been an alternate path to my survival,**
> **I would have jumped for it.**
> **My country intentionally provides no alternate paths.**
> **All other roads lead to poverty.**

Girls come to the tourist resorts to make money for their families—not themselves. Sometimes the money is a lot better than at other times. In high season, when the tourists are plentiful, it seems that money is "Falling from the trees." A girl doesn't even need to sleep with very many tourists to make good money. Tips from the bar, as well as commissions from the drinks (30%), reap us huge rewards. Tourists are exceedingly generous with their money as they unabashedly compete for our attention, taking great pleasure in luring us away from other men. I was always in high demand and loved every moment of the attention and the power it gave me over men. Some of us have looked for work in other fields but the income does not come close to the money we earn in our profession. Even if we were willing to settle for far less pay, we would be hard-pressed to find good work. I was lucky when I became older; I found a position as a tour guide, an actress, a model, and a translator; and I introduced men to girls.

Walking ATMs: Thai bar girls

In the eyes of our families, we, the bar girls of Pattaya, Bangkok, and Phuket, have become nothing more than walking ATM machines. Our families no longer look to manage their own lives on their own funds. Rather, they simply wait until the family bar girl sends money home through the postal system; or with present-day technology, receive a phone call learning that a deposit has been made from which they can make an ATM withdrawal. Our families constantly hound us for more and more money. They believe that the money coming from Farang, through us, is simply falling from the sky, without understanding the true costs we pay.

Walking ATMs: Farang

In our eyes, the Farang are also walking ATMs. We have no idea what the Farang have done to earn their money, but instead of seeking to understand, we have chosen to learn every way possible through craft, cunning, or guile, to deceive the tourist into relinquishing every dollar possible. In effect, we see the tourist as our families see us. How I disdain my mother for her behavior, valuing the money I earn more than she values me. As a girl from Isaan, I cannot openly show it. On the other hand, I exhibited that identical behavior toward my clients. I did a lot of harm to the men I met, and I didn't care.

Did my customers think that Bt 1,000, the price of sex with me at 15, 16, or 17-years old, was adequate compensation for the true mental and emotional pain that I suffered from sleeping with them? If they did, they were sadly mistaken. It was not! That may have been the price that I quoted, but there were additional charges. *They never saw the fine print!*

By the time I turned 18, I was one of the hottest dancers at my GoGo. I earned a lot of money, lived well, helped my family, and was lucky enough to have very naive men send me money when they returned home--believing that I would quit the bar life, and that I waited with bated-breath for their return. I never really understood how an older man could believe that an attractive 18-year-old whom he had just met, living the life of a prostitute, would remain true to him. But, young men were also taken-in and proved equally as gullible, although with far shallower pockets. I was interested in every one of them--the part of them that paid me. I can only make the assumption that most men have egos the size of "all outdoors."

I was satisfied with my life, my job, and my income until my salary at the GoGo abruptly changed. I was angry with the way that it happened more than the actual money involved; I was angry enough to quit. These situations are all-too-common as *mama-sans* are frequently jealous of the pretty young girls in their bars who are earning far more money than they ever had. On one occasion, my bar-fine was paid by the man who "bought me out" for two weeks. Upon my return to the bar, the *mama-san* claimed that it had not been paid. At the end of the month, she deducted the bar-fine, Bt 7,000 ($175) from my salary, plus Bt 150 for every day that I had been absent from work, leaving me with almost nothing from the GoGo. I quit on the spot. I moved to a new GoGo. *I had the most readily-portable skill that had not gone out of fashion in 5,000 years.*

It wasn't long before I was, once again, the number one dancer. There were many other attractive girls there, but I was fortunate that men liked me. I was small, outgoing, and charming which attracted them to my dancing talent. I also spoke English very well. In Thailand, many of the girls cannot speak English, so those of us who can have a great advantage.

I had a lot of spare time during the day and I decided to go back to school. In Thailand, as so many people are unable to complete 7th to 9th grades, especially females, the government makes middle-school available in the afternoons, early evenings, and on weekends. I decided to attend a school in Naklua, Pattaya's sister city, and I didn't have to go very often. I would pick up my books and then turn in the assignments every couple of weeks. I had begun to think that it was time to make more of my life.

All this at only 4' 9"

Age 18

Chapter 11

"18 Rain"

"18 Rain" speaks of 18 rainy seasons

In my life, men have been solely a means to an end, and I do not expect my views to change anytime in the near future. I have always pushed them as far as I could in the knowledge that any one of them could be easily replaced around the next corner. Once I tricked men into giving me every baht that I could, it was still never enough. I was never satisfied. Regardless of how difficult, inconvenient, or even painful it was for them to satisfy my insatiable lust for money, I didn't care. I always wanted more!

The Culture of Pattaya Beach: An Addictive Lifestyle

Pattaya City is different than the rest of Thailand, with the exception of the tourist areas of Patpong, Nana, and Soi Cowboy in Bangkok, and the islands of Koh Samui and Phuket. It was built for and thrives on sex-tourists. Most of the girls working in the city are from Isaan. There are many girls who work "real jobs" and also see tourists for money "after hours." These girls work as waitresses, shop girls, and maids. There is so much more money in sleeping with tourists that a salary from any other job cannot begin to compete. A day job provides girls with the avenue to meet men that being unemployed, or only going to the discos, never would. There is no limit to the number of men that one can meet at the discos or by simply working at a bar or GoGo. But working a normal job, however demeaning and low paying, can often assist a girl to meet nicer "day-time men," rather than "late-night drunks."

Everyone in the city knows that their livelihoods are dependent upon the Isaan-born bar girls attracting tourists. The unkempt beaches littered with garbage, plastic, and animal waste; a polluted bay; and the lack of infrastructure; offer little to the tourist who seeks a tropical paradise. Promoting Thailand for its beauty, making it appealing to the rest of the world, and thereby attracting the tourist dollar is important. It is for this reason that the Social Minister of Thailand has declared that she sees no signs of prostitution in Pattaya. *Even the most naive tourist knows that prostitution is the glitziest sign in town. Its glow radiates from the luminous neon signs of every bar, every GoGo, every street corner, and in the shameless costumes of the thousands of girls who work the city's streets by day and after dark.*

The advantage of being a bar girl in Pattaya is simple. There is virtually no stigma to my line of work here--absolutely none! You could not say that of any Western country, nor of most nations. At 18, I can openly walk down the street, hand-in-hand, with a 50+ year old man, enter shopping centers, banks, restaurants, government offices, etc. and few will raise an eyebrow. Approximately 20% of the female tenants in apartments are bar girls. Everyone else who lives in the apartments and works in the shops and restaurants knows who generates the money that keeps the city afloat. Tourists do not come to Pattaya for its beaches; the inexpensive, yet tasty food; nor the temples and cultural dances. They come for the girls who trade sex for money. There is not the same disdain for us in Pattaya, Patpong, and Nana Plaza, as there is in the rest of Bangkok and in many other parts of the country.

When not working in the GoGo bars in Pattaya Beach, I spent most of my spare time in the afternoon staying home with Sai, watching TV, and waiting for work to start in the evening. I was generally too tired to do much during the daylight hours as dancing all night took a lot of energy. I also had a sister for whom I was responsible. I worried that she might some day end up like me. This was my greatest fear. This was also the reason that I continued to work as I did, so that she could finish her education and would never feel compelled to see sex-tourists for money. I needed to keep my eyes on her and on her friends. I wanted to make sure that she would never develop a circle of friends who were like me. I felt about my sister in her selection of friends, the same way that Bangkok John felt about his teen-aged daughter and boys in general. *Neither of us wanted our loved ones to develop relationships with people like us.*

One day, I was in the Royal Garden Shopping Center, the nicest shopping center in Pattaya. While buying a coke on the third floor Food Court, I walked into the man next to me and spilled my drink all over him. I was very embarrassed and I didn't know what to say or do. I thought about pretending that I didn't speak English. But even though I lived the life that I did, I was responsible and really didn't want to lie to him—at least not yet. I apologized to him in English. I was surprised that he wasn't angry. Instead, he laughed about it. He told me not to worry and then began asking questions. He wanted to know where I worked. I told him, *"I go with men."* Now it was his turn to be surprised. He asked, *"What are you doing now?"* I said, *"Nothing."* He asked if I would go with him. I agreed. I thought, *"That was an interesting way to get a client."*

Meeting Dave

I met Dave a year or two earlier. He had been referred to me by a former client. Dave had a friend in Bangkok who was trying to locate more girls to work in her beer garden. I told him that Nan and I couldn't work in Bangkok. He returned to his country for work almost immediately after speaking to me, but I got his address and decided to write to him as he spoke Thai well--very unusual for a Farang. Dave and I became friends and he seemed to be there for me whenever I was in need. He loaned me money and he gave freely of his time—listening to me complain about men, money, my mom, and a great deal more.

203

Several years later, during one of Dave's holidays in Thailand, I learned that Nan, my former roommate, had been in a motorbike crash. I thought that she might be in Chonburi Hospital, about 30-kilometers away. It was 6:00A.M., and I hadn't yet been to sleep. I went to Dave's house, waking him up, and begging his help. He reluctantly got out of bed and took me to the hospital on his motorbike. It was a 40-minute trip and I slept leaning on his back all the way. Upon arriving, we saw the receptionist and asked for Nan. Thai people, especially those from Isaan, call everyone by their nicknames. That's when I realized that although I had known her for four years, I didn't know her real name. I described her to the receptionist and gave the few details I had learned about the accident. The hospital didn't have a patient fitting her description, but they had recently admitted a male patient who had been involved in a motorbike accident. Dave and I went upstairs to find Nan's amphetamine-dealing boyfriend wired together and bandaged like a mummy. Although I would never want to see Nan injured from an accident, I must admit that I wasn't sorry that her boyfriend had sustained such serious injuries.

Happy in Pattaya?

The relaxed lifestyle of Pattaya, easy money, and good beach weather, in contrast to Bangkok's heat, humidity, and pollution were enough to keep any Isaan girl very comfortable. This is the reason that I stayed so long and why my sister was so happy. In Isaan, we speak a lot about being happy. We will do whatever it takes to make our families happy, until our sacrifices become so great that we begin to look for a way out.

My Suicide Attempt

I was only 18 and I had been working in the sex-trade for four years. My daily liaisons with literally hundreds of men over my teenage years finally became too much for me. I no longer wanted to see them, speak to them, nor have sex with them; neither did I want to see, nor speak to anyone else. I was exhausted; I hated my life and even worse, I hated myself. *The rules of my culture did not allow me to hate my mother.* The past four years had been filled with men falling all over me and my mother's incessant demands for more money. For four years, I had lived in the dark shadow of emotional sickness. I was desperate to escape and I knew of only one way out.

Although Pattaya had a lot to offer a bar girl fresh from Bangkok, it also had its drawbacks. During one of my worst periods of depression, I drank bleach in a frantic, but futile attempt to kill myself. My neighbor took me to Pattaya Memorial hospital where my stomach was pumped. I recovered after a few days and returned to the darkness of the GoGos and the discos--clubs that now seemed to reek with the nauseating odor of stale alcohol and stung my eyes with the dense fog of cigarette smoke. As dark as these clubs were, there was no darkness greater than that which I felt in my soul.

Soi 8, Bars from top to bottom

Typical of the bars where I made my living

This Thai song could have been written for me.

"18 Rain"

I am confused sometimes,
If anyone would be patient to listen to all of my stories
They are home, but empty-nothing, it's absolutely hell!
Sometimes it is painful
I've kept watching, and am jealous of those who have normal
and perfect families
While I am so lonely and scared
My heart is crying and longing for someone who can console
and understand me
I won't require more than this
It has been the past 18 rainy seasons, 18 winter seasons
They were very hard and painful days
Do not forget me
Do not walk away from me
Today, I am crying from the depths of my heart
It is a wall that blinds the mind
It's so cold and heartless
It's a problem
It's just like this
It is the past 18 rainy seasons
It is a dangerous fork
It is just like I have no future
Everyone looks down at me, but who knows my insides
Do you know my heart is longing for someone
Someone who can console me
Someone who is understanding
I do not require more than this
18 years of age
It broke my heart
Don't forget me
Don't walk away from me
Today my heart is confused

Chapter 12

Cedrik and Switzerland

Cedrik had a friend who worked in Bangkok. On the occasional weekend, he would venture down the two hours of highway to Pattaya. About a month or two after Cedrik left, his friend told him that he had seen me walking with another man in Pattaya. I immediately received a phone call from Switzerland. I quickly assured him that I was just talking to someone and that I was faithful. I told him that I was in love with him and that I would never return to the GoGos. I would keep my promise to him. *The only promise I will never go back on is the one "To take care of my family."* As long as Cedrik continued to send money, he believed that I would not cheat on him. That was the greatest error in his thinking; it is the flaw in the thinking of most Farang. They believe that we hold the same value system as they do and that prostitutes are faithful. I can't imagine where they get this idea. I doubt that they would have the same confidence in prostitutes in their own countries.

Cedrik and I stayed in touch on the phone for a couple of months. At first, he would call in the daytime, but after he heard that I might be playing around, he started to call at night so that I would have to be home to answer his calls. I would simply wait for his call at 11:00 P.M. or midnight, and then I would "go to work." After a while, I told him that his phone calls were waking my sister who had to get up early to go to school. He believed me and started to call earlier. This allowed me to go out earlier as well.

A gift from Cedrik, I named him Tim, a girl's best friend

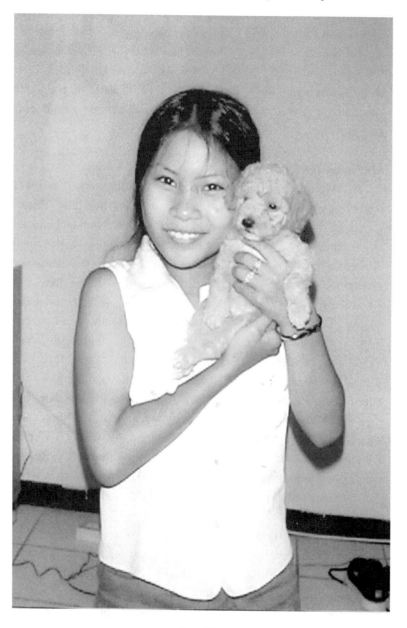

Age 18

Cedrik returned to Pattaya a few months later. Prior to his arrival, I had been working and earning from Bt 40,000 to 50,000 each month and receiving his generous contribution which brought my income to nearly Bt 75,000. This income was in addition to selling his computer. Poor Thai women will do anything to keep cash flowing into their households. I had created a profitable situation for myself and for my family, and nothing would ever keep me from continuing to do so.

My Swiss Marriage

My luck was about to end when Cedrik returned and was ready to get married. We went to Ubon to get a Buddhist "Paper-marriage." To me, it was like an employment contract with an initial bonus and a monthly retainer. He was happy and excited, bringing a few friends with him from Bangkok to my village for the ceremony. He paid my mother a Brideprice of Bt 50,000 ($1,250). He also gave her an additional Bt 20,000 ($500) in gold and spent nearly $1,000 on the wedding. This is a lot of money for a wedding in rural Thailand. His extravagance allowed my mother to *"Make face"* in the community. Not only had she made *"Face"* for years, from all of the money that I had sent home from work as a prostitute, but now she was also able to benefit from my marriage. No Thai man would ever pay that kind of money to marry an "ex"-prostitute. Thais know that the purpose of the "Brideprice" is to buy a Virgin! Farang do not! Thai men in Isaan marry prostitutes only to access the money the girls have saved. Generally, Thai prostitutes in Isaan marry Farang only to access the money *they* have saved.

While in the village, I sent Cedrik to the shop around the corner to buy a few bottles of Coke. He paid for the Coke, picked up the bottles, and walked away. The 12-year old counter girl flew out of the shop, screaming at him in Isaan. He didn't realize that she was yelling at him and he kept on walking. She then began to swear, *"You thief, white pig..."* and worse. I heard the commotion

210

and knew there could be only one person in town that she would speak to in that way. This led me to go out and investigate. Cedrik did not realize that within these little shops, Coke is bought and poured into bags with ice. The bottles are not taken from the shop. I quickly returned the bottles and resolved the misunderstanding. Day after day, the neighbors would come to look at Cedrik--the only white man in Boontung.

At the wedding, dozens of family members, along with friends and neighbors—most of whom I had never met, arrived from all over the province. Some of them even brought their daughters to meet Cedrik's friends. Once my mother informed them of my marriage and of the free food and drink, they appeared as if by magic. They celebrated all day and all night, drinking until they could no longer stand. My family was actually celebrating the new source of income that I had found.

A marriage to a Farang meant that there would be a stream of monthly payments to my family's household--forever. My mother would never have to "work" again, as if she ever really had. She could not only hold her head high, she could be arrogant. She was no longer just a village woman with a daughter surreptitiously *"Working"* in the city. She was now the mother of a girl married to a Farang. The marriage ceremony itself was a success. Cedrik became a happily married man. He could boast to his friends back home that he had married a petite and beautiful Thai girl. Little did either one of us know of the fate that would soon befall us.

It was time to plan for my departure. I had to send a TV, video player, kitchenware, and light clothing to Ubon as they would be of no use in the cold weather of Switzerland. I rented a truck to send all of it home--some 10 hours away. The costs were minimal. Of course, they were borne by Cedrik.

More importantly, I had the human element of my sister who would have to return to the province. This became a serious problem as she no longer wanted a life in a poor, rural village. I had already made her travel arrangements to Ubon. She could not remain in Pattaya by herself. I would not allow her to stay where Farang prowl day-and-night, seeking out girls her age as trophies, and trading them as baseball cards.

It didn't take long for the letter to arrive from the Swiss Embassy informing me that my Visa was waiting to be picked up in Bangkok. It was all so easy. I was ready to go to Europe for the very first time and I was very excited. I eagerly dashed off to Bangkok to pick it up, returned to Pattaya, packed my suitcase, and ordered my ticket to Zurich. In less than a week, I was on a plane bound for Switzerland.

As became the custom, I would pray for my father every time I would board a plane for Europe. I don't know how far prayers can travel, but I think that Europe is too far away from which to pray. Also, spirits do not live in Europe, but in Thailand, Cambodia, Burma, and Laos.

Upon arriving in Switzerland, I discovered that even in the summer it was cool and dry. I couldn't imagine what it might be like in the winter. Little did I know that I would never be so fortunate as to find out.

When the plane touched down in Zurich, I was tired and disoriented. The airport signs were in German, English, French, and Italian, but not in Thai. Switzerland is not only very far removed from Thailand in distance, but also in culture. Cedrik met me outside of Customs. The first thing that he did was to drive to a "short-time" hotel for sex. He never asked if I was tired or hungry. He didn't seem to be concerned about me at all. Sex was the only activity on his mind. It was the last activity in which I wanted to engage at that moment, and I refused. He was rather annoyed, to say the least; our marriage was not getting off to a very good start. He didn't want to introduce me to his mother until he had romped between the sheets. I was also very annoyed; I refused to give in.

It was an hour's drive to his home. I thought his home was lovely and that it was incredible that I would soon be living here. There were not any houses like this in Ubon. Cedrik's home had beautiful white carpets, and his mother had three cars. I had entered into a wonderful new world, one that was clean and comfortable. I knew that his father had committed suicide when the family's business went under. I knew what it was like to lose one's father. But fortunately for Cedrik, his mother still loved him; she loved what she could do for him, and she looked out after him. She was rather unlike my mother who cared only for what I could provide for her.

The Swiss are deliberate about keeping everything precisely in its place. Thais live in a never-ending, cluttered state of chaos where everything they own is on display. I didn't know how well my Isaan philosophy would adapt to this world, but I was certainly going to give it a try.

I was meeting Cedrik's mother for the first time, face-to-face, although we had already spoken on the telephone. She spoke English well, unlike her son, and she was far wiser. Although our introduction went well, I could see even at this early stage of our relationship that at sometime in the future she might become a problem for me. We talked about my future and my whole-hearted affection for her son—the latter topic was of primary importance to her. We spoke about how I would adapt to Switzerland; learn French; attend school to educate myself; and become a productive family member. I was not in the mood for this conversation,

213

although I made every effort to be pleasant. I had just traveled from Thailand to Switzerland--a 10-hour flight, and I was very tired. I couldn't understand why no one gave any thought to how I might be feeling after such a long journey. I didn't want to talk; I only wanted to sleep. I felt that his mother was taking advantage of my vulnerability to learn of my motives in marrying her son. I couldn't have been happier when she stopped talking, and I could go to sleep.

Each morning, Cedrik would go to work, leaving me at home with his retired mother. She and I would talk about a lot of things, but mostly about my relationship with her son. She was sincerely worried that I was a terrible girl whose intention was to hurt her son. Nothing could have been further from the truth. I really wanted Cedrik, although a callow young man and a "Mama's boy," to be as happy as possible. She didn't believe me. I also had to make sure that nothing, nor anyone, impaired my true purpose in life--to provide for my family. This is where we would ultimately find disagreement.

I really wished that his mother had been employed outside the home; then I would have been able to spend more time in their house alone. I wanted to explore its many rooms and the shelves with all its knick-knacks. We didn't have money to buy so many pretty things when I grew up. We had enough money for food and only the bare essentials; but not enough for me to attend school and certainly never enough money for the purchase of beautiful hand-painted ceramics.

A couple of days each week, I would take the bus into town. Even during the summer, it was uncomfortably cold for a Thai native used to the glow of the sun's warming rays, 365 days a year. Passengers stared; I certainly didn't look like the ordinary passenger. I was short, petite, and dark-skinned, and as tall as a 10-year old Swiss. I would pay my fare and sit down. It could be that everyone

214

wasn't staring, but many were. At least I think they were; Thais are suspicious people.

When the bus arrived at my destination, I would hop off and wander around the most immaculate country in the world. I had never imagined that any city could be so clean. Not only were the streets swept free of litter, but the buildings looked as if they were freshly-painted, cars gleamed, and everyone was impeccably-dressed. I wondered how they did it. Cars and trucks emitted no visible pollution. I couldn't believe it. Why did the cars, trucks, and motorbikes in Thailand emit black smoke, making the air impossible to breathe, leaving soot on one's skin, and burning one's eyes? What could Thai engineers learn from this refrigerated and mountainous land?

I was able to enjoy many tall, beautiful, snow-capped mountains while sight-seeing around the city. I wished I could show my mother and sisters how beautiful Switzerland was. We had nothing like this in Ubon, nor anywhere else in Thailand. The air was cool and dry; it was like opening a refrigerator door. I fantasized about staying here for a very long time.

Switzerland was not only cold; it was expensive! How did they earn enough money to be able to afford everything here? I knew that the Swiss were big spenders in Thailand. Later, I learned how...MONEY! The Swiss have very large banks and they take care of money for people from all over the world. As my interests were also in making money, I felt that the Swiss and I, most definitely, had something in common.

Every time I returned home from exploring the city, I always found Cedrik's mother waiting for me. She was anxious to hear what I had discovered and to question me. I was reasonably truthful; I spoke about the expensive prices, incredible cleanliness, and the exquisitely beautiful mountains. I didn't tell her what really opened my eyes and sparked my interest more than anything else; *I didn't tell her that I saw MONEY!*

Cedrik came home each day at 5:00 P.M. The only reason I was "happy" to see him was so that I could avoid his mother's incessant questioning of my plans for the future. But communicating with him was difficult; his English was very poor and he wasn't interested in any further study. Instead, he gave me books to learn French, a language in which I had no interest. I thought that it would have been a lot easier for him to learn English than for me to learn French. In Continental Europe, English is the one language that pervades every country even though it is not the native language of any one of them. It doesn't take a scholar, nor a world-traveler, to realize that English is the universal language. I had learned to speak English and I expected the same effort of Europeans.

I slept with Cedrik every night, but our sex was antiseptic and boring. He even wanted to wear a condom for oral sex. He was inexperienced in the bedroom and knew nothing about foreplay or sexual pleasure--except for his own. I was sure that he had never even seen a porn movie. Maybe, I should have suggested one?

After a week, I started to see a pattern emerge on the subject of finances. While I had been living in Pattaya, Cedrik took very good care of me—financially. I also received money from other men who had returned to their homes overseas, all the while I had continued to work. I asked Cedrik about continuing his payments to me. He responded that I was now in Switzerland, I was his wife, and he would take care of me and all of my needs. He said that I no longer needed an income to take care of myself. He didn't understand that without warning, he had just eliminated my family's only source of income. He was placing himself between me and the money I knew was due me. He apparently thought that I was sleeping with him for my room and board. *To a girl in my profession, sex is never free!*

Cedrik was under the impression that the money he sent to me was the only money I received, and that it was for my care alone. In fact, the money he sent every month was little more than one-third of my income; it was less money than I sent to my mother and sister in Ubon. I couldn't tell him that I had also lived from the generosity of other men while I had also continued to work, and I had been doing extremely well financially.

I felt that I had lost my freedom; I definitely had lost my income. All of this left me at a loss as to what I could do *legally*— to create a new source of cash. I had married a young Swiss boy for the purpose of improving my life and my financial situation. Although Switzerland was lovely, and I had a comfortable house in which to live, I couldn't understand the language and I was very bored. I was also 5,000 miles from home; sticky rice; som-tum; spicy food; warm weather; and the nightlife to which I had become accustomed.

After discussing these issues with Cedrik, difficult at best considering his limited English skills, I was forced to make a decision. I felt that I had no other choice. On my 10th day in Switzerland, I told him for the last time that I needed to send money home every month. He was unyielding. He said that he had sent money every month while he was in Switzerland; paid a Brideprice; bought gold for my family; and a laptop computer for me. As this was his final answer, I told him that I needed to return home and to my former career as he was denying me my only income.

Marriage Curtailed

Cedrik was not only heartbroken, he was terribly angry. He was about to lose the sex for which he thought he had paid in advance. Further, what could be more humiliating to a newly-married young man than his new wife choosing prostitution over him? He was awash with emotion—embarrassed, even mortified, deeply enraged, and even more deeply hurt. He said that after he had already spent so much money on me during the past year, he would not allow me to return to Thailand. I would remain his wife, and I would remain in Switzerland. Unfortunately, his social maturity was decades younger than his chronological years; he also had no understanding of women--especially Thai women. More at issue, he certainly knew nothing of Thai women working in the sex-trade. Although we had known one another for quite some time now, he had acquired virtually no understanding of me, nor I of him. Our life experiences were polarized at 180 degrees. We couldn't have been further apart, and our differences were seemingly carved in stone.

I grabbed my passport and began to pack my bags. I didn't know exactly how I was going to return to Thailand, or even how I would reach the airport. These issues were of less immediate concern to me than the issue of my income. If Cedrik would no longer provide money to my family, I would no longer provide anything to him; I would return to Thailand. He didn't realize that I married him to ensure that money continued to flow to my family and for no other reason. It became apparent that he believed that I was truly in love with him. He had a great deal to learn about life and even more to learn about bar girls.

I had a grip on my passport, but Cedrik tore it away from me and a struggle ensued. I bit his arm as hard as I could. When he screamed and finally let go of my passport, I released my bite and grabbed it. I apologized. I told him that he had no right to deny me

218

my passport—it belonged to me! As far as I was concerned, he did not buy me; he had only made an initial deposit and leased me, and his payments were past due.

His mother heard the commotion and came running in. She was in shock when she saw that I had bitten him so badly that he would require emergency medical care. Of course, neither of them could understand my feelings of desperation. They would never understand that Cedrik's control of my passport meant my family would do without the basic necessities of life. I could not, and I would not allow that to happen. I had been sleeping with men since I was 14 to care for my family. I was not going to stop getting paid for it now.

At first, we went to the hospital's Emergency Room to seek treatment and to suture the gash in his arm. His wound was deep. I stayed in the waiting room while his mother went into another room. Everyone was speaking French and I couldn't understand them. If I had married an Englishman, I would have understood. Why did I marry a French speaker? I waited while Cedrik's injury was treated.

Cedrik's mother finally returned; she was irate, an emotion that I could understand. I imagined for a moment that my son had been supporting a girl for many months and then brought her home to be his wife. But since her arrival, she had demonstrated nothing but her ingratitude and after only 10 days, she physically attacked my son and wanted to return to her home country. I could completely identify with her feelings for me. She told me that I had to see a psychologist. As far as I was concerned, I was just fine. But, I was willing to do anything that would expedite my leaving Switzerland and allow me to return to Pattaya, where I could once again see that my family received the funds they required. Begrudgingly, I went to the psychologist's office.

Immediately following treatment to Cedrik's arm, the three of us sat down and talked with the therapist. Cedrik's Mom thought I was crazy, not only because I had behaved so violently, but she couldn't understand how someone could not love her son--not unlike most mothers I suppose. She also would never understand that my behavior was related to the unexpected loss of my monthly allowance that kept me from supporting my family.

The psychologist spoke at length. Cedrik and his mother spoke to him in French, and he translated into English for me. I explained that I wasn't crazy, but I simply wanted my passport and to return to Thailand. He agreed that this was the best solution and explained our discussions to Cedrik's mom. I had my passport and the arrangements were made.

We returned home from the hospital and I packed my clothes. Although we all agreed unequivocally that I should leave, I was not entirely prepared to depart without a "golden handshake"— or even a silver one. The accepted practice in Pattaya is that when a Farang breaks up with a bar girl, she receives something for her time and effort as a departing gift, regardless of what she has already received. Cedrik and his mother, both being unsophisticated to the ways of bar girl/Farang relationships, knew nothing about this standard policy. I left with nothing more than the few items I had upon my arrival except for a one-way ticket back home.

Cedrik's mom took my bags, believing that I would try to go to another man instead of returning to Thailand. She called the police to take me to the airport. I was detained in a small room for about four hours before I boarded the plane which would carry me home. On Swiss Air, it was wonderful to be served by Farang rather than serving them.* It was a fantasy come true. Landing at Don Muang Airport in Bangkok was like returning from a long and disastrous holiday. But, I would once again be my own master.

*After I had been working in Pattaya for about a year or two, I decided to apply for a job as a waitress. I learned that waitresses earn every baht they receive and more. They deserve to be tipped well. My career as a waitress was short-lived, lasting less than a day. This was not due to the very hard work, the serving of Farang, nor even the extremely poor salary. The issue of salary could have been easily corrected by my seeing men whom I had met at the restaurant after I completed my day job. Tourists will pay more to a girl they believe is a waitress (a straight girl) than they will to a bar girl. I could have made 100% more from each client and seen a lot fewer men. The reason employment as a waitress did not fit my lifestyle was that I would have been required to labor at a boring and repetitive job for 8 to 9 hours each day, 26 days per month.

In Thailand, like most poor countries, people who have power and money often exploit it in cruel ways, i.e. Thai employers. The owner of this restaurant was no exception. He treated all of the employees very poorly. After he shouted at me one time, I shouted back-- swearing at him in English, and then I left. The tourist-patrons were shocked to see a waitress snap back at her boss in English, with no concern for her job. Little did they know that I could earn so much more money simply by meeting men, while partying the night away at a disco, although eventually at great emotional cost.

I dreamed about returning to Europe, the land of the Farang. They lived so well and were so courteous. How different it was from my country. I wondered why my people could not be as considerate. But for now, I would need to remain in Pattaya and return to work. I could wonder about why my people behaved so differently at some other time and in some other place.

221

Chapter 13

Broadening My Horizons

Returning to Pattaya

I arrived in Bangkok the next morning and in Pattaya that afternoon. I dropped my suitcase at an apartment that I liked and quickly darted over to see Dave who was very surprised to see me. *"What the hell happened? I expected you to be in Switzerland longer than 12 days,"* were the first words to come from his lips. I told him that I really didn't know how long it would last, but that I would have stayed as long as the money continued to flow. It didn't, and neither did I! Instead my income suffered a reversal; therefore, so did my stay. *I was there to maintain monthly payments to my family--and for no other reason!*

I told Dave that I needed to borrow Bt 6,000 to pay for the apartment; rent a motorbike, and head up to Bangkok to locate Steve. (I had met him a few years earlier at Thermae and we spent a great holiday together in Chiang Mai). Immediately upon my return to Pattaya, I called him and we arranged to meet. I had always thought he was the long-term type of a guy for me. With cash in hand, I jumped on the bus. Upon my arrival, I found a cheap room and waited there until late in the evening to head over to Thermae. While looking for Steve, I saw Jorg once again. He was exactly the wrong person at the wrong time. He looked at me and said, *"You have AIDS! Why are you working here?"* I said to him, *"Why not? I still need to eat, pay my rent, and send money home for my sisters."*

After hours of waiting and consuming non-alcoholic drinks, Steve finally arrived. His very first words to me were not at all what I expected. He said that I looked fat. I thought, *"He has a lot of nerve!"* If nothing else, I had confidence in my appearance! I was stunned but my response was immediate. *"Ha! Nobody has ever said that to me before!"* I was petite, with the firm body of a GoGo dancer, and I was very, very sexy! I knew better! Even after our rather turbulent reunion, we spent a lovely few days together in Chiang Mai. After a month, he returned to work, and so did I. Up to that time, Steve was the nicest relationship I had ever had.

I settled into my small, new apartment and began to think about my next plan of attack. I knew that financially, I was no better off than when I left for Switzerland a couple of weeks earlier. The upside was that I had just come from a rich and beautiful country and experienced Europe for the first time. I knew that I would find a way to return—*somehow!*

My first night back in Pattaya was like any other night. It was like I had never left. The weather hadn't changed. In fact, Pattaya's weather changes little throughout the year. It is always warm even during the cool and rainy seasons. My friends were still there and so were many of the tourists I had seen just a little over two weeks earlier.

I began making my rounds of the bars; I wanted my next job to be at a bar filled with customers. I didn't want to sit in a bar and work to bring in patrons--my future clients. Attracting customers was the responsibility of the bar. Once they sat down, I would take over. There are bar girls who bring customers to the bar --generally the youngest and prettiest; then the most devious girls try to get drinks and bar-fines. I could perform either duty, but I decided to let the "young blood" do the work while I concentrated on separating the customers from their money. After all, I had already been in the business for many years and I was a pro.

Soi 7 nightshift

Bringing in the trade

I decided to work at a bar in North Pattaya. Being 18, I was legally allowed to work in a bar; but even if I had been 16, as when I first arrived in Pattaya, the police would have looked the other way for a price--one that was included in the bar owner's monthly bribe. The government's efforts have done a great deal to remove girls under 18-years of age from plain sight in the bar and GoGo scene. I would never have believed that I would see it in such a short period of time. Yet, there are still many policemen who are more than willing to look the other way and allow these girls to remain—for a price. Their extra drawing-power and increased revenue more than compensates for the additional kickbacks that the bar owners are forced to pay.

Pressure from local-and-foreign NGOs and foreign news services brought an ugly fact-of-life "to light" in Thailand, and more precisely, in Pattaya. The government wanted to remove this

"*Loss of face*" quickly, and it succeeded, although its efforts served only as a facade. Younger girls are no longer *easily-visible* in the bar scene. Yet, there are still countless poor girls in Pattaya who find a way to meet men for money. There is an equally endless number of sex-tourists and sex-retirees looking and/or waiting at home for those *very* girls. Now, these girls more easily function simply as "*Room service*" rather than "*Take out.*"

Doorknockers

Many underage girls still continue to work in Pattaya. Although they cannot legally work in the beer bars and GoGos due to the government's much-improved enforcement of the "No one under 18" rule, this has done little to thwart their liaisons with their customers. Underage girls still meet men in the malls, markets, food courts, and on Beach Road.

During my time, "Knock, knock, knock" was the sound of underage girls looking for customers. Although more and more mobile telephones are in use today, for the girls who still cannot afford one, they go around to the homes of past customers looking for a "short-time." Girls spend the early afternoon and/or evening strolling through the condominium blocks and nicer housing developments full of Western retirees and (s)ex-patriots, if they are not successful in finding a customer at the mall or at the beach. They are no different than "Door-to-door" salesgirls. Nan and I occasionally solicited our customers in this manner. If one of our past customers was available, then we would see him; if not, then we would make the rounds, knocking until we found someone.

Pattaya's infamous Beach Road:
Underage street girls looking for foreign customers

Clockwise from upper left:
Ages 16, 15, 14 and 14

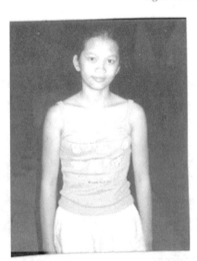 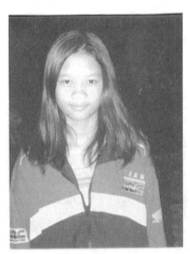

Despite the efforts of the government and the NGOs,
there is still no shortage of underage girls--or customers
prowling for them--by night and by day

226

Beach Road mom (left) pimping her daughters
Age 17 (center), age 15 (right)

While most Isaan mom's receive their cash via the ATM,
this one gets involved in the sale

16-year old girl lies about her age, steals mobile phone from foreign punter

An Australian tourist who marched a girl to Pattaya police station for stealing his mobile phone while he was in the bathroom, prior to having sex with her, received a shock when officers advised him she was only 16-years old.

Groski Koming, a 60-year old Australian national, told the duty officer that he had been taking a walk along South Pattaya Beach when the girl, who cannot be named for legal reasons and has been given the alias Wan, came up and invited him to go to bed with her for 500 baht. Koming said he asked her how old she was because she looked so young and she told him that she was 20. Satisfied, he accepted her offer and took her back to his room.

He went to the bathroom to take a shower while the girl sat on the bed. While he was in the shower, she took his mobile phone and fled. He followed her and shouted to a motorcycle-taxi driver to help. They stopped the girl, and Koming decided to take her to the station so that the police could give her a warning. Wan said that she was only 16 and had lied about her age. She admitted snatching the mobile phone. The police warned her and reminded her that it is illegal for her to perform sexual services because she is still a minor. No action was taken against the foreigner for taking an underage prostitute to his hotel room.

PattayaMail June 10-16, 2005

Aussie punter and 16-year old Beach Road prostitute

Photo courtesy of PattayaMail

No action was taken against this foreigner
for taking an underage prostitute to his hotel room.

I was living in the central part of the city and working in North Pattaya, only a short commute. It was not much of a bar-- although it had enough customers, but I would also not have much competition while working there. I was there only a few days before I was struck by "luck"—both good and bad. I ran into Paul, an old acquaintance. Paul was a photographer for whom I had frequently posed. He paid very well, Bt 2,000-3,000 ($50 to $75) for a two-hour session. We had not seen one another in a long time, primarily because we greatly irritated one another. But, I made the decision that this time it would be different. I had no one sending me money while believing that I belonged to them. I needed money, and if it meant I had to work with Paul, I would. We made arrangements to meet the following day and I began my modeling career once again.

"Ms. Photogenic"

Paul asked if I were interested in earning more money than I would normally make by going with men. I was always interested in making money. He asked if I would be interested in, once again, posing for nude photographs. I was used to being seen without clothes on stage and in hotel rooms, and I didn't mind the work or the money. There was no sex involved and I would receive twice the amount of money I earned sleeping with men. This was a very good deal.

The cash Paul paid me for photographs was a lot more than the Bt 1,000 ($25) that I would receive for a couple of hours with a client. I thought I was on to a new career or at least a sideline, once again. Paul would photograph me for a couple of hours and quite often take me to eat. He had lots of sexy clothes and jewelry to model. He would also give me money to buy clothes for our photo shoots. He paid me very well, and I would always bring him the change, unlike other men for whom I had worked. These were men to whom I told I needed more money for everything even if they had already given me enough. My stay at the bar in North Pattaya lasted no more than a few days. I didn't need the bar to meet men, and I didn't want to show up 7 hours/day, 28 days/month. I could spend my time in ways far more financially rewarding. Better yet, I was a model!

I would pose for Paul two or three times a week for a month or more, and I'd see men when convenient. He took hundreds and hundreds of photos that would tempt almost any man. I would begin partially-clothed, and then my clothing would drop away until I was naked. He had a myriad of colorful and revealing costumes for me to wear--and not to wear. He also had a treasure-trove of lovely jewelry. Some of his pieces contained real stones and were very expensive; other pieces were of the costume variety. All of it was beautiful. Towards the end of every session, Paul's

230

jewelry was all that touched my flesh.

He took provocative photos of me while showering, bathing, and while sitting or lying down. Every pout and every pose were choreographed to arouse the "Animal instinct" in men. I excited and I enticed them, and then I lured them in. Flirting with the camera was second nature; it was no different than what I had been doing on stage and in hotel rooms since I was 14. We took photos in every milieu—from his hotel room to some of the most exquisitely beautiful beaches in the world—including Phuket, Koh Samui, and the Similan Islands. I was also earning greater money than I had ever earned in my life and I wasn't selling sex.

I have been featured in *"Oriental Dolls," "Oriental Women," "Asian Beauties,"* and *"Asian Hotties."* Paul loved my look and he was a good photographer. I was making so much money that I didn't have to look around for men--unless I wanted to. I was able to live comfortably and send money home on my "modeling" income alone. For now, I didn't need money from men other than Paul. I was doing very well on my own.

After a couple of months, Paul had taken more than enough pictures of me. He needed new faces, but he found that he was unsuccessful in his pursuit of Thai girls to model for him. Most Thai girls, even those who danced naked in the GoGos, would not accept his offers even though he agreed to pay them more money than they could make going with men. Pornography is so disdained in Thailand that his offers frightened them from accepting "modeling" jobs. It is really difficult to scare a bar girl into turning down money. The irony in their refusal to model is that they earn their livelihoods by dancing in the nude for less money, and they never become rich. Yet, when offered an opportunity to model in the nude and substantially increase their income, they refuse.

231

Pornography is not only unacceptable in Thailand, it is also illegal! Prostitution runs amok, but photos are taboo! We like to hide everything unacceptable and present a facade. Photographs completely destroy this possibility. They are a record which we cannot deny. Paul's difficulty in hiring new faces led to my new career.

Modeling Agent Extraordinaire

As Paul was having so much trouble getting other girls to model for him, he asked if I would help. I explained that his problem had nothing to do with his salary offer which was extremely good, but it was because *"He"* was making the offer. I knew that I could easily convince girls to go with him on photo shoots, and I could earn a commission as well. Even though he didn't need any more photos of me, I could still make good money from our new arrangement. I quickly became a modeling agent.

Paul and I would walk to the bars and GoGos in Bangkok and Pattaya to find the prettiest girls with the best bodies. We visited dozens of bars night after night. He was extremely selective. I would see girls who I knew would be great for his photos, but he was never satisfied, and we would continue to scour every GoGo and every bar until closing time. He couldn't make up his mind. When he finally found a girl he wanted, he would buy her a drink, and I would talk to her about his proposition. Although at first the girls always refused, I was generally able to convince them to accept his offer. I explained that she might not receive another offer that night. Or, if she did, it would be one-third to one-half of ours. I still had great skills of persuasion. She would usually accept. I also reminded her that she could not get AIDS or another Sexually Transmitted Disease (STD) from photos, and that she might be able to take more photos and make more money in the future.

It was during this time that I recruited girls for the photo shoots that I would reflect on my arrival in Bangkok and my first jobs--mopping floors, washing dishes, slicing limes, and squeezing oranges. I remembered Thermae Bar, the discos in Bangkok, and the GoGos in Pattaya. I also thought about my short, yet highly-profitable modeling career. Now, I was working as a modeling agent, earning Bt 1,000 for every girl I recruited, and I was very successful in supplying models to Paul. Not only did I convince girls to come pose for him, I also served as translator during the session. The money was pretty good for the work and I would do it again--any day. It was a lot better than going with men for money.

Film Career

After we had developed a large "stable" of girls who were both pleasant and photogenic, we pursued another form of media-- film. At first, I was the sole performer. I would talk seductively to the camera while undressing provocatively. I had thought that the photo shoots paid well, but I soon learned that there was even more money in films. I was paid Bt 3,000 ($75) for a one-hour performance.

I had a starring role in *"Amazing Bangkok 1999"* and I narrated *"Sex! Sin! And Sun! In Phuket."* Paul had taken thousands of pictures. He had some really beautiful girls--including me. Some of the girls were easy to work with while others were really difficult and in a hurry to leave. The girls who were amiable and photogenic received return offers for work. Those who were trouble didn't receive another opportunity to make easy money!

When I made videos, I pretended that I was a woman whom I had seen in sexy or X-rated American and European videos. It wasn't difficult and it was a lot of fun. I wouldn't want my little sisters to do it, but I didn't mind. In fact, it became so routine that I had forgotten that I came to Pattaya primarily to see men for money. I would never have thought that I could make so much extra money for being pretty and allowing someone to video my performance. I continued posing and pouting, bathing and showering, and bouncing around the room—all for the camera.

Before long, Paul began filming two girls on camera at a time. All of the girls received the same salary. Paul didn't tolerate "Prima donnas." Filming is a lot of work, and Paul was the director and the camera man. As long as he was paying the models, they would do exactly what he and I demanded of them.

I was now on film with other girls. It was the same as when I was filmed alone. We would shower and bathe together, slowly caressing one another from head to toe. While appearing casual, we would towel-dry each other, teasingly drop our towels and sway over to the bed—ever so seductively. Then we would continue to perform for the camera--creating lust and desire. At least, that was our intention. Sometimes there would be two, three, or even four of us. It was an excellent business arrangement for everyone. The girls would each receive Bt 3,000 ($75). That is three times as much as a man would pay for the night, and as much as our brothers or sisters earn in one full-month of back-breaking labor in the provinces.

Paul would make a one-hour video for Bt 12,000 ($300). He sold these soft-core porn videos overseas that featured only alluring and captivating sun-tanned Thai beauties. Farang men exhibit great interest in exotic and mysterious Asian women. Paul made a lot of money; we made a lot of money; and all the while Western men fantasized over the petite, dark-haired, bronzed-skin beauties they would never have.

On several occasions, we traveled to the islands off Pattaya Beach and to those in the south of Thailand—near Phuket or Koh Samui. We rented a speedboat, sent the skipper off, and filmed for hours. We ran on the bleached white sand and frolicked in the white-capped waves. These were uninhabited islands where tourists seldom wandered. We must have made a dozen videos over the course of a year. I loved to make these videos because the money was so good, and I had fallen in love with the camera. I was Paul's first starlet, and I never worried about my competition.

Paul told us that it was every man's dream to be on a tropical island with so many exotic and beautiful naked girls. He just put their fantasies on film; his sales were proof that he was right. Orders for the movies came in like never before. Thailand is full of beautiful islands and even more beautiful women. As young Thai women, we didn't understand the fantasy, nor the business end of Paul's efforts. We didn't have to. If Farang men were willing to pay Paul a lot of money for his videos, and he was willing to pay us a lot of money for running naked on the beach, we were willing to play. We would have been willing to run for hours at a time and days-on-end--as long as the money followed.

We made a lot of island movies. It was a great way to spend the day. All of us would have gone to the islands to spend the day for free if we had been asked. We were used to receiving money for taking off our clothes, but receiving a lot of money for taking off our clothes, playing in the surf, and having a wonderful time was even better!

Tour Guide

I have also been a travel-guide for videos filmed all over Thailand that were sold around the world. It is amazing what a young girl can accomplish when she puts her mind and body to it. Sadly, the industries of prostitution, pornography, and the sale of a young girl's sexuality are the only ones available in Thailand where we can be fairly-compensated for our efforts. I left a village in Ubon when I was *only 13*. I had no idea what I was going to do except I knew that I was going to help give my family a better life, as my father had tried so hard to do.

My entire life had been about earning money through the sex-trade. Later, I moved on to soft-core porn in print and on film. Although I would still see tourists for money, I began doing more. I began making clean, legitimate travel videos that one could show to their mothers.

I made travel videos for Bangkok, and the beautiful beach resorts of Phuket and Koh Samui, as well as the less attractive beach resort of Pattaya. I was paid many thousands of baht for each video, and the best part was that I could keep my clothes on. These videos would take three hours and they required more from me than the earlier videos. But, they were clean and they were fun. I was lucky enough to land this job because I spoke English well, I was pretty, and I had a good sense of humor. If I had spoken perfect English and was of only average appearance, I would never have been offered the opportunity to appear in these travel videos.

To make the first video, I was flown to Phuket. Many more flights were to follow. I was a poor girl from the province, flying to a beautiful exotic isle to make a travel video that would be sold all over the world. I was living a dream far greater than I had ever hoped for. *I was living a dream come true!*

Helping Another Girl Get into the "Trade"

While I was doing everything I could to stay out of the business, a neighbor told me that her friend wanted to start making the kind of money that I did, and she wanted to know what I could do to help. I told her that she knew exactly what I did, and that it was no different than the other 10,000 bar girls in Pattaya. She admitting knowing that, but she thought I could help her out since I already knew so many men. Shortly thereafter, I learned that not

236

only did this 16-year old girl want to become a bar girl, more importantly, she wanted to sell her virginity. I did not really want to become involved, but they continued to press the issue and told me how badly *her family* needed the money; so I agreed. *Once again, a daughter was selling her virginity to help her family,* providing additional evidence for the Thai proverb shared earlier, *"Thai women are just another kind of crop."*

It did not take more than a few days for me to meet a guy who wanted to buy a girl's virginity and pay a "Fair price." There is no shortage of these kinds of guys in Pattaya because they flock here from throughout the world for this very reason. This man offered to pay Bt 20,000 ($500) for a 16-year old girl's virginity. I felt that this was a reasonable offer. It was not the same amount that I had received a few years earlier, but it was a lot of money in Pattaya. I informed the girl of the offer and she readily accepted. After she received the money, not only did she pay me a Bt 3,000 commission, but he paid me Bt 2,000 as well. I made Bt 5,000 out of the whole thing. I really didn't want to get involved in the first place, but I did it to help the girl make money, not because I was going to receive anything in return. Now, I wish that I had turned down the commission I received from the young girl, as well as the tip from the man. Or, that I had thought about giving the tip to the girl. I was now no better than the *mama-san* who helped to sell my virginity four years earlier.

I did everything I could to make sure that my sisters would never get involved in the sex-tourist trade, and here I was helping a 16-year old get involved in it. It was one of the worst things that I had ever done, and I have continued to regret that decision. I will always feel the need to make-up for my terrible lack of good judgment. I want to devote the rest of my life to protecting and saving young girls from the "Sex-for-sale" industry, not facilitating their entry into it.

Chapter 14

So Many Suitors, So Little Time

Johan from Sweden

The first time I saw Johan, he was eating with a friend outside of the 19th Hole Super Pub near Walking Street. Although I wasn't working that night, I still went to that location to buy fruit and to watch Farang. I saw Johan watching me and we exchanged smiles. I knew that he was new to Pattaya because of his lack of casual attire and his apparent discomfort. I had seen his friend who sat by his side many times before. I offered some bananas to Johan, but he refused. I was not used to being turned down, and I really wanted to meet him. I decided to push over my motorbike, hoping that he would help me stand it back up. Before he could get up, a Japanese tourist came to my aid. I was angry that Johan didn't have the opportunity to help me. I was also angry with myself that Johan had not "taken to me" right away. Men generally did! I learned later that he was very shy.

Two days later, I saw Johan and his friend sitting two bars away from the one in which I was working. I told my friend to tell him where I was the next time she went to the lady's room. Moments later, he waved and came to see me. We enjoyed a few beers while I convinced him that I was worth his time so that he would pay my bar-fine. I tried to get Johan to pay my friend's bar-fine and take us both, but he refused, causing her to cry. She had the ability to feign tears easily. In our profession, this talent comes in handy. She really didn't care about going with us, but she really wanted to get off from work that night, and get her commission from the bar-fine he would have paid.

I spent the next 12 days with Johan during his first trip to Thailand. He paid me Bt 1000/night ($25) and complained that it

238

was too expensive. I didn't offer him a discount because I knew that he could easily afford it. Yet, after we had spent 12 days together, I had begun to develop some feelings for him. He was different from other men I had met. He was nice to women and to people in general; he was kind, polite, and well-mannered. His traveling companion, Jesper, never paid a woman more than Bt 500 ($12) per night; he even cheated a young girl by paying her only Bt 2,000 ($50) for her virginity. The normal price for a girl, still untouched, was approximately Bt 20,000 ($500). I thought he was the worst kind of human being. Only an evil and loathsome individual would take away a poor, young girl's most valuable and saleable asset and not pay her its true value.

On Johan's last day in Pattaya, the Foreign Exchange counter had closed and the nearest ATM wasn't working, so he couldn't access any more money. I still don't know why I felt I could trust him, but I lent him about Bt 5,000 ($125) so that we could have a "Bon voyage" party. The following day, Johan had to return to Sweden and I took him to the airport in Bangkok. We took our photo and we stayed in touch. Every couple of weeks, I placed an international call to Sweden. I stopped calling Johan when John, a former client from England, returned to Thailand.

John from England

The first time I met John, I was working on Soi 8. John walked past the bar, saw me, and immediately changed his direction. He returned, sat down, and bought me a drink. He quickly decided to pay my bar-fine. After only one day, he wanted me to stay with him for a long time. He paid me Bt 2,000/day for six months—the entire length of time he stayed in Pattaya. That is a great boyfriend! He finally had to return to England, but only for three months. When he left, I moved to the Nirun Condotel.

After three months in England, he returned to Thailand. He

spent a lot of time looking for me and finally found me at my new apartment. John knew that Sai would be staying with me. He thought about establishing a business here. But, he didn't know how to go about it or what business to pursue. He considered an ice cream shop on Second Road, but instead we made a little restaurant on Soi Buakhow. It was a lot of work! As he was in a spending mood, I also convinced him to buy a motorbike for me.

John once gave me Bt 250,000 to buy a business, but I wasn't ready to buy anything and I gave the money back. *Now I know that the reader may find it very difficult to believe, but I actually gave the money back!* He gave me money again to make my own restaurant on Soi Buakhow, but not nearly Bt 250,000. He also found Dave to return to him the Bt 6,000 that I had borrowed upon my return from Switzerland.

Our relationship lasted a couple more months, but problems started to arise between us because he didn't get along with Sai. Few did! He was always fighting with her as did nearly everyone. Because I loved Sai, I always took Sai's side. This led to John's decision to finally separate from me. I was broken-hearted for a while; I really did like him, and he was extremely generous. But to be perfectly honest, I didn't stay broken-hearted for long as I knew that Johan was just around the corner.

Johan and I had been out of touch for a couple of months even after he returned to Pattaya. He contacted Dave to try and find me, and he sought me out at every GoGo and bar in the city. Since Dave knew that I was with John and wanted to stay with him, he claimed that he didn't know where I could be found. One afternoon, I saw Johan on Soi Buakhow; neither of us spoke. I was embarrassed that I hadn't contacted him for a long time. I told Sai to tell him that I missed him and wanted to know his hotel. I was at a loss at what to say. I knew that Johan had planned to stay for six more weeks; so, after learning of his hotel, I decided to surprise him. He was delighted to see me and we decided to stay together until he returned to Sweden. He even asked me to go to Sweden for a holiday. I told him that I'd think about it.

Jurgen from Germany

Not long after Johan's departure, I met Jurgen. We spent a couple of weeks together and got along really well. On Jurgen's second trip to Pattaya, he said that I could make a lot of money in his country, and he would arrange for me to go to Germany to work. He promised to marry me if I would return with him to Koln. I had no other prospects in Thailand other than working in Pattaya, so I agreed. It didn't take long for me to decide that I would make Germany my next home. Jurgen filed the Visa application at the German Embassy in Bangkok.

When the time had arrived to go to the Embassy, Dave took me and helped me to complete more paperwork. It was a lot more trouble than I had anticipated. We took the 6:00 A.M. bus from Pattaya in order to arrive early, but a queue was already in place when we arrived, and we still had to wait our turn in-line. Wading through the "Ribbons of red tape" took the entire day. After spending hours in line, we had to give up our place because we didn't have a duplicate copy of one of our forms. It would have been much more efficient, a characteristic for which the Germans are well-known, to have made a copy for us. I would have expected this act of courtesy after meeting the Swiss. In this case, they abruptly refused. Instead, Dave had to leave the Embassy and locate a copy shop blocks away. Upon his return, we had to take a new number and start again. It was the end of the day before we had completed this long, tedious, and infuriating process.

First, we had a bite to eat to fortify ourselves for the two-and-a-half hour ride home. To my surprise, Dave made me pay for lunch. He was angry because this process consumed the entire day and was made more difficult by the lack of cooperation from the Embassy staff. Actually, I didn't mind because I used Jurgen's money. The anxiety of submitting the paperwork was finally over, and I could concentrate during the next couple of weeks on working in Pattaya. I would also think a lot about how life would be in Germany. I called Jurgen "collect" the following day to tell him that I had submitted the required forms to his Embassy in Bangkok. He was thrilled. In time, I would learn the true reason for his unrestrained delight. It took about two weeks for my Visa to arrive. When it did, I felt as if the pressure had been lifted and I could relax. I was really going to Europe--again; I knew that this trip had to result in far happier experiences than my first one.

Once again, it was time to arrange for a ticket and prepare to leave Thailand. I had a 15-year-old sister to send home to Ubon, who as before did not want to leave Pattaya--Thailand's humble answer to Las Vegas, Hollywood, New Orleans, and Atlantic City all rolled-up into one exciting 24-hour sex-tourist resort. But, Sai was adamant about staying in Pattaya with her friends. I was worried that she might run away and be on her own. She had worked twice, once for a few months operating a photo sticker booth in a shopping center and another time as a waitress in a late-night restaurant near our apartment. She used this income as her spending money. I always took care of all of the bills. I was worried that if she ran away, she would eventually take up the life I led and sleep with tourists for money. *I had done everything all of my life to make sure that she would never have to live MY life! This had always been my greatest fear and a recurring nightmare.*

Sai refused to return to Ubon, instead opting to stay with her friend in an apartment and keeping her job as a waitress. I worried that she might not remain a waitress. There is so little money working in any normal job in Thailand, and Thai employers are notoriously unkind and unfair. This is the reason so many Thais want to work for foreign companies, so many maids want to work for foreigners, and why many ex-brothel girls end up going to Pattaya and Patpong to sleep with foreigners. I was frightened that she would decide not to work the long hours for such little money. I was frightened that she would do as I had done and start making real money sleeping with tourists. But, I felt that I had to move to Germany, and I had to leave her in Pattaya—alone.

Sai building her own sandcastles on Pattaya Beach, Age 14

What My Sister Means to Me

If anything that my sisters do makes them happy,
they should just do it.
I will take care of all of the painful parts of their lives myself.
They can take the happy path on their own.
I have two sisters, but no one ever thinks about staying with me.
My little sister, Joy, Do you know yourself at this moment?
You are like a cracked glass waiting to break at anytime.
You must be careful.
The roads have many directions.
Some are bad, and others are good.
Some roads are even cut off.
Dead ends.
I am not able to know all of the roads before I take them.
Where will they lead or will they be dead ends?
And you, which road will you to take?
The road on which you choose to stand right now
does not know where the end lies or how it will end.
Actually, each woman has her own life, walking different ways.
Joy, you have your own sister, but you never love her.
Joy, you never can understand my feelings.
Because you never love yourself,
You will never love a sister, not even me.
You have large round eyes.
When you were little,
They were very beautiful and lovely eyes for me.
But now, your big beautiful eyes do not look soft anymore.
(Not from a nice person)
Plants come from the ground
Your eyes are like this from hate and pressure.
These are eyes without happiness for a long time.
When I look at your eyes, I see a lot of sadness and pain.
You might need love and understanding from someone
And, I am sure that that someone is not me.

Right now, you are 15, going on 16 so soon.
Joy, Nong Lak, "younger loved one,"
If someday you are lonely, and need someone,
I ask you to look at the mirror.
To stand in front of the mirror and look at yourself.
That is the person you need.
You are going to live like a child but as a teenager.
The age of the path of danger,
This age you can see is quite dangerous.
One little child used to sit on my lap, I used to hug and kiss her.
That child has changed to another person already.
You are the one, the most important one to me.
You are the one closest to me.
Joy, do you remember we used to go take the shells from the rice fields,
looking for fish and frogs?
And swim in the stream, racing the buffaloes?
I was the one who would take everyone to school every day.
Now, there are three of us including Joy, Nong Ying, and me.
The life we had as children
was the happiest time that we have ever had.
Don't you think so Joy?
If I could stop time, or turn the clock back,
I would like to stay in that time once again.
The time when we would go to the rice fields;
Hands dirty with mud; drinking water from the pond
In the middle of the fields; looking for mushrooms;
Taking the sap from the tree to take home to make candles.
It was better for me to do that than to put on a short skirt
And high heels, going to the discos to meet men for the night,
Because all of these do not make me be myself.
How I loved being a child.

One Vast Blur

These years have passed quickly. My birthdays, from the age of 14 through 19, seemed to have come and gone as if by overnight; I often have trouble remembering those years. It has been *"One vast blur."* I was out all night, every night, and often saw nothing more than the sunset, or an occasional sunrise. In Patpong, the constant flickering of the blinding strobe lights, and the blare of the computerized music, left me feeling battered and lost in the emptiness of their din. For five years I have lived like an owl--rarely seeing the sun. My life was no different than any other dancer, except that at the beginning of my "career," I was younger than most. As I grew, I became more emotionally and psychologically in-sync with the rest of the dancers. I was a little more self-assured as I approached men and less crushed by rejection. I saw other 14-year old girls fearfully drop into and then fall out of the business.

I had hoped that sending Sai money every month from Germany would prevent my fate from becoming hers. I hoped for the best as I prepared to leave. Once again, I said my last prayer at the airport in Thailand. I will always believe that praying in Thailand is different than in a Farang country. Once again, we have different spirits in our world. I do not believe that the spirits would have heard me, nor answered my calls, from Germany. I took advantage of my last chance *"to be in the neighborhood."* And, just as when I flew to Switzerland, I prayed for my father.

Finally, I arrived in Germany. Again, I had traveled a long way from home. I was there for one reason and one reason only--to make money. I was honest about it from the beginning, and I never misled Jurgen. Jurgen was honest with me as well--or so I thought. He wanted me to work to make money. We were in full-agreement. I would work in a massage parlor in Germany and make a lot of money because men would believe that I was much younger than I really was. They would flock to buy my services for that reason. I would tell them that I was 16 in order to get bigger tips, although I was actually 19. Once German men believed that I was only 16, they wouldn't look at another woman. Jurgen and I would split my income 50/50, and from his share, the utilities, rent, and food would be paid. At least, this was the unwritten contract to which I had agreed.

Our misunderstanding occurred when I learned that Jurgen expected me to sleep with him as well. In addition to having sex with men from the massage parlor and giving him 50% of my earnings, he also expected sexual favors. I was willing to split the money that I earned 50/50, because I would earn five times more in Germany than I could in Pattaya. I would also not have any financial obligations other than my family. But, if he wanted sex with me, he would have to pay for it. Once again, *Sex was not free!* Sex was my only way of earning an income. We had a serious conflict which required an immediate resolution.

I told Jurgen that if he expected to receive 50% of my salary, he would have to forget about sleeping with me. He was hurt; he felt that I had not lived up to my side of the bargain. As far as he was concerned, he was entitled to one-half of my income and free sex. In my mind, he was demanding more than 50% from our arrangement. *Sex had a price tag and it wasn't cheap!* I couldn't believe that he would expect so much.

Soon after I began earning money, Jurgen took it to pay for my air ticket to Germany. I couldn't believe that he now expected me to pay for my flight. Our arrangements were becoming increasingly ugly. He paid for the ticket in the first place so that he could take 50% of my income and get free sex. When he took money from my earnings to pay for my flight, I knew that I needed a way out.

Germany was too cold for my Thai blood, even though I had already experienced the chilly climate of Switzerland and that was in August. Now, Jurgen wanted to go to Spain. Since I didn't speak Spanish, I was concerned about how I would communicate. I didn't think that Jurgen could speak Spanish either. I was a little hesitant about the trip, but it was far better than giving him half of my earnings in Germany, and the weather had to be an improvement.

While in Spain, I was really unhappy with Jurgen. I had also been unhappy with him in Germany—but our situation was reaching the "Point of no return." I remembered Johan, we had known one another for a while by now, and he had always treated me very well. I wanted to see him again, and I definitely wanted to get away from Jurgen. I called Johan in Sweden from my hotel in Spain. I didn't care that the calls would be expensive; Jurgen would pay for them.

I told Johan that Jurgen planned to use me to make money for himself. In my eyes, the flow of money between Farang men and me travels only one way. Money leaves them and comes to me, not the other way around. Johan really cared about me and he was concerned for my welfare. Although I was in Spain with Jurgen, Johan came to see me for a week. Jurgen was angry, but there was nothing he could do about it. He didn't have any rights to me in Spain, nor as he would soon learn, anywhere else either.

Spain--and Germany, too

From Germany, and my short-lived career as a "masseuse," I traveled to Spain to seek relief from the cold and from payments to Jurgen. Spain was a most welcome change. I had now lived in Switzerland and Germany knowing only the chill of Europe. In Spain, I was enjoying its warmth. When Jurgen learned that Johan was coming to Spain to meet me, he locked me out on the balcony until 3:00 A.M. He was very angry about not being able to "Cash in" on what he had intended to be his little brown "Cash cow."

Sunny Spain

A smile for Johan

While in Spain, Jurgen did not have enough money to pay the hotel bill, and he told me to go out and make some money. Since I had gone to Europe to make money "that way" anyway, it didn't matter to him whether I made it in Germany or in Spain. He always said that I had such an easy life as I was able to make money with so little effort. He could not possibly have fathomed how difficult it was to earn each and every baht. He knew nothing of the sacrifices I had made, nor did he care!

I was very happy when Johan arrived in Spain, and I went to his hotel to meet him. We would have a week together and I was going to make the best of every moment. I told him that I didn't think that I would be able to get myself out of the mess in Germany without returning to Thailand; so, we examined the possibilities. We also talked about the good times we shared and the fun we had together in Thailand. This was my second trip to Europe, and I really wanted to make it work. The last thing that I wanted to do was to return to the social and economic ruins of Thailand and the life of a bar girl—poorly-paid relative to European standards. I also didn't want to compete with all of the young and pretty Thai girls anymore as I was already 19, although I was still highly-competitive.

After a few days together, Johan made a snap decision; he would take me to Sweden. Of course, that had been my plan all along. I had every intention of spending my time with someone with whom I could share mutual affection. I also knew that I had to liberate myself from my disastrous situation with Jurgen, although I never gave a thought to Sweden's climate. I would soon learn the true meaning of the word "Cold!" At the end of the week, Johan returned to Sweden, and I returned to Jurgen's hotel.

Jurgen cried over my decision to leave. He said that he loved me, and that I was breaking our agreement. I told him that I was neither his employee, nor his lover. He expected both and ended up with neither. I later learned that he had previously brought a Filipina girlfriend to Germany for the same purpose. He was now 0 for 2!

Immediately after our return to Germany from Spain, I excitedly boarded a plane bound for Sweden. When I left, Jurgen said, *"You are so lucky to have me. You will come back to me."* I ran into him a few years later in Pattaya. He asked if I would like to return to him under the same conditions as before. Without a second thought, I adamantly declined his offer feeling as if my self-worth had reached the heavens—at least for that single moment in time. I was feeling very good about myself!

Upon my arrival in Stockholm, I learned that the German airline ticket agent should have required me to present a Swedish Visa prior to issuing a ticket. Europeans can travel around Europe without Visas, but Thai people cannot. I had traveled to Spain without a problem. The Spanish were used to receiving tourists from all over the world, so they allowed me to enter unquestioned. But upon my arrival in Sweden, the Immigration authorities, although polite, refused me entrance. I was in the Swedish airport, but I couldn't enter the country. Johan was waiting for me outside the Immigration area. He was allowed to enter to speak with the officials, but as long as I didn't have a Visa, I wouldn't be allowed to enter Sweden.

Immigration informed me that I needed to return to Germany to apply for a Visa with the Swedish Embassy. They said it was a simple formality and that it would not be difficult as long as Johan was my sponsor. Johan said that he would buy round-trip tickets for us, Sweden/Germany/Sweden. It would only take one day for the Swedish Visa to be issued. I was really angry about this sudden "State-of-affairs." I was standing inches from entering Sweden and beginning a brand-new life with Johan. Unfortunately,

I was forced to turn around and fly away—to Germany.

Upon leaving the airport in Koln, I immediately rushed back to Jurgen's apartment to pick up some more of my clothes. It is common behavior of bar girls to leave some of their things at the homes of their ex-boyfriends when they leave. That way, they will always have a reason to return. The usual explanation is that they were simply on a trip and had every intention of returning. But this time, I had no intention of returning. I would sooner return to Thailand than live with Jurgen and share half-of-my-earnings.

I took a taxi from Jurgen's apartment to the hotel Johan had chosen for the night, and then we went to the Swedish Consulate in Hamburg to apply for a Tourist Visa. They politely accepted my application. Europeans are very polite to pretty, young Thai girls. I would never receive the same gracious treatment in Thailand unless I stayed at a Five Star Hotel. Tourists in Thailand can be the recipients of great courtesy, but it does not come from the heart of a Thai. Thai government employees also have no vested interest in the customer accomplishing one's goals and dreams or not. Rather, it is only in the interest of receiving financial rewards that they provide service. Europeans provide good service because they actually want to help.

The following day, Johan and I flew to Sweden. Not only was I excited about entering into a new life with him, I had also fled Germany and Jurgen. Upon landing, I approached Immigration and proudly showed them my Swedish Visa. Immigration graciously welcomed me into Sweden, *"Varsagod!"*

Chapter 15

Finally, Sweden

I could not have been happier. I had just arrived in Sweden, a rich European country, and I was with a young, attractive man who really cared about me. But, no sooner had I walked outside the airport than I was numbed by the biting cold. This was not even winter, but the bitter and icy winds chilled me to the bone. I never knew that it could be this cold anywhere on the planet. I knew that I would probably never again leave the warmth inside of my new home.

Upon arriving at Johan's apartment, I ran inside and left my bags in the car for him to carry. I was too cold to think about anything other than seeking the warmth of his living room. I already missed "Som tum," a very spicy green papaya salad indigenous to those from Isaan. We believe it is essential to our very survival.

Sai in Trouble

It was shortly after I had begun my new life with Johan, when a friend of Sai's contacted me. Sai had refused to return to Ubon when I left for Germany, and I had genuinely worried about leaving her with her friends in Pattaya. I had worried that she might become involved in something illegal. Trouble was and remains easily available, just for the asking, in Pattaya. She had begun using Yabah, a popular amphetamine in Thailand. She was now in jail. Through a friend, she reached me and asked for help. I wired non-refundable "Bail" money which amounts to no more than a bribe to the police. Upon receipt, the case against her was discharged and she was free to go. The cost was Bt 5,000 ($125). It would have been worth twice that amount to release her from jail. Paying the bribe also allowed me to sleep at night. Pattaya is filled with people

253

living on the edge. The attraction to that exhilarating life-style was too much for a 15-year old to resist, particularly without any adult supervision.

A Woman of Leisure

As I held a Tourist Visa, I was not allowed to work. Instead, I lived the life of *"A woman of leisure."* I did the small amount of housekeeping required for two people; this left me a lot of time to watch television and go to the gym. I also visited Johan's parents on many occasions. But, I was bored with being home alone. I asked Johan if he could get a Swedish Visa for my friend Bee.

Bee: A "Fish to Water"

Several months prior to my trip to Germany, I met Bee, one of Ying's high school friends. The first time she came to visit me in Pattaya, she asked how the girls owned so many nice things like motorbikes, gold, and pretty clothes. Most importantly, she wanted to know how they had so much money. I told her the truth, *"They slept with tourists."* She said, *"Is that all?"* She went after it like a *"Fish to water."* She was much more interested than most girls who come to Pattaya for the first time, but it usually doesn't take a lot of prodding to get girls into the business when they see how much money is available. The fact that one no longer needs to work long hours, for meager compensation from a Thai employer, is more than adequate motivation. Shortly thereafter, she moved to Bangkok to work the scene.

In no time at all, Johan had succeeded in getting her a Visa to visit me; Swedish Immigration is rather liberal. They not only granted me a three-month Tourist Visa, but when I became bored, they even allowed a friend to come and stay with me. I was thrilled to have someone with whom I could share my native dialect and eat my native food.

Bee and I enjoyed the cooler weather and had a wonderful time touring the countryside. As I had come to know the city of Stockholm, I served as Bee's tour guide. I couldn't believe that I was serving as a guide in a European country and taking my friend to the best places to shop. I felt as if I were living a dream! We were two poor, young girls from the lower class in Thailand; touring Sweden; and being recognized by Swedes as "equals"-- more or less. Maybe our appearance had something to do with it, at least when it came to men. This could never happen in Bangkok, nor in any region of Thailand. I could travel to Laos and be viewed as an equal in the ethnic sense of equality, but I would still be only a woman. In Sweden, I was an equal—to both men and women.

One day, while Bee and I were seeing the sights, we got into a cab with a driver from Morocco. He asked where we were from. I told him, *"Thailand."* He asked if I would go home with him to meet his friend for sex. I said *"Absolutely not."* He was under the impression that all Thai females worked as strippers and all Thai strippers were also prostitutes. He was very mistaken. I was no longer a bar girl. Bee, on the other hand, asked me in Thai, how much she could get from his friend for a short-time. I was a bit surprised, but I told her to tell him the Swedish Kroner equivalent of $300. Surprisingly, he agreed. That was Bt 12,000 for a short-time--12 times the going rate in Thailand. Bee jumped at the chance.

Bee came to Sweden with the intention of finding a husband. But it wasn't until she returned to Thailand, while on a holiday in Phuket, that she met a wonderful Dane who took her home to Denmark. Maybe it's true, *"That which we seek is in our own back yard."*

Return to Thailand: A New Visa

After three months in Sweden, I returned to Thailand to obtain a new Visa and to Ubon to see my mother—where I remained for five weeks. For any girl who has lived outside of her village for an extended period of time, returning to her roots—particularly a rural, primitive, and provincial countryside, is extremely difficult. Five weeks after my return, I realized I needed the fun, music, excitement, and nightlife of Pattaya to which I quickly fled, and where I stayed for two more months.

In Pattaya, I stayed in a hotel owned by Johan's friend. I also spent some time teaching Paul to speak, read, and write Thai. My mother came to see me, and she even *"worked"* at the hotel for a month. Although she was willing to occupy her time in the hotel temporarily, she had no interest in Pattaya, in living in this resort city, nor in actually working for a living. She was simply waiting with bated-breath for me to return to Sweden, so that she would reap the rewards of my new life.

I would regularly go to the Food Court in Royal Garden to eat and talk to old friends. I was just burning time until my new Swedish Visa was ready. I led a rather quiet and sequestered life compared to my previous one as a well-paid harlot, although on occasion, I would go out in the evening with Paul. I didn't come to Pattaya to meet men. After five years, I had a man of my own who was happy to care for me emotionally, physically, and most importantly--*financially*.

I had more time to spend with my mother than I had in the past five years. She knew nothing about my Visa, nor all of the paperwork required, but she knew that my leaving the country meant more money for her. She always knew that I would provide for her and my sisters.

I brought Ying to Pattaya for the first time to see where I had lived for so many years. She had always wanted to see Pattaya. She was my only full-blood sister. She was also only 18 months away from her high school graduation. I had worked so that she could complete her high school degree and gain the education that I never had. No one ever gave me the same opportunity. I was very, very proud of her. I always hoped that she would be very proud of me, too. She didn't exactly know what to think about Pattaya. It was far from the provincial village she called home. She liked the easy access to movie theaters and modern, air-conditioned shopping centers, non-existent in the villages and virtually unknown to the majority of its residents. The city was abundant with our favorite Isaan food. She also enjoyed the warm tropical breeze and the sound of the sea as it gently brushed against the shore. Other than these few pleasures, there isn't a lot to do in Pattaya when not pursuing an income by night.

My Return to Sweden/Sai's Return to Trouble

The Swedish Embassy notified me that my Visa was available and that I would be heading off to Sweden, once again. So, I packed my bags and prepared for my flight. This time I didn't have an apartment full of furniture and electronics to ship home. This time I was off to Sweden in a "New York minute."

I had not been in Sweden long when I received a phone call about Sai. I learned that she was in jail for taking Yabah. I was asked for money in order to secure her release, once again. I was at a loss. I had thought that she was no longer using Yabah and had straightened-up her life. I was very much mistaken. I realized that as long as she remained in Pattaya, she was ripe for trouble. This time I sent money to my mother to pay the bribe for her release, although I had no guarantees that she would be released as this was her second arrest. It was very painful to learn of my little sister being in the Juvenile Ward. I felt that if I paid yet again, one more

257

bribe, she might still return to a life with her delinquent friends—
one fraught with drugs and possibly crime. I really didn't know
what to do and I didn't see any other solution. I sent the money to
my mother, money to secure the release of my 16-year old sister
from jail. Instead, my mother kept the money and spent it on
luxuries and *"Making face"* in the village, leaving Sai to rot in a
Thai jail for the next six months.

Upon Sai's release, she knew that she never wanted to
return to the cold, hard confinement of this juvenile prison. She
was forced to return to Ubon. My mother was not going to allow
her to remain in Pattaya without a guardian. I wished that she could
have been more like Ying, a good student, and already in the 11th
grade. She would have made my life and that of my mother much
easier. If she had never learned that she was adopted, she might
have ended up more like Ying, but I will never know.

Sai nearly finished the 9th grade, an accomplishment that
would have given her access to decent employment. With a 9th
grade education, she could have found employment with a large
company that would have provided her with health insurance, four
days off each month, and other benefits. She quit school when she
was so close to achieving this end and immediately got into trouble.
She had wasted a golden opportunity. I had invested a lot of time
and money into giving her a good life, paying for her education, and
helping her to create her own successful future. All of this was lost
when she dropped out of school and started using Yabah. I was
very angry and terribly hurt; I felt that my efforts had been wasted.

Dancing Again

My life in Sweden was going well. Thanks to Johan's
generosity, I was sending some money home every month to my
mother's delight; but I couldn't stay in the apartment all day and be
unproductive. I soon found a job doing what I did best—exotic

258

dancing. The money was far more than I could ever have earned in Thailand. I soon learned that I was not the only Thai girl dancing, but I was the smallest, the youngest, and therefore I attracted a great deal of notice.

My first day at work was my opportunity to show-off my stuff on stage, a rather flashy act that I had refined during my tenure as a hotshot little dancer in Pattaya. I danced the very same way I always had in the GoGos of Thailand, the same way that brought me so many customers. To my surprise, customers and dancers alike were all laughing at me as I unknowingly made a fool of myself. I was used to being one of the hottest girls on stage. Suddenly, I was the laughing stock. I knew that I would have to change whatever it was that I was doing wrong. I wasn't about to lose this opportunity to earn great money in the form of Swedish Kroners (SEK).

Strip dancers in Thailand perform more like gymnasts and keep their bikini panties on--most of the time. Swedish women do not like Asian women working in their clubs; they "Play dirty" in an effort to expedite our failure. They think that we all come to Europe to pursue our earlier professions. We are also generally far better dancers than they are with the exotic look, tan skin, and tiny bodies that their European men prefer. On my very first day, one of the dancers stole my bra; I was not off to a great start. Later, my name was written into the schedule book and I wasn't told. I lost 600 SEK ($60) because I didn't come to work. Some of the girls just wanted to make my life as miserable as possible, and they succeeded.

One day, I was madly running around in the locker room of the club. The manager came in and told me to get out on the floor and asked me what I was still doing in the locker room; it was time for me to be on stage. I told her that I was looking for my costume which I soon found in the trashcan. A Swedish dancer had thrown away my clothes; she was not fond of little tan Asian dancers stealing the limelight and the attention from customers that she thought were rightfully hers. It took a long while for the other dancers to realize that I was sincere about dancing for a living. Eventually, some of these girls became my friends.

"Bait and Switch"

I couldn't speak any Swedish other than just the few words that Johan had taught me. I needed to communicate with the customers in English. I would lie about doing everything for them to encourage the customers to buy a private room and get a private dance. After they paid the fee of which I would receive a healthy percentage, and we went to the room, I would then relent on my promise. I just did what every other girl in the club did—a strip dancer's version of *"Bait and switch."* In the bar, I would tell a customer *"Come to the private room, I lick you."* Once in the private room, I would tell him that I had said *"I like you,"* or *"I will lick your fingers and nipples only."* Many of these men were angry as one would expect. Surprisingly, not all of them were. If they became irate, the bouncers asked them to leave the club. If they became volatile, they would be assisted out the front door.

We would normally dance all night, receiving a break at Midnight. I was always happy to go to the 7-11 convenience store to buy food and snacks; noodles, BBQ chicken, sandwiches, drinks, and the like. We needed this to keep our energy-level up as dancing and misleading customers were exhausting. Few of the Western girls ever offered to go for snacks, but generally the East Asian and South American girls were always more than willing. One night, after receiving a few Kroners from each of the girls, I brought back all of the food and put it on the table. One of the Swedish girls asked how much her food cost. Like every other girl there, she ate the same thing every night and knew exactly how much her food cost. On this particular occasion, I had forgotten the receipt. She and a few of the other Western girls said, *"How are we going to know how much our change is?"* In an instant, I pulled all of the change out of my pocket, threw it on the table with the food, and told them to figure it out on their own. Swedish women were not as fond of me as Swedish men were.

On another occasion, a Swedish man spoke very degradingly about Thai girls. *"They're all whores. They only want money. They're all liars and thieves."* Regardless of how accurately he described my past, I managed to hide my emotions, despite my simmering anger. *My sisters most definitely weren't whores!* I told him that if he came to the private room, I would give him a *"Blow job"* for the lowest price possible, 1,500 SEK ($150). This was the price generally charged for a private-room lap dance and entitles the man only to watch the girl strip-dance. When we went into the private room, I gave him a nice smile and left. Then I told the bouncers that he spanked me. He was told to leave the club immediately. Men are not allowed to touch women in the club. I knew that my behavior was wrong, but speaking badly about Thai women—to a Thai woman—could be considered none other than incredibly stupid. He received exactly what he deserved!

At the club, I would irritate men intentionally, and mislead them as to the sexual encounter that they would enjoy in the private rooms—all the while being paid handsomely for this deception. I really loved my job. I could treat them like so many of the girls in Thailand had been treated by sex-tourists and be financially rewarded.

Not all men who come to exotic dance clubs are stupid. Some come for the pure pleasure of watching sexy girls perform, enjoy the feeling of being aroused, and are willing to pay for the pleasure. One customer watched me dance for a while and talked to me during my break. He finally asked for a dance in the private room. After a rather long dance, and more small talk, he tipped me 10,000 SEK ($1,000.) Four days later, on my day off, he came in again. When I arrived the following day, I discovered that he had left an additional $500 tip for me. *He had actually paid another 5,000 SEK ($500) tip to show his appreciation.* It was wonderful to earn a substantial amount of cash without having to go to work. It made me feel as I had never felt before--so extraordinarily special. I was experiencing pure, unadulterated ecstasy to earn so much money without having "to sell my flesh" in the true meaning of the word. There are strippers in Sweden who also serve as escorts on their days off, making as much as 2,000 SEK ($200) for a simple dinner date; that does not include any sexual favors. Those are negotiated separately. But, this was no longer my line of work.

Working in Sweden has allowed me to save a bundle of money while also preparing to bring my mother to Europe. I've assisted Ying to attend college in Korat, purchased a couple of plots of land, begun building a new house in my village, and generally made a better life for myself and my family. Nearly everything has gone well. The only real problem I have experienced, besides the freezing temperatures, has been with Sai to whom I have given so much. She started seeing a worthless guy and eventually became pregnant. She became a mother at 17. I have agreed to assist her one last time by financing a little clothing shop for her at the Lotus Superstore in Ubon.

Upon Reflection
I have a friend living in Germany who grew up as I did, selling her virginity at age 16. She worked in the sex-tourist havens until she met a very nice German who took her to his country. We share our feelings about our past and our relentless shame. We were desperate for money and subjected ourselves to every obscene and lewd desire that perverted Farang tourists could afford. The

general public knows little about the lives of bar girls after they have left the trade; they also have little reason to care. But for those who have studied our plight, it is well known that we require long-term psychotherapy if we are to resolve our emotional suffering and maintain a life that can be called even remotely normal. Sadly, few girls have the knowledge that psychological help exists. Even if they do, they do not have the inclination, nor the resources to afford such a luxury.

When I visit Johan's family, I become keenly aware that I missed something in my life while "growing up," a family that cared about my welfare. I know I was so very fortunate to move to Sweden. I live a life that is an impossible dream to most girls who are born to the rural countryside of Thailand. My life in Sweden is relatively easy, safe, and comfortable; not unlike heaven, although certainly colder.

After now being in Sweden for a while and dancing at the club, I am earning more than I ever thought possible. I am performing, working at a profession I enjoy, and I am the center of attention. I am also not selling my dignity to support my family. This feels like the opportunity of a lifetime, and it's happening to me. Yet, I realize that this isn't enough. I want more; more money and more from life. I want to live and work in an exciting city where the weather is warm; its inhabitants speak English; and the money flows as easily as it does here. My Isaan blood is used to warm weather 365 days a year. The temperature at noon, on a warm summer day in Sweden, is as cold as the coldest day in Pattaya or Bangkok. Las Vegas seems to be the only answer. I read about Las Vegas after listening to girls at the club. Its residents speak English; the weather is warm; and it's filled with a never-ending array of colorful attractions and exciting people. Most importantly, the money doesn't just flow; it gushes!

I know that I cannot easily get a Visa to visit America. I have thought long and hard about my many options—one of which is marrying an American. There are hundreds of thousands of Thai people in America; if they found a way to get there—so can I! The U.S. is a lot closer to Sweden, than Sweden is to Thailand, and I found a way to get here. There must be a way!

Dreams of Las Vegas or Something Greater?

It has been a little while since I wrote the last paragraph. I have since vacillated a great deal about going to Las Vegas. I have remained in Sweden where I continue to save money. Whether or not I move to Las Vegas, the epitome of a nightclub dancer's career remains an unknown.

I am incredibly happy and so very fortunate that I have been given the chance to come to Sweden. I have earned a great income, provided for my family, and saved for my future. My stay in Sweden has improved the quality of my life and that of my family, now and for many years to come. I must admit that I've never made much effort to learn Swedish because it's a difficult language. I've never really felt the need to do so because my "sales pitch" goes beyond words. I am a successful communicator in most any language whether at work or at play—as communication involves a great deal more than just words. In addition, the chilly weather is always a great challenge to someone from Thailand, and I don't handle it very well. I intend to spend a little more time here and then pack my bags for my next adventure. I'm destined for a location where the sun shines more than six months of the year—*Las Vegas?*

When I was 13, and I boarded the bus for Bangkok, I had no idea where my life was headed. After experiencing a lifetime of very "Hard living" in a short seven years, and surviving and overcoming the life of a young girl in the flesh-trade, I know that there are no obstacles great enough to keep me from my dreams. I have been fortunate in that I have been able to lift myself from a life with no future, in the poorest region of Thailand, to one of living and traveling in Europe. All things considered, Las Vegas is not too wild an idea when looking at it from my perspective.

I have read that dancers in Las Vegas actually pay $40-$60/day to the club in order to perform because they receive so much in tips from the customers. I can't imagine paying to work in a club. The GoGo bars in Pattaya have a hard time finding enough girls to fill the stage. But, if in Las Vegas, the tips are so good that dancers are willing to pay for the privilege, who am I to argue? I wouldn't mind getting in on some of that action.

Since the age of 13, my life has revolved around very bright lights, a tiny stage, ear-shattering rock music, and nights so late that they often saw the sun rise. These nights were filled with vile old men, teeth stained yellow from nicotine, and their breath fouled by alcohol. The opportunity of never again having to sleep with disgusting or depraved men lies ahead in Las Vegas. Like Sweden, it appears to offer great money without ever having to sell my flesh. This could certainly be something of which I could be very proud and still earn the money I need to send home. Then again, I seriously question if I really want to use my body, or continue as a club dancer, to reap my financial rewards at this stage of my life. *Maybe, I am destined for something even greater.*

Short-Lived Sabbatical

I finally stopped working in the strip club and I have begun studying Swedish; I have also become very serious about changing the direction of my life. Writing this book and remembering so much of my life has motivated me to stop dancing. I plan that my next career, whatever it is, will be far more respectable. Returning to school was my first step. Although a strip-dancer's salary is

265

significant, particularly considering how little education most of the performers have, I know that I am capable of more. *I have proven that I can have everything I want and need without ever having to sleep with sex-tourists again!*

In the first four months of 2002, I sent Bt 500,000 ($12,500) to my mother. Of this amount, Bt 200,000 ($5,000) was for land purchased in my name, and Bt 300,000 ($7,500) was destined for my savings account and my mom's living expenses. I discovered that my mother spent the entire Bt 300,000 in a short four months, and she still wanted more. The amount of $1,875 a month is more than 18 times the average family's monthly income of $100 in my rural village.

My mother was angry with me when I stopped working at the club, and she demanded more money. During our phone conversations, she would talk about the homes of parents of other bar girls in the village, stating that these girls send their parents more money than I do. I knew that she was lying. Although other Isaan women would tell my mother that their daughters in Pattaya, Bangkok, Europe, or the U.S. would send home $2,000/month, I knew that this wasn't true. In truth, they were comparing their daughter's earnings through prostitution while never admitting it. What is also true is that their lies are typical examples of trying to see who could attain the greater *"Face."*

Ying has been gifted with a motorbike, attractive clothes, a mobile phone, a high school education, and so much more, yet she is never satisfied. She has followed in my mother's footsteps—an insatiable desire for material goods. She lives as if she were the daughter of a middle-class family. She is anxious to reap the rewards of my income, regardless of its source. She also makes every effort to distance herself from the embarrassment of being raised in a poor backward village, from our family, AND most of all from me and my former profession. She will not speak to me in our native dialect of Isaan if there are men around who would then classify her as a "hillbilly." She doesn't care what women think of her. I compare Ying's life at 17 with that of my own. She could never fathom the life that I endured in order for her to have the life that she now enjoys. She has no understanding of just how fortunate she is, and she doesn't even care.

Farang have told me for years that my family was "Bleeding me dry." Swedes, with whom I have shared my story, have confirmed their statements. As a result, I have recently made the decision to send my family only Bt 5,000/month. This amount is as much as my two sisters would earn if they had jobs in our village. I am presenting them with a gift of Bt 5,000 ($120) each and every month; they will not have to work for it. No one ever gave me that kind of money for doing nothing. As a result of this decision, my mother has also made a decision. Once again, after sending money for seven long years, I am no longer welcome in *"her home." "Her home?" This is "My Home!" It is the home that I bought, and I furnished, with proceeds from years of physical and emotional sacrifice. Sacrifice that I will have to continue to pay for the rest of my life!*

My mother has no desire to ever see me again unless my return is accompanied by Bt 200,000 ($5,000). I was the black sheep in my family until I began sending money home. Little did I realize during all of these years, I was *still* the black sheep of the family who just happened to be sending money home. For all of those years, my mother led me to believe that I was welcome back into *our* home and I had made up for the death of my father. *Once I reduced my monetary gifts, she treated me just as she always had. I was an outcast!*

My mother's lack of gratitude is the common response among Isaan mothers to their daughters, who, after years of sacrificing their young lives for their families, decide to limit the gifts they send home. Or, they may also choose to leave the sex-trade in which case their generous monetary gifts must stop. Parents, particularly mothers, will continue to live in the houses provided by their daughters, while those very same daughters may need to seek refuge in thatched huts, supporting one child or several, on Bt 70/day earned in a factory making shoes, clothing, or accessories. The millions of baht they earned from the sale of their bodies were long ago squandered by their parents and extended families. Once the money is gone, so are their families and all of the friends who had benefited from their earlier earnings.

These young women are now often very sick from years of abusing their bodies and they are also very much alone. To add to their suffering, their children are often denied legal status and an education if they were born overseas. Those who earned the greatest amount of money (generally in Japan) and return home, also appear to suffer the greatest disappointment and have the most critical adjustment to make to village life. Some are unable to adjust and become alcoholics; others commit suicide. *Like me, their only desire was to become a "Good daughter." We were all simply following the rules of our culture that told us we had to do anything necessary to take care of our families—Anything!*

Her only remaining treasure from her years of sacrifice in Japan

Photographer: Sanitsuda Ekachai   *Photo courtesy of Bangkok Post*

Retired sex-worker, Duangjand, shown with her 13-year old Thai-Japanese daughter

Traveling to Japan when she was 18, this young woman earned millions of Thai baht in the sex-trade even after paying off her traffickers. Following many years of servicing men, she returned to her home in Chiang Rai with a toddler and a Japanese (trophy)

269

husband, only to be abandoned by him two years later. Penniless, she remarried and gave birth to three more children.

A "Good Daughter's" final reward

Photographer: Sanitsuda Ekachai   *Photo courtesy of Bangkok Post*

Thatched hut belonging to Duangjand, where she now lives and cares for her bed-ridden husband and four children, serves as an everlasting reminder of a destiny far from the one she dreamed her sacrifice would take her. It sits across the street from an elegant, two-story, well-landscaped, gate-enclosed Bangkok-style mansion, similar to the one she bought and furnished and where her mother presently resides.

Bangkok-style home

Photographer: Sanitsuda Ekachai *Photo courtesy of Bangkok Post*

This home bears striking resemblance to the one from which Duangjand was banished once this "Good daughter" could no longer provide her mother with money after leaving the sex-trade and being abandoned by her Japanese husband. Her tragic story of being disowned by her mother when the money disappeared is all-too common. It is also my story.

It has taken me many years, but I have finally come to the conclusion that the Farang who told me *"Your mother treats you like you treat your clients; like a walking ATM,"* have been right all along. For the past seven years, I have been nothing more than an inexhaustible money supply for her and my sisters. I could be well-off now if my family would have practiced some form of financial responsibility instead of spending my money so frivolously.

Thoughts of Spain, Again

It is May and the weather in Sweden is warming up; it is up to 40°F at Noon. Sweden has become very accommodating; and I hope to be issued a Swedish passport next year. Few foreigners, maybe 100/year, are allowed a Thai passport with only a few of those being Westerners. This is just one of a myriad of differences between our lands. On the other hand, U.S. and European countries allow many foreigners to become citizens in their respective countries. Asian counties will not allow other people to become citizens quite as readily.

Once I receive my Swedish passport, I will be able to work in Spain—another member of the EU. Sweden has been wonderful and I am very appreciative of their liberal Immigration laws, health care, and educational system. Yet, a Visa, good health insurance, and a language school cannot protect me from the savage, unforgiving cold. Spain offers many advantages, two of which are a warm climate and Mallorca, a tourist city like Pattaya where a night-owl can flourish. The Spanish like to party all night, every night. The Spanish and I definitely have something in common. It is not so improbable a thought that someday I might also be able to acquire a Spanish passport.

Another advantage to Spain is that tourists spend a lot of money there, especially in the strip clubs. I could very easily adapt to the Spanish lifestyle. I would be able to dance there the way I did in Thailand and not in Sweden, and it would require no change in my persona. I often consider the easy money; the lure of tourist money being almost irresistible. Yet, I know that this move would be a step backwards as I remember my long-term goals. These are far more meaningful to me than any money that I could ever earn, or anything else that I could ever accomplish. If they weren't, I could simply become a hooker in Sweden and make a bundle. Clearly, I am confused and even conflicted about my future. I know

272

what I want for my life; attaining those goals without dancing is my greatest challenge.

I am in an industry composed of young sexy girls and I am bringing in more money than I ever dreamed of. All the while, I know that there has to be more to life than this. Here in Sweden, girls come from Eastern Europe, South America, Thailand, and the Philippines—all impoverished regions of the world. In Thailand, they are from the North and the Northeast. Thailand appears to be but a microcosm of the entire world's sex scene. These girls, including myself, come from equivalent ghettos of the world.

Johan in Crisis

Johan has lost his job. As a computer professional, always in demand, his loss of employment has been a huge blow. He spends every waking moment looking for work—to no avail. Understandably, he has become increasingly irritable; difficult to live with; and of greater concern--he has become depressed. He has been used to living the comfortable life of a young professional, whose income bought him everything he wanted. He has exhausted his savings and can no longer support us. I have never been comfortable with him being the sole provider, primarily because he has been so very generous. Beyond my need for the basic necessities; I truly want to help him through this crisis. I have returned to dancing—consoling myself with the fact that dancing in Europe is not the same as dancing in Thailand. *In Sweden, I am only selling a sexual fantasy; I am no longer selling sex.*

Shortly thereafter

Johan has become very angry about my sending so much of my income home--until very recently. Although I made the decision to decrease my remittances home, it seems that I made this decision too late. His strong feeling about this issue, in addition to his loss of employment, has led to our break up. I have lost the best boyfriend that I have ever had because of the monetary demands made upon me by my mother. My willingness to feed her insatiable hunger for money and accede to her voracious desire to *"Make Face"* are issues for which I must bear full-responsibility.

Johan has sublet his apartment and moved to his parents' house because he could no longer afford the rent. I have moved into a little house just outside of Stockholm owned by the Thai manager of my club. She came to Sweden about 12 years ago for reasons similar to mine. She just wanted to save some money and improve her life and that of her family. Now, she owns a couple of houses and manages a profitable club. Someday, I would like to emulate her success.

I'm in Crisis
Text messages to Dave from Johan: Prior to his departure for Spain

Lon has been talking about taking her life. Her behavior is frequently Manic-Depressive although she has not been diagnosed as such. She is ecstatically happy falling to thoughts of suicide. She tried to open the car door on the motorway. On another occasion, I found her standing next to an open window in my apartment on the 5th floor. I wasn't amused.

Not long ago, she went to visit a friend about 150km outside of Stockholm. I had gone out with a friend and was at a hotel bar when she called me. She freaked out because she felt that I didn't care about her; she told her friend she was going out for a walk and disappeared. Her friend became worried and called the police. I received a call from the police early in the morning when they fetched her at some woman's house. Apparently, she just started to walk aimlessly, throwing away everything she had including gold and money. A woman found her, brought her home, and also called the police. She said that Lon had been talking about jumping into the cold river below. Lon gave them my address in Stockholm.

Later yet, my notes to Dave

Johan left for Spain to help his friend build a business. His departure has left me alone, and I miss him terribly. I've become severely-depressed and I've now started to smoke. My life consists of double-shifts at work, and I'm dancing 16-hours a day. I return home briefly to sleep, and then I go back to work again. As I'm no longer living with Johan, I've no desire to go home. I often catch a few winks at work between dances when the clientele is low.

I've become dysfunctional and I can no longer care for myself. I'm heartbroken over Johan's leaving me to work in Spain. I feel abandoned although I know that this was never his intention. I've been admitted to Karolinska University Hospital, in Solna, Stockholm, and I'll remain here for several weeks. I'm heavily-medicated and will remain so for many months—even following my release. I'm totally unable to work. Diagnoses: Clinical Depression and Schizophrenia.

I've finally made the decision to return to Thailand in late August of 2003. There appears to be no further reason for me to remain in Sweden; Johan is gone; and I can no longer work. I hope that returning to the country of my birth will heal my heart and nourish my soul. I need to move on with my life. Never before has everything in my life gone so well, only to fall apart so rapidly.

The Swedish government has taken care of me for a couple of months and will continue to do so until I am well enough to travel on my own. I would never have received the same treatment in my own country, and I've not even earned permanent Swedish residency. I'll always be grateful to Sweden for allowing me to regain my dignity by giving me the opportunity to earn and save

275

money without having to sell my body, for the medical and psychiatric assistance I've received from their health care and social welfare system, and for the economic assistance that continued into my first month in Thailand. To my surprise, a check was deposited into my account after I had returned home. Sweden's generous social welfare system has allowed me to receive medical care and disability insurance at $1,000/month, as long as I am a resident of Sweden. But, now I'm also labeled Clinically-Depressed and Schizophrenic. I've become physically ill and gained a lot of weight from the many drugs prescribed to reduce my symptoms. It's time to go home; Johan is gone; and I can't be alone. I need help for the simplest of tasks.

Chapter 16

Home Sweet Home?

Returning to Thailand

I returned to Thailand on August 29, 2003. I had arranged for my brother who was living in Bangkok to meet me at the airport; he didn't appear. His behavior was typical and should have been expected. The responsibility displayed by men from the village leaves everything to be desired. If he had thought that I had brought something for him, he would have been at the airport on time. Still heavily medicated, I managed to reach a hotel on my own from where I contacted him. It wasn't long before I found myself paying the round-trip transportation costs for my brother and his wife to travel to Ubon to visit my mother. In the 11 hours that it took for me to travel from Sweden to Thailand, I became my family's "Walking ATM" once again—nothing had really changed! I had returned to become the same major source of income they had known for over seven years and their financial savior!

I hadn't sent my mother any money for a few months because I had been ill and hospitalized. Upon my arrival, I learned that she had borrowed Bt 30,000 ($750) that she fully-expected me to repay, plus the interest charges of 5-to-10% per month for three months. My sisters have never contributed to my mother's welfare, and now at 43 years of age, it would never occur to my mother to work. She has become used to automatically receiving all the money she has ever needed to live a comfortable life—through me and me alone!

September 2003
Lost land

My mother informed me today that she gave land to my brother, the land that had been promised to me by my grandfather in

277

exchange for taking care of my grandmother after his death. I had kept my side of the bargain, and I had even gone above and beyond my original promise until her death. But, that made no difference to my mother. Nothing has changed regardless of all that I have done for her and the family. She said that she gave the land to my brother because he has children, and they will need the rice that they will grow in that soil more than I ever will.

Medication and Never-ending Torment

I am still haunted by my past during every waking and sleeping hour. I continue to have dreams of suicide, jumping from tall buildings, and of being attacked by large dogs. I am a chronic insomniac. When I can sleep, frightening and repetitive nightmares awaken me throughout the night. During afternoon naps, I talk in my sleep about my past. While still in Sweden, I began sleepwalking. Long walks in the middle of the night resulted in the police picking me up and driving me home.

I cannot rid my mind of my past. I take a pharmacy of psychotropic and other drugs in order to survive from one day to the next. *This is not living.* I feel like a zombie. These drugs include Haldol: an anti-psychotic for treatment of hallucinations and delusions; Imovane: to induce sleep; Chlorpromazine: an anti-psychotic for treatment of hallucinations and delusions; Perphenazine: another anti-psychotic; Fluoxetine: Prozac, an antidepressant; Anta: an antacid; and Povanic: an enzyme for digestion. One might wonder why someone who is psychotic would require antacids and enzymes. The reason is that all of these drugs make me violently ill; nausea and vomiting are a daily occurrence. The enzymes are to aid my digestion and the antacids speak for themselves. The anti-psychotic drugs intended to eliminate my hallucinations intensified them. The warning that *"Haldol can cause psychotic behavior and hallucinations"* describes just one of Haldol's side affects. *In other words, Haldol can and does cause the same psychotic reactions it is prescribed to treat.* The litany of adverse reactions to these drugs reads like a shopping list for Disaster—with a capital "D." One Haldol website alone lists more than 100 adverse reactions. Other psychotropic drugs are equally debilitating and even dangerous. I am physically sick most all of the time.

Some of the adverse side effects from which I personally suffer read like a textbook of reasons not to take these drugs:

- Insomnia
- Lethargy
- Panic attacks
- Hating people
- Hallucinations
- Self-mutilation
- Loss of sex drive
- Tremors in hands
- Inner-restlessness
- Complete paranoia
- Severe constipation
- Feeling like a zombie
- Severe mood changes
- Nightmares and flashbacks
- Manic/Depressive episodes
- Obsessive and Suicidal thoughts
- Flash anger and verbal aggression
- Sudden and excessive weight gain
- Urge to jump out of a fast moving car
- Mind racing and inability to control thoughts
- Fear of doctors admitting me to a psych-ward

October 2003
My First Job

My first job in Pattaya was in a British restaurant. I agreed to work 6 days/week, 8 hours/day for Bt 4,500/month ($112) plus tips. Within the first week, the owner increased my base hours to 10 hours/day and then the following week to 12 hours/day. He offered me Bt 17/hour (43¢) over-time, over 60 hours/week. My base hours kept growing and growing. I vehemently declined the over-time and was promptly fired. The owner also didn't pay me for the days that I had worked. This is one of the many reasons so many "straight girls" change career paths after arriving in Pattaya. *At least, in the flesh-trade, agreements for payments of services are not broken, sparing us the headaches of arguing over money.*

On Dating Andy

It was about this same time that I really wanted a new boyfriend. I had been in Pattaya for over a month, and I had been without a boyfriend for several months since Johan had left for Spain. I believed that a new man would help me forget about Johan. I applied to a dating service. Their staff ignored the stated preferences that I ticked off on their standard application, including height, age, hair color, religion, hobbies etc. Instead, they matched me with Andy, a 49-year old, 6'1" gangly Brit, whose education must have stopped somewhere in the neighborhood of the 9th grade. He was ignorant to any topic in which he might be engaged other than that of house painting. He lacked people skills; he argued with everyone; and he didn't have a clue as to what the term "Social graces" might include. He also had poor communication skills, not only because he stuttered, but because he was learning impaired (developmentally disabled), which accounted for his inability to make any new friends, or find a woman on his own.

The main reason Farang sex-tourists come to Thailand is that they lack the ability to develop mature female relationships in their own countries. They are less-threatened and less-intimidated by Thai women. The fact that Andy was unable to find even a poor village woman, without the benefit of a dating agency, speaks volumes about his fear in relating to the opposite sex. His feelings of inadequacy and his low self-esteem were readily-apparent to anyone with whom he came in contact. Instead of helping me to forget about Johan, this new relationship caused me to miss him even more.

While dating Andy, I located another position as a waitress at Chantilly's Restaurant in Jomtien Beach, an upscale tourist resort just south of Pattaya. I enjoyed my work, and the surroundings were well above the types of establishments in which I was used to working.

Nightly, Andy came into Chantilly's to see me although I had asked him not to. Worse was the fact that by the time he came to visit me, he was drunk and obnoxious, causing me great embarrassment and threatening my job. I needed to take a couple of days off because I was sick. The owner used this opportunity to tell me not to return. I believe the real reason was that Andy had been a nuisance and he took my time away from other customers. Andy had cost me my job!

Changing Jobs Again

I took another job as the cashier at a small take-out pizza shop. I enjoyed the work, but I didn't get along with the staff, especially one female cook and her boyfriend--a motorbike delivery boy. He and the other delivery boys would consistently ask for gasoline money from the register--up to Bt 100/day, even though I knew they only needed Bt 20. I refused and they were angry! The cook would constantly antagonize me for not giving her boyfriend, Dom, extra money. Our situation was approaching one of violence. Dom was only too eager to become involved. I knew that I would have to quit. I hated going to work because I couldn't stand the ongoing arguments anymore. I told the owner that his staff had been cheating him. His response was far from what I expected. He said that he was willing to tolerate their theft because the business was earning good money.

About five days after I left the pizza parlor, I was still enraged over the way Dom had threatened me. I won't tolerate abuse from any Thai man and I knew how to get even. I called the pizza parlor and arranged to have a pizza delivered. My replacement answered the phone; she didn't know my voice, and the restaurant didn't know my address. I ordered a pizza and waited for Dom to deliver it. I planned to stand in the back of my apartment and ask him to come inside for payment. Upon entering, I would slash him with a knife and allow him to run away. I didn't believe that there was any way a Thai court would convict a woman in her own home. Dave tried to talk me out of it, but I wouldn't listen! When the deliveryman arrived, Dave met him at the entrance to my apartment building in an effort to keep me out-of-trouble and from doing something stupid. It was the wrong deliveryman. I know that Buddha sent Dave and the wrong deliveryman to protect me from my own undoing.

Changing Jobs Once Again

It wasn't long before I found a new job as a bartender/cashier at Golden Gate Bar and Grill. One day, my previous employer (the owner of the pizza shop) came into the bar and noticed me. He asked how I had been and how I liked my new job. He told me that he had shut down the "Pizza take-out" until he could find other staff because their stealing had finally gone too far. I wondered how far is "Too far" before a business owner takes action against his own staff—and then it was not by firing them, or reporting them to the police; it was in shutting down his business. The reason was that the owner was a Farang who should not have been physically operating a business. He can own one, but he is not legally allowed to work on the premises.

Andy Costs Me, Yet Another Job

Andy has become the most difficult man I have ever known. I lost my job as a waitress at Chantilly's because he kept coming into the restaurant while drunk. I lost my next job at the Golden Gate Bar because he nearly came to blows with the owner—a fight that caused me to reach for a knife—a knife with which I accidentally cut myself causing me to go the hospital for stitches. After I went to the hospital, I went to the police station. The police forced my employer to pay for my medical expenses and my "Pain and suffering." He was very angry as he blamed the altercation on Andy and me—*Rightly so!*. Yet, he didn't have a lot of choice, but to pay! He was another Farang, operating his business from behind the cash register--prohibited in Thailand.

Although Andy may be difficult, I am becoming *his* worst nightmare!! There are many reasons I continue to go out with him, even after I quickly learned that he expects me to pay 50% of our restaurant checks and all mutual expenses incurred, while *he* "courts" *me*. I think that somehow he fills a need in me to help. I see someone whose situation is worse than my own. Many of us in the flesh-trade tend to be rescuers as we have already rescued our families. From a less than benevolent perspective, this relationship also gives me a feeling of tremendous personal power. I feel that Andy is a man I can control. I can do anything I want, act-out as much as I want, treat him badly if I feel like it, and he will always be there. He needs me and he knows there is no one else to help him. He is even more desperate for a relationship than I am!

To be brutally honest, I am 23; three years older than the average 20-year old GoGo dancer. I have gained more than 15 pounds—a lot of weight on my now fully-grown 4'9" frame; I am smoking a pack per day and taking a number of psychotropic medications. I am not the same sexy beauty I was less than a year ago. I desperately want someone to love me. Andy must love me because he puts up with my wicked behavior and my outbursts. We are made for each other.

Besides, who else will have me? Most importantly, when I look at Andy, I see **"BRITISH VISA"** written all over him in BOLD CAPITAL LETTERS!

My Puppy, Beach

While walking on the boardwalk recently, I saw a little puppy no more than a couple of months old. She had a moment of good fortune; she found a piece of grilled chicken on the ground. While preparing to sink her tiny teeth into it and nourish her apparently voracious hunger, which had no doubt received little nourishment throughout her short life, a larger dog stole it from her. At that very moment, I no longer saw a puppy, but a powerless little girl. That little puppy was me just ten years earlier, when at 13, I was alone on the streets of Bangkok. Neither of us had a roof, nor food, nor anyone to help us. I was not going to let what happened to me, happen to this puppy, if I could do anything to stop it. I slowly walked towards her, bent over, and opened my hands to pick her up. I was surprised that she didn't run away. She eagerly responded to a little love and affection. If only I had been as lucky 10 years ago as she was at this moment. She licked my face, and made soft little puppy sounds. I took her home and named her "Beach."

Beach learned the difference between the roars of the various motorbikes that sped down my street. She also knew the sound of my motorbike. When I pulled in, she would always run out to greet me; she was excited about my return and it was often difficult to avoid hitting her. She was not waiting for tuna, chicken, or beef; she was waiting for me to hold her close and give her my love.

It had only been a few months since I found Beach, when one day I returned from work and found her sick; I immediately took her to the Vet's. He gave her a shot, but the medicine she received was too late to help her. She died in my arms on the back of Dave's motorbike as he drove us back to my apartment.

Beach was the closest that I had ever come to having a baby, and she was gone forever. I would never again see her tail wag, feel her warmth, or sense her love. She was the only one who ever truly loved me, other than my father; neither asking anything in return. *At that point in my life, she was all that I truly loved.* Juk, Dave, and I buried her near a pond on the vacant land beside my apartment building.

January 2004
Too Many Pills—Once Again
One early morning, about 7:00A.M., I got up from another night of too many sleeping pills and not enough sleep. The pills had left me feeling dizzy. I should have learned to follow the dosage, but I simply kept taking them until I finally fell asleep. While making my way to the kitchen, I fell down through my glass table. I didn't know what to do next, so I called Dave. I didn't care that it was barely daybreak; I never really concerned myself with others when I needed something. Dave came over to find blood splattered around my room and on my sheets. He wanted to take me to the hospital, but I refused to go. Instead, he applied band-aids to wounds on my head and my hands. They eventually healed pretty well and the scars are no longer visible. Thank goodness, he did a good job. I am still pretty!

February 2004
Thoughts of Johan

The very unhealthy and destructive relationship I now have with Andy leads me to think more and more about Johan. He was wonderful to me and tolerated my poor and childish behavior. I didn't take care of his feelings in the way that he deserved. As a result, the abusive relationship I have with Andy is all that I deserve.

To Johan

It is a nightmare come true
Yesterday, I lost you
I have good memories and happiness with you
I cannot forget those memories
I know I cannot have you anymore
You don't know how much I hurt
I want you to know that I will always need you
I know it is too late
I always understand
I would like to have everything return to how it once was
I want you to know that you will never die in my heart
The sea and the sky are as far apart as we are
Don't know when we will meet again
But, I want to make sure that we will
Right now, all I can do is beg the stars and the sky to be your friend
when you are sad
and take care of you when I am not there.
From the one who cannot forget you.

February 2004
Gay and Juk

I had already known Juk for a while when she and her friend Gay moved in with me. Gay had ideas for being in Pattaya other than working a normal job. Fortunately for her, although she didn't know it at the time, she lacked the physical attributes necessary to earn good money in my profession. She was full-of-energy and very eager to find a foreign boyfriend; she was also short and heavy-set. She never found a boyfriend, but she found a job at a 7-11 convenience store. She finished 9th grade as did Juk, but she was 23 while Juk was 28. The 7-11 would not hire Juk because of her age. At only 28, she was already "over the hill." Not being employable by 7-11, left Juk to continue seeking work. She found a much better job at an upscale pool hall. In order to locate the lowest rungs of decent employment, not only does one need to have a 9th or 12th grade education, denied to many girls based on school fees, one must also be young--under 25. Many of the signs for work have the maximum-age posted.

Juk

Sometimes I think about Juk who is five years older than I am and also from Isaan. At the age of 15, when she finished the 9th grade, she began working at a shoe factory. She earned a total of Bt 95/day ($3.80), for 8 hours/day, 6 days/week. Three years later, she changed jobs and began working for a clothing factory earning Bt 145/day ($5.80), 8 hours/day, 6 days/week. On Sunday, her only day off, and after work, she went to school--eventually finishing 70% of the work required to complete a high school diploma.

Two years later, when Juk was 20, the baht took a downturn and dropped to Bt 40/$1. She changed jobs again and began working at Seagate, earning Bt 163 /day ($4.00), 6 days/week. When Seagate closed seven of its nine factories to avoid the "high" costs of Thai labor, choosing to manufacture abroad, she relocated to Advanced Technologies where she assembled thermostats for Bt 150/day ($3.75), 6 days/week. She finally decided to quit the electronics factory and move to Pattaya with her friend, Gay.

Juk now works as a waitress and a markee (one who maintains a pool table) at MegaBreak, an upscale Australian owned pool hall in Pattaya. She earns Bt 5,000/month ($125) for 6 days/week, 8 hours/day, and from Bt 2,000 to 3,000/ month in tips. That is a very good income for a girl not employed in the flesh-trade. The downside was that she had to work 30-straight days before receiving a day off during her first month of employment.

I write about Juk because although we are only a few years apart in age, I compare her life to mine. She also comes from poverty, although unlike me, she is fortunate that both of her parents are still alive. Also unlike me, her mother has been the primary breadwinner for her family throughout her life. She is 4' 10" tall, 86 pounds dripping wet, and pretty. She has never traveled to Europe; she has never traveled anywhere other than Singapore to work as a cook's aid for two weeks. She has little experience of the world or of men. She never seems to do without anything she really wants because she doesn't want very much. She always appears to be happy; she is definitely content. She has friends who really care about her, and her relationships seem to last a long time. She is also healthy, mentally and physically. She has no need for psychotropic drugs, sleeping pills, or any of the other medications that I must take to maintain emotional stability. She lives a "normal" life for a young woman not involved in the sex-trade, a life I wish were mine.

Juk once made the mistake of telling Ying, *"You have a great body and could make a lot of money working in a GoGo."* She was unaware of my past. She also had no idea that I had lived the way I did to ensure that my sisters would never have to endure the same form of employment. I didn't speak to her again for at least two months. She never learned the reason for my silence.

Juk's sister, Yen, became a GoGo dancer like me. Although she no longer works, she doesn't have to. She lives off the money sent to her by Farang, one a Brit employed in Oman and the other, an American. Why do two girls from the same loving family, lacking the same opportunities, go their very separate ways?

Two Sisters, Distinctly Different Destinies
What causes two sisters raised in the same home, with the same adult supervision, to develop distinctly different personalities and contrasting lifestyles? Childhood experiences, as different as night and day, might serve as one explanation. Although I can't explain why Juk and her sister are so very different, I can explain the family dynamics that have driven both Ying and I in opposite directions. Although Ying was struck from time-to-time, it was never with the same frequency, force, nor malice as when that same stick left welts on my tiny frame. Ying did not live 24-hours a day-- day-in and day-out--in fear of being constantly hit, as I did.

As early as I can remember, the adults in my family beat me with a stick for the slightest infraction. In fact, they needed no provocation. I was brutalized by those who were supposed to look after the helpless little ones who had been born and entrusted to their care. The blows could come at anytime and from anyone-- anyone but my father. I lived in fear of being chased around our one-room house and of being caught and hit. There was nowhere to run and nowhere to hide. I hated those who constantly hurt me. The only way that I could save myself was to run away. I knew that I didn't deserve to be beaten time and again. Although I never understood the reason, I always felt that my family was ashamed of me. But I was a good girl, albeit mischievous, not an uncommon trait among children who are seeking to explore life to its fullest.

All I ever wanted, from the time I was in primary school, was to be able to go to school and do nice things for my sisters whom I loved. I had a good heart that over the years filled with rage for those who had caused me so much pain. It was only though the blessings of Buddha that a tiny space in my heart remained open to love, and to the knowledge that there was a worthwhile human being buried deep-down inside--wearing my skin. I knew that I was worth saving. But upon the death of my father, I felt responsible. A black cloud of guilt followed me wherever I went. I knew that my family would suffer even greater humiliation at their poverty. My culture ingrained within me that I owed it to them to provide the finances that my father no longer could—and I have always met my obligations. I knew that I was willing to sacrifice my life--to die physically, emotionally, and spiritually, in order to compensate my family for his death.

Ying, on the other hand, never had any reason to feel the responsibility, nor the blame, that I did. As a result, she could pursue her innate artistic talents and her scholastic abilities at which she excelled, and for which she often received recognition. I could have as well, but I was never given the opportunity. She was acknowledged as being a "Good girl," clever, and she was well-liked. She never had any reason to prove herself; she already had. She could live her life almost the way it was intended that a child should, while within the confines of an ignorant and unfortunate family, in a poor village in Northeastern Thailand. *She could have that life only because I sacrificed mine.*

Chapter 17

Misguided Matrimony

March 2004
Marrying Andy

Andy and I were married in Pattaya on March 6, 2004. Almost immediately, we applied for my Visa, but I was not given an interview at the British Embassy in Bangkok until three months later in late June.

May 2004
Andy and Me in Pattaya

Andy and I have been married only a couple of months and we are getting along worse than usual. The other day, I asked him to get me some water from the kitchen. I could have easily gotten up to get it myself, but I was used to simply asking him to do everything for me. I knew that I was just testing him to see how far he could be pushed before he had had enough. It took less than a moment for me to find out. He returned with water and poured it all over my head. I was furious and told him I wanted a divorce. I stormed from the house to stay at a friend's apartment that night. I thought I could pressure Andy into learning that everything would go my way, and that if he didn't do as I asked, he would return to England a single man. He would also return lighter by Bt 30,000 and the small amount of gold that he had given to my mother as a Brideprice. My temper tantrum intimidated him and he called almost immediately to apologize. I returned to his apartment the following night, fully-satisfied that I had both him and our relationship under control.

June 2004

At Dave's house yesterday, I told Andy that he had not been a good father and that he had not taken care of his children.

291

Hadn't he chosen to come to Thailand with his savings rather than spend it on them? He was irate! He said that if I believed that he had not taken care of his children, I could use his phone to call his ex-wife or his ex-girlfriend who were both in England. I promptly picked up his mobile phone and threw it across the room, bouncing it off the wall and watching the cover break-off. I believed that I was right and that was all that mattered. Whether I was right or wrong was irrelevant; it was what I believed. As it turned out, I was wrong, but I never apologized.

For most of us who have survived in the flesh-trade, our rage knows no bounds. We have repressed so much anger throughout our young lives that when given the opportunity to vent that anger, we are like animals just released from a cage and our energy explodes. As a rule, we look for any and every opportunity to lash out, particularly when we know we are in a situation where we have nothing to lose. I never felt that losing Andy would have been any great loss. I also felt that I would never lose him, nor the impending Visa, as he would never leave me.

First Visa Interview

My first interview was initially conducted by a highly-educated British woman who not only spoke a sophisticated form of English, far from that of the men who frequent the bars, but she also spoke with a heavy British accent. I didn't learn English from watching the BBC, but from speaking and listening to mostly American men in Thailand. They were neither British, nor were they educated. As I had difficulty in understanding her, I asked for a Thai woman to conduct the interview. I thought that we would have a more personable conversation based on our mutual language and culture.

My request was quickly granted; I thought that I was now on my own territory, and my skills of friendly persuasion would shine through. When the new counselor approached, I realized that I received more than I had bargained for. She was equally as educated as the first. She was used to interviewing bar girls just like me, who, in order to access Visas to the UK, marry unsuspecting, gullible Englishmen who desire wives less than half their age. She spoke sophisticated Thai to me as if I had a college degree. She had to have known that it was difficult for me to understand her legal jargon. This was her way of keeping me in my place and reminding me of her elevated position. She also knew that she was making it difficult for me and for all bar girls to get their British Visas. *"Little did she know who I really was or of how much I was capable."*

I was clever, yes, but my skills and "education" had been well-honed for street survival, not for bluffing my way through an Embassy interview. I could "pull off" anything that I set my mind to, but I couldn't speak Thai at the sophisticated level that she did. I had only six years of formal education. I was sitting there thinking, *"0 for 2, don't they have any Isaan people working in this Embassy?"* Not only was I unsuccessful at securing my Visa, we were also told to return in a couple of weeks with Andy's "Proof of Employment." Andy wasn't employed, but he had been offered a job by his previous company upon his return to England. He contacted his former manager who faxed him the offer for verification.

July 2004

We returned to the British Embassy in mid-July, holding the required documents, only to learn it was necessary that Andy immediately fly back to England and fax his banking records. Confirmation of his financial assets was also required prior to the issuance of my Visa. From England, he sent me all of the required paperwork. Only a couple of weeks later, I was off to the British Embassy once again, a trip that I expected would change the recent downhill course of my life. With documents in-hand, Dave and I waited in line in front of the Embassy for over two hours. When we finally reached the counter, the financial documentation was immediately accepted; I had a brief interview and my Visa was approved. Andy and I made plans for me to go to England!

Whose Gold is it Anyway?

Shortly before going to England, I went to see my brother in Bangkok one last time. The first thing I noticed was that he was wearing the gold that my mother demanded that I purchase for her upon my arrival from Sweden, only 11 months earlier. My mother has cavalierly given away to my brother so much that I have given to her. She has never given anything to me other than Bt 300 to send me away when I was *only 13*. What is wrong with me that I continue to give to her—that I allow her to manipulate me and to intimidate me? *Then, I remember. Of course, I am the eldest daughter and I am from Isaan. I am a daughter of Isaan and I am a product of my culture!*

> ### "Man is paddy, Woman is rice."
> Thai proverb

My Mother—Nothing Has Changed!

On my family's last trip to my apartment in Pattaya, prior to my departure for Europe, my mother once again came begging me to reimburse her for the transportation costs for her and her grandchildren (my brother's children), from Ubon to Pattaya. During their stay, I watched as my two year-old nephew repeatedly hit his four-year old sister. His mean and aggressive behavior brought no response from my mother nor from my brother. It did bring a response from me. Never again will my nephew strike his sister, at least in my presence. This is why the majority of Thai men grow up the way they do, expressing little to no respect nor concern for women. My mother babied my nephew as if he were an infant, while leaving my niece to bathe and dress herself.

Finally, Off to England

As of this moment, I have no idea what my future holds. Will I get a normal job and settle down to a normal British life, earning £5/hour at a shop or a retirement home caring for the elderly, or will I return to my dancing life? I only know that Andy is my way out of Thailand and far from my life as a bar girl. I have learned that in England, there are clubs where I can dance in front of men while still dressed. That would be a first for me. The money is not as good as from stripping, but Andy would never allow me to do that again. Dancing dressed in England will pay far better than working as a cashier in Thailand. *Everything pays better than working in Thailand.*

Late July 2004

I left Pattaya once again for the chance to live in Europe, but this time in an English speaking country. Dave and Juk sent me off to the airport in a taxi. I prayed for my father and family at the airport in Bangkok, boarded the plane, and prepared to begin my new life in England. At least, this was a country where I already spoke the language, unlike Switzerland, Germany, Spain, and Sweden.

England

My arrival in England went rather well. I passed through Manchester Airport's Customs and Immigration very quickly. Andy had left for England earlier in the month and he was eagerly awaiting my arrival. He hadn't had sex in weeks and I expected that would be the first thing on his mind. His tall, lanky body was outside of Customs where hoards of English people were waiting to meet their loved ones. When I saw him, I worried that it would be a repeat of the situation that we both endured in Thailand.

In England, life with Andy didn't get off to a roaring start. He was earning less than £1,000/month ($1,880); rented an apartment; didn't have a house phone; owned a used Volkswagen; and little else, other than the clothes in his closet. I was aware that he didn't have much, but I had expected more. I certainly wanted more than this. The truth be told, I am never satisfied! What might be enough for someone else is most definitely not enough for me! *I always want more, more, more!!!*

Just a few days after my arrival, I needed my meds and I needed them immediately, but Andy kept finding excuses why he couldn't help me buy them. *"The Pharmacies are closed;"* or *"It's Sunday, you can't see a doctor on Sunday;"* or *"It's Monday, I am at work today."* If you have ever been in need of medication, and your husband refuses to make any effort to help, don't argue about it! *Find a new husband!!!* I was finally able to find a doctor, a pharmacy, and bought my medicine—all on my own.

August 2004

I hadn't been in England more than a couple of weeks when I got a job as a cleaner at Stoke-on-Trent College. The pay was £4.85/hour ($9.50) full-time. This job paid enough for me to save some money based on my original arrangement with Andy. We had agreed that I would pay for the food and he would pay for everything else. It was not like I was earning the great money I had earned as a dancer in Sweden, but it was enough for the moment. Slowly but surely, I knew that I would be able to improve my life here.

I couldn't open a bank account because I didn't have an apartment lease or a water or power bill in my name. Therefore, my electronic paycheck went into Andy's bank account. It soon became very apparent that "food," for which payment was my responsibility, encompassed "anything" that could be purchased at

296

the market. Andy also had monthly payments to make on credit cards and bank loans. He informed me that he would use more than just the "food" money to pay these debts. He gave me a minimal stipend to feed myself at work and have a cup of coffee. He said the rest would pay for the TV, car payments, rent, etc. This was most definitely not our arrangement; and I was very definitely not happy about this change in the state of our financial affairs.

Ramblings of a Clinically-Depressed Schizophrenic—
On and Off My Meds
Text Messages to Dave
August 6, 2004

Hi Dave,

How are you? I feel like I want to kill myself here with Andy. I have never met anyone like him. I miss Johan a lot now. I talk to Tony in London, my ex-boyfriend from years ago, almost everyday. Andy gives me only £3 per day. That is not enough to buy Thai food; a banana is all that I can afford. Tony has told me to come and stay with him as soon as I can if I ever need to leave.

Sometimes, Andy was not able to stop work to take me to the doctor, so I had to go by myself. Anyway, I do like my job a lot as it makes me feel a lot better. But when I get paid, I will have to give Andy an additional £20 per week. I have never had to give money to a man before. Sometimes, I don't know what I am doing here with him.

September 2004

Besides paying for a lot more than I had planned from my small salary, I am also Andy's cook and cleaner. I come home from work after 9:00pm to find the house a mess, his dishes from a snack in the sink, and him watching TV, asking me what I am going to cook for dinner. Between this kind of behavior and the changes he

297

underwent upon arriving in his country, where I guess he felt more at home, I have finally had my fill. I told him that I wanted out. The last thing that any man wants to see is his sex, cook, cleaner, and most of all his additional income, walk out the door. He told me, time and time again, that he spent so much money getting me to England. The Visa and the ticket combined were approximately $1,000, but he complained that there were other expenses involved in staying together and supporting me while we were in Thailand.

October 2, 2004

I have not been taking my medication, and in my state I believe that he has been whining too much. I got so tired of hearing him that I threw a wine bottle across the room towards the TV, but I didn't break it. He responded by calling the police and telling them that I was violent and that I had hit him two weeks earlier. I had, but he hit me as well. "She hit me last time," he told the Bobbies. The officers took the report and asked me to come and talk to them at a later date. I could see the look on their faces and read their minds. "She is 4' 9" and he is 6' 1"—and he is the one who called us?"

After a few more days of living with him and refusing him sex, he told me to sleep in the other bedroom where there was no mattress or blanket. I had a pillow and only a towel to keep me warm. I lived like that for a few days. During that time, he told me not to use "his" TV or "his" stereo or anything else that was "his." I was not going to stay with the kind of man who would refuse me a blanket for warmth. That was the last straw!

More Phone Calls to Dave
October 5, 2004

After Andy had given me £250 to move out and get my own apartment, I abruptly changed my mind about leaving because I now had money in my hand. I wanted to stay in his house and keep the money instead, and I wanted him to pay all of the bills. As far as I was concerned, leaving his home would have left me totally without funds, with the exception of £250 ($480), the difference between me and being on the streets. This was not enough for an apartment, a security fee, and food until my next paycheck. I wanted to stay in "our" home, and I did--for a few more days until the state of our relationship made that impossible. I knew that I would have to look for another place to stay, even if it meant eating only noodles twice a day.

Andy wrote to Dave about the decline of our relationship, thinking that Dave would tell me to keep my word. Both Andy and I have been calling Dave and sending him text messages since our return to England. From the moment of my arrival, our relationship was on the skids. Although I wanted a relationship that worked, I didn't want one with Andy. Fortunately, from my earlier days in Pattaya, Tony was in London with a standing invitation to come stay with him.

Moving Out

During the few hours I had in between work in the morning, English school in the afternoon, and work again in the evening, I found a student apartment for £40/week ($75). Each resident had a private room, but the best part of this new housing situation was that this room belonged to me--and me alone! I would never have to allow Andy entrance.

I have not been taking my medicine lately, and I feel that I am losing my mind. I believe I heard a friend of Andy's talking on the radio; he was speaking about a Thai girl who left her English husband, violating her Visa obligations. I am afraid that Andy is sending others to harm me. I send text messages to Dave and he tells me to take my medicine. He reminds me that I don't have a radio. He is worried because he says that I am not thinking clearly, that the stories I tell him can't be happening. He says that I am hallucinating more and more.

Andy still calls me throughout the day; he comes to my room looking for me--*at least I believe that he does.* I have told him, time and time again, that I am not going to move back with him. I would sooner leave England and return to the poverty of Thailand than spend another minute in his company.

I had always thought that the men I met at the bars were bad, but those who frequent dating services are even worse. They are like the men in the bars, but they pretend to be different. The Swiss, German, Spanish, and English men I have met while in Europe are nothing like the men from these countries who visit Pattaya Beach on their sex tours. Pattaya attracts the lowest form of Western men that I have ever met. Thai bar girls get the wrong impression of foreign men, while sex-tourists also receive the wrong impression of Thai girls, believing that they are all devious bar girls—like me. We think that they are all old, fat, drunk, unkempt, and mentally and/or physically disabled. We also think that they are not the brightest men to walk the planet. Referring to them as "average" would be a compliment. Some of them are so physically-impaired that they are unable to take care of themselves, and they are seeking a caretaker in the form of a Thai bride. As for the emotionally-impaired, Andy is a perfect example.

Day-in and day-out, I worry that I will be awakened by Immigration at my door, telling me that I am in violation of my Visa by leaving Andy's home. Although it concerns me, and I sometimes lose sleep over it, I would rather worry than spend another day with him. My friends warned me that he was not the right man, and that I should definitely look elsewhere, but I felt sorry for him. Then, there was that "British Visa" he so proudly wore. He knew what I wanted and that I would put up with a lot to get it. My friends also told me that he feigned ignorance to avoid paying his share, but I excused his bad manners by stating that he simply didn't understand. I couldn't have been more wrong.

November 8, 2004
Three Weeks at Harplands Hospital

I had been working at Stoke-on-Trent College as a cleaner for three months when I stopped taking my meds. Several weeks passed, I had been hallucinating, although as with any psychosis, hallucinations are real to the one experiencing them. A co-worker finally called the hospital; I was picked up and immediately hospitalized. *I went willingly.*

November 15, 2004

I have been in the hospital for approximately a week now. Andy called me, he wants to talk; he is in dire straits. He has been asking Dave to access my medical history in Sweden so that the English doctors can help me. Dave has been willing to act as an intermediary, but he would never give Andy personal data even if he knew it. Andy is sending Dave three or four text messages every day about the problems that I am causing him. Yesterday, I told Andy that I wanted to go back with him, but when he arrived at the hospital to see me, I told him that I would never live with him again; then I hit him.

Andy told Dave that I would have a government-appointed lawyer appear with me at the tribunal. The purpose of this hearing was to determine whether, or not, I could be released from the hospital on Monday. The lawyer would put forward my case that Andy was abusive based on my statements. But, I didn't tell the attorney how I created situations intended to incite Andy's wrath. I can be a real bitch when I'm off my medication--or even when I'm on it. The psychiatrists have now taken me off of anti-psychotic drugs and are only prescribing sleeping medication.

November 18, 2004

I had been in the hospital for over a week when the social worker spoke to Andy on the phone, asking about his financial status and if he had any property in Thailand. In his need to present himself as someone of greater means, he said that he owned property overseas. Realizing later that his lie would lead the hospital to believe that he was able to pay for my care, he became worried that the hospital would bill him. At this point in time, I had not paid enough national insurance to gain access to England's system of Socialized Medicine.

November 22, 2004

The hospital held their tribunal to decide what to do about me and about Andy and me. The hospital's psychiatrists and social workers spoke with us individually. The government lawyer asked Andy if he were able to assist me financially; he said that he wasn't. He stated that he was more than willing to get back together and pay for rent and bills, if I would pay for food.

Andy told the doctors about Dave, and that he had been like the father I didn't have. He said that Dave had helped me out in the past; he also told them that I had money in a Thai bank account for which I had an ATM card. The government attorney asked if Andy had started proceedings against me for divorce. He hadn't; he was waiting to see what I wanted to do about our relationship. He was worried about the position my hospitalization had put me in, regarding my ability to remain in England. He believed that I had dug a hole for myself, which I had. He was also worried that he might be the one who would have to pay to dig me out.

November 26, 2004

I phoned Andy last night from the hospital again and told him I wanted to see him. He came to see me, but kept a little more distance for caution. I was nicer to him this time than the last. I

302

told him that I didn't love him, but I cared about him. I cried and cried about my situation, that of being hospitalized in a psychiatric facility in England. This felt like a re-run of my experience in Sweden, except I was no longer on anti-psychotic medication.

November 28, 2004

Today, I was released from the hospital into Andy's "care."

November 29, 2004

I am out of the hospital and feeling better with new medication. I still miss my friends in Thailand. I asked Dave and Juk to come to England, but that request fell upon deaf ears. Neither of them has any interest in coming here. England is really a good country. It's not fun; but the government has assisted me through its medical system, as well as given me disability checks. It has also provided me with free English classes, and I am not even a citizen. A foreigner in my country would never be so fortunate.

December 31, 2004
Home with Andy

I've been with Andy for a month now. I received my monthly sick-leave check of £400/$750. Andy needed £220/$400 to pay bills; many of these were debts he had acquired prior to my arrival in England. I am back in the same situation that I was before I moved out on my own. I gave him half of the rent because he asked for it. If I hadn't given it to him, he would have said things to hurt me. I hate giving him my money, but I want to stay in England so badly, and I can't live alone because I'm not well. I have no home, nowhere to go, and no family here. My sisters never even write or call. I don't know what I'm going to do with my life. I would leave if I had someone else to care for me in England. I could go to Tony's; he continues to offer to care for me, but I haven't as I worry about losing my Visa and the opportunity to stay out of Thailand, forever!

January 1, 2005

After only four weeks back at Andy's home, I am already considering moving out again and getting a new room. I've also arranged a date with another man; Andy has arranged a date with another woman.

January 3, 2005

It hasn't taken long before I have come to realize that I can't leave him; I am in too much pain—emotionally and physically. In England, men do not give money to their girlfriends like in Thailand. They won't even buy cigarettes for their girlfriends, or as in my case—a wife! I tried meeting two men; they were both the same. English men are nice, but they don't pay for anything except the first meal they share with their date. I could find a new man, but I am fed up with trying. After all I've been through, I believe that if I am married for life, I will never again feel any more pain.

January 4, 2005

Yesterday, Andy lost his job as a driver for a construction firm, but today he got it back. This brief lapse in his employment and in the security of our finances may have led to my being more depressed than usual. This afternoon, I felt so badly. I miss Johan a lot more when I feel down, as he would always cheer me up. I wanted Dave to ask him to contact me. If he contacted me, it would have made me feel a lot better. All I needed was just to hear his voice. If he called, it would probably make me cry, but if he wants no longer to be my friend, that would make me cry every day. I do love him. I still show Johan's photo to all of my friends in the college where I work. I miss him more and more every day. While crying at work, one of my friends said that she believed he still loved me. I want to believe it, too! I always wonder, if when Dave E-mails him, *"Does he ask about me? Does he have a new girlfriend?"* And then, I also feel sorry for Andy. I should never have left Sweden for Thailand. *I should never have met Andy!*

January 5, 2005

I am so sorry that I've caused Dave and Johan so much trouble and that I've been such a burden to them. I know I will never meet men like them again. They always helped me to help my family. I will never forget that. I wish I could take care of myself and my sisters on my own, but I have neither enough money, nor the emotional, nor physical strength to do that anymore. Hopefully, in the future, I will be able to help my sisters once again. Andy has been trying to get government money for taking care of me through my illness for quite some time. He is also trying to get a government apartment more quickly for the same reason. Andy is experienced at applying for government assistance. Hopefully, he will be successful very soon.

A little while ago, Andy said it was okay for me to start dancing again. But in the past, he had told me that there were not any strip clubs in our town. I will still try to find a place to dance; the amount of money that an attractive 4' 9"Thai can earn in England is very high. I also worry that Andy would expect half of it. That is just how I am!

Andy is not too happy about how our relationship is going. He is really stressed out and upset about the whole situation with me. He has finally had enough of me and he needs to get on with his life. But, he is in a dilemma. He wants to do the right thing by me. He wants me to be able to stay in England, while at the same time he wants to see about getting a divorce. That is the tricky part in regards to my Visa.

January 8, 2005

Andy asked my biographer to write a short-story version of this book for us to submit to a contest put on by the magazine *"Take a Break."* The best submission wins £500 ($950). He thinks that we could win and we really do need the money now.

That request was ignored as it would have taken a great deal of time. It was also really none of Andy's business.

Later, Andy called Dave to request a loan of £500 ($950) for us to pay a surveyor to get a mortgage for a house. Andy promised Dave that we would return the money upon receiving the mortgage money. Andy thinks nothing of asking anyone for anything. He feels "Entitled." He always has his hand out.

January 12, 2005
Andy once again called Dave to ask about a loan. He has lost his job--again. He is no longer interested in money for a surveyor, but now he simply needs to make payments on the bills which are overdue.

January 13, 2005
I called Dave twice today to discuss my returning to Thailand. I must have cried to him and Juk for 30 minutes. I am tired of England and of not having any friends here. It has not worked out as I had planned. I asked if Dave would be willing to open a small shop for me to run in Ubon, or one for Juk and myself to operate in Pattaya. I am so miserable that I am willing to trade England for a little shop in an Ubon village; that is exceedingly miserable. I never thought that I would want to leave England or any European country for Thailand. Dave and Juk talked me out of leaving England. Dave even mentioned that maybe I should look at dancing again, and that it might cheer me up. This idea infuriated Andy! Dave also suggested that if I am feeling this depressed, I should consider re-admitting myself to the hospital. I told him that I had gone yesterday and that the doctor said that I was *"Just having a bad day and would be better in a day or two."* The doctor was wrong! I wonder what he would say now. I can't overcome my deep sense of sorrow and loneliness. I feel empty inside. This pain is more than I can bear!

Later the Same Day

Andy called Dave to inform him that I had just OD'd. He yelled, *"Lon is lying on the floor! She overdosed on her sleeping pills and medicine. The ambulance is on its way now!"*

January 14, 2005

They were unable to pump my stomach as it needed to be done within one hour of my ingesting the drugs. I took a lot of them. The doctors are worried that my kidneys and heart might have been damaged, but I am resilient. My blood pressure is only 84 and I am on a drip, trying to bring it back to normal.

I woke up a lot more stable. My blood pressure is approaching normal. The doctors are still waiting to see the results of the blood tests. Last night, I lied to Andy—again. I told him that Dave had offered me Bt 50,000 to return to Thailand and set up a small shop. I wanted to make Andy jealous; I wanted to see if he would let me keep more of my money and not ask for so much.

It is nearly 7:00 P.M.; I am being allowed to leave the hospital. My blood pressure and heart rate have normalized. I am returning home with Andy. I am in a better frame of mind.

January 17, 2005

I called Dave to tell him that I met a man who wanted to make contact with Ying as soon as he saw her picture. I wanted him to set up an E-mail address for her so that this man could contact her. I am always trying to improve my sisters' lives, in this case by finding Ying a foreign boyfriend--a potential husband. I also miss my family a lot and I desperately need their company.

January 22, 2005

I sent a text message to Dave asking him to tell Andy to take better care of me. I am sick and can't take care of myself. I need someone for all of my life. For now, I have decided that this person will be Andy.

January 23, 2005

I am feeling up today, but I still miss Dave and Juk. I know more about Andy everyday and I am learning to understand him. I can accept him and live with him--for now!

January 26, 2005

I love Andy. He makes me love him because I feel sorry for him. I don't know why people always do bad things to him. He doesn't know how to hurt anyone. I want to put my whole life with him. I know he's not a bad man, but he doesn't understand things and I don't know how to do everything here. But everything he does, he does his best.

January 27, 2005

Andy always forgives me; he needs someone; that is all that he wants. I feel the same way and that is why I love him. I want real love; that is what I'm looking for. Now, I believe that I have it. I know why others don't like him, but I'm with him for a long time now. Do you know what I see? I see myself when I look at him— somebody who no one loves! I can't leave him because it will make him feel badly. And, it would make me feel badly to hurt him.

February 5, 2005

Andy knows that Dave has never been fond of our relationship. This prompted him to send Dave a message concerning the advantages of my being here. *"Even though we don't have much money, compared to Thailand, Lon has a better life in England with free doctors and better health care. When Lon receives permanent residency next year, she will be able to claim a lot of money for her disability. So in time, things will improve for her through me, and I will see to it that she receives all of the*

308

medical help that she requires." Although, all of the government aid I will receive will come through his efforts, everything I receive will benefit him as well—as it already has!

March 9, 2005
Marriage Counselor

We are going to see a Marriage Counselor to try and sort things out. Our relationship is like a roller coaster; it is very high when we have a lot of laughs; and very low when it costs me too much. The laughs are not that frequent anymore.

March 11, 2005

I may have finally brought my marriage to an end. I have not been treating Andy very well for a while. My nurse found a women's shelter where I can stay for a few days. Her idea is that it will give us a rest from each other; she has seen the tension going on between us. The real cause of our conflict is that I want to live a single life. I like to go out and meet other men, and I am. Andy found a list of men in my purse that I had taken from the Personals.

Andy now thinks that he will do better in his life without me. He believes no man will want to have a long-term relationship with me because I treat all men badly. He also thinks that I have no self-respect. I disagree.

March 17, 2005

Andy phoned a solicitor this morning. He made the call right in front of me; he wanted to prove to me that he was serious about dissolving our relationship. He made the appointment for next week to discuss initiating divorce proceedings. He feels that I have used him and he isn't happy about it. Shortly after listening to him, I left the house in a hurry. My friend came to pick me up. We were going to see a government-provided attorney to see where I stood in this situation. Andy has finally had enough of me—again!

March 19, 2005

I decided to play a game with Andy. I made up with him on the surface, convincing him that we could give our lives together another try. I even pretended to like his children—*yuck!* I have been acting since I was 14—this was an easy role. He was so very happy about it. He now thinks that he can prove Dave wrong and that we can work things out together. He wanted Dave to send his congratulations for our reconciliation. Dave neither believed it would work out, nor cared. I immediately sent Dave a text message assuring him that things were not great. I told him that I was just being calm for the time being for the sole-purpose of making my life more comfortable with Andy. I also told him that I was still looking for a way to live my life in England without Andy, while still maintaining my Visa status. My Visa is all that I care about. It will not only be of great benefit to me personally, but also to my sisters when I am finally able to bring them here.

March 21, 2005

Today was a great day! I was awarded £62 /$118 per month; the disability allowance that Andy had previously applied for has finally come through.

March 24, 2005

Maybe I shouldn't have played so nice to Andy as now it's starting to cost me once again. He wants £110 ($190) from me because I am still with him. All he asks for is money, money, money, money--not so unlike me! I can understand that. Dave tells me not to worry about the Visa, and that England will not kick me out of the country. But, I do worry. I do not want to go back to Thailand—ever!

I had a job interview today at a hotel. The job is 48/hours per week, but I don't think that I will get it. I will still keep looking. I still need Andy to show me how to do things. Fortunately, I learn fast! If I want to stay in England, I have to know how to survive here. And, I also want both of my sisters to come and have a good life. Everyone brings their families here and I don't want to ruin this opportunity, so I have to be careful. That's my dream. I love my sisters. I desperately want to leave him. If I go slowly, I will—and I will take my sisters with me. Believe me!

Ying, age 19 and me, age 23

March 27, 2005

 I asked Dave to send me some clothes from Thailand. They are too expensive here. And, there are not many beautiful things here like in Thailand. Thailand is the best place for shopping and finding my petite size.

 Dave urged me to contact a social service worker in Stoke-on-Trent to try and iron out some of my problems, and also to learn more about my standing in regards to the Visa. Because I didn't know who she was or how she could help me, I never followed through. I've talked to four Thai girls here and they have all told me the same thing. If I am not with Andy, the government will send me back. But if I have a baby here, they can never send me back and they will even help me support it. Thai women have told me that English men don't give their ladies money. So, I need to get a full-time job and then take care of my Visa. Finally, I need to find somewhere else to stay, but now is not the time.

March 28, 2005

 The job that I applied for last week came through. I now have a new job as an operator/receptionist. No longer am I a cleaner. I haven't been this happy in many, many months. This is the most honorable employment I have ever had in my life. The salary of £5/hour ($9.50) will be enough for me to apply for Ying's Visa and to support her, but it will be tight. All I have ever wanted was to make life better for my family and primarily for my sisters. Once I experienced Europe, I knew that this was the place for my sisters and me, where we could all live with dignity.

April 1, 2005

 I learned today that my written English is not good enough to perform the duties of a receptionist. I was transferred to work as a bartender. I couldn't have been happier with the change. I now have a little black uniform with a white shirt and bow tie. I look great and enjoy the work much more; it suits my personality because I am a "people–person." Two weeks of training and I will be a full-fledged bartender.

The dancing club to which I recently applied called me. They want me to dance ASAP. I plan to work two or three nights per week. Now, I will be able to save enough money and have a high-enough income to apply for Ying's Visa so that she can get out of Thailand. I have lost the weight that I put on with the medication; now I weigh only 39.5 kilos (87 pounds) which means I can fit into my sexy clothes and look good. I will have Dave and Juk send me some dancing costumes to get started. In Thailand, one costume costs $5. In England, one outfit costs £21 ($40).

April 15, 2005

The new dancing costumes that Dave and Juk sent me still sit in the bag….

June 2005
A New Job, A New Apartment and…

The differences I have with Andy have become irreconcilable. We fight constantly! He has relegated me to another room in our townhouse and he refuses to pay for my food or do anything to help me. Fortunately, I am working and can take care of myself. I have a new job at a "Fish 'n Chips" shop owned by a Chinese woman. The bar couldn't give me enough hours as a bartender, although I loved the job. I just need to find my own place.

The Following Week

My new employer has offered me a room in her house. I've also learned from the Thai Embassy that since I will soon be in England for one year, I can apply for a Visa that will allow me to remain here. I am leaving Andy for the last time. I have a job, some money, and a place of my own. I will also be able to get a British Visa based on my employment rather than my marriage. I did it!!! *I knew that I could, that I would, succeed in Europe this time!* I'll pack my bags immediately. Can't wait!!! Andy will have mixed feelings about my leaving, but mostly he will feel relief.

"The peace I never found"

Painted in England

Chapter 18

On Reflection: A Decade Later

June 2005
Sai

Sai's rejection by her mother at birth, and learning of it years later, has had an enormous affect on her character. Later, when she learned in such a cruel manner that her 18-year old sister was a prostitute—by having it literally "thrown in her face," her heart was broken. This knowledge, added to her earlier rejection, destroyed the last of her self-esteem. Her suffering is displayed in the tattoos covering her entire back and in her tongue ring—hideous and blatant examples of her anti-social behavior. She also manifests her anger in her defiance of the rules of society as in her prior use of Yabah, quitting school, and getting pregnant. Yet, the sadness and rage that she feels has helped her to understand my position better than Ying, my blood sister, ever could.

Currently, Sai, at 19, cares nothing for her baby. She gave it to her natural mother to care for. Why would a young woman give her baby to another woman who has proven herself an unfit mother, one that tried to kill her years earlier? My feelings are that she doesn't know how to love her own child at this point in her life, nor is she willing to learn. She thought that she could force her mother to love this infant; love that she had never received. On the other hand, the only reason that her mother takes care of the baby is because Sai sends her money every month. She refuses to allow me to buy presents for my niece. She even denies her baby small tokens of love from another. She hates the fact that she has given birth to this child in the very same way that her mother hated having given birth to her.

Sai recently lost her job at Pran Talay's shrimp factory because her boyfriend consistently came by to see her. He had previously lost his job at the same factory for being argumentative. She was living in a small room and was desperate for work, so she did what any innovative and industrious girl might do; she forged a high school diploma. She learned this skill in the juvenile detention home while serving time for using Yabah. Few Isaan girls are able to attend high school, and fewer yet manage to graduate. Her struggle to survive was not terribly different from mine nearly 10 years earlier. She took the only way out that she knew. I am proud of her for doing so. She now has a good salary Bt 5,500/month ($137) base pay for 8 hours/day, 6 days/week. When overtime is included, her salary is approximately Bt 10,000/month ($250) which equals 12 hours/day, 6 days/week with health insurance, four days off each month, money for lunch at the company food court, etc. Those are benefits that few girls in Thailand ever have, and she has them because she forged a high school diploma. *In Thailand, the vast majority of girls do not have the opportunity to receive benefits by following the rules and doing the right thing. We have to find an alternate way if we ever want to get anything approaching a fair deal.*

Ying

In July 2002, Ying graduated from 12th grade! She was the first one in our family ever to graduate. Only an extremely small percentage of girls from poor Isaan provinces graduate from high school. The plans I made at the age of 13 for my sisters' education became a reality when I was 21. I understand and apply economics in Thailand far better than Thai government economists. I have been able to lift my family from the abject poverty into which we were born—and I did it alone! *Although, I never really saved much of what I earned; I saved my sisters from the same peril that befell me. No one will ever tell me, as they did Sai, "Your sister is a prostitute!" I did what I intended to do; and I succeeded!*

318

Ying (center) with friends in her graduating class.

Both of my sisters had been living with their boyfriends for many months. After enduring physical and verbal abuse, Sai and Ying decided to leave. They moved in together and so did both of their ex-boyfriends. I helped Ying plan for college. My mother was opposed to Ying's intention to further her education because that would mean that she would not see any money from Ying's employment until she graduated—at least four years away.

Shortly before leaving for England, I visited Ying. She told me that she believed I should continue to send the same money home that I had sent in the past while I worked as a bar girl and a dancer. She had grown to believe that it was still my responsibility to provide for my mother and her. She believed that being a bar girl and a dancer was *Who I was*, not *What I did.* She believed that I owed it to her to continue to support her.

Dave is now paying for her college tuition and he also gave her a motorbike; the same one that he had made available to me upon my return from Sweden. Whether or not she ever understands how fortunate she has been or expresses any gratitude remains to be seen. Her sole-purpose in living is to maintain the facade of not being a poor girl from Isaan. She does this primarily by maintaining an impeccable personal appearance.

No Escape

When I think about my seven years in the sex-tourist trade, my pain is often unbearable. I want no part of my past. I desperately want to sever my memories from my mind, my mind from my body, and the body that I sold for so little—from the truth of who I am. *But, there is no escape!* My life has been exceedingly difficult since I decided to turn it around. I live in the constant belief that the worst will befall me, and that everyone will cheat me in the same way that I was cheated of my youth—and in the very same way that I cheated so many men.

My paranoia is a common disorder among many bargirls. We suffer for every baht we send home to support our families. In return, we receive little appreciation and more often--outright ingratitude. We are cheated by our families and by society in general. We believe, and rightly so, that no one loves us and no one cares. Our value to our families is in the money that we send home; to our country, it is in the tourist revenue that we create.

We are sick, mentally and physically. As much as I want to recover and be happy, somewhere deep down in the recesses of my soul, I don't believe that I deserve happiness. Of the stories of young bar girls who finally leave the profession, few of them live happily ever after. We have a very poor rate of success.

I am one of the few, but fortunate girls, who found the opportunity to move abroad where I was paid far better for my talent and my looks--work that didn't include a humiliating romp, or tussle, between the sheets in a sleazy hotel room. But, that doesn't mean it was easy. Changing countries, cultures, and careers, and earning an adequate salary have been a daily struggle. I have been disappointed time and again by jobs that appear one moment and are lost in the next. Everyday, I must remind myself that I am a valuable human being with special inherent gifts. Most importantly, I am strong and more determined than ever to succeed!

If one were to ask me what I envision for my future, I would say that I want to be a role-model to other young girls. I want them to know that they can and will survive after leaving their lives in the sex-trade behind them. It takes only one single "leap of faith." They just need someone to tell them, maybe for the very first time, that they are worth the risk! They need to be reminded that they already have value simply because they exist. This belief is not intrinsic to Isaan culture, and therefore, it is not instilled during our childhood. Each girl must discover for herself that the truth is she doesn't need to sell her body to prove her worth—a worth her family doesn't even value. I can help her to make that discovery.

As I remind them, I am also reminding myself. Who is in a better position to assist these young women? Who could possibly know better about the lives they have felt compelled to live? Only someone who has walked our path and suffered our fate could possibly understand the depth to which we have fallen.

It has been a long journey from my poor, dusty village in Ubon, to the refined culture of Europe. I have lived in Sweden, Switzerland, Germany, and England. I have also lived and survived a nightmare in my 24 years. Now, I intend to live my dreams. *I finally know what it's like to be valued for no other reason than "I am."* I want to help other young Isaan girls feel this wonderful too. I have already received the education of a lifetime in only 10 years. I still have a lot to do and also a lot to learn. But, that's okay, because I have a very long life ahead of me. *I am only 24!*

REFERENCES

Chapter 2: *Bangkok, My New Home*
1. Trink, Bernard, Bangkok Post

Chapter 3: *Isaan Family Values: A Contradiction in Terms*
1. Thai.sex.net

Chapter 5: *Education*
1. Bangkok Post   05/13/03
2. The Nation   05/15/04
3. Bangkok Post   05/14-05/19/03
4. The Nation   05/10/04
5. Bangkok Post   07/01/03
6. Bangkok Post   07/29/03
7. Bangkok Post   05/12/03
8. Bangkok Post   06/23/03
9. Bangkok Post   06/29/03

Chapter 6: *Exquisite Beauty, Rustic Charm, Unimaginable Corruption: The Unabridged Truth about Thailand*
1. Bangkok Post   08/27/03

Social Values Need To Be Re-examined
1. Bangkok Post   07/29/03

Thailand: Sex Capital of the World
1. Dr. Chutikul, Saisuree, Thailand's Minister for Women and Children,
2. Ehrlich, Richard, *"Health Officials Say 1,000,000 Thai Men Bed 26,000 HIV–Infected Prostitutes Every Night,"* 1993,
3. Stickman.com, Bangkok
4. Ehrlich, Richard, *"Health Officials Say..."* Ibid
5. Thai Red Cross
6. Thai Red Cross
7. Stickman.com, Bangkok
8. Ehrlich, Richard, Ibid

Sexual Slavery

1. Son, Johanna, *"Changing Attitudes: Key to Ending Child Sex Trade,"* InterPress Service, 01/23/95.
2. U.S. State Department 2002
3. ECPAT Intl. (End Child Prostitution in Asian Tourism), "www.hrw.org/about/projects/traffcamp/intro.html"
4. Thaisex/Chulalongkorn University
5. CATW Fact Book (Coalition Against Trafficking in Women), *Asia Pacific Newsletter,* Volume 1.2, Winter 1998
6. Bangkok Post   05/08/05
7. Brown, Louise, Sex Slaves, Virago Press, 2000
8. Bangkok Post   05/27/03
9. ABC (Australian Broadcasting Corporation) 07/05/03
10. Brown, Louise, Sex Slaves, Ibid
11. Thaisex.net
12. Brown, Louise, Sex Slaves, Ibid
13. Johnson Tim, *"Child Trafficking On Rise Due to Weak Laws,"* Kyodo News Intl., 03/09/00
14. Jones, Arthur, *"Global Slave Trade Prospers,"* *National Catholic Reporter*, 05/25/01
15. Son, Joanna,   *"Changing Attitudes...,"* Ibid
16. Guardian Angel, Jubilee @ St. Johns U.K
17. *"A Samaritan's Quest to Save Children,"* InterPress Service 10/16/04
18. ECPAT INTL., *"Child Prostitution and Trafficking Prevention Program in Northern Thailand,"* 10/07/02
19. *Peace and Environment News,* July and August 1994
20. CATW Fact Book, Ibid
21. Ashizuka, Tomoko, *"Women Trafficked from Thailand to Japan"* TED Studies, 10/2000
22. CATW Fact Book, Ibid
23. Bangkok Post   01/28/06 (Alexandra Hudson)

Job Slavery

1. Johnson, Tim, *"Child Trafficking on Rise Due to Weak Laws,"* Ibid.
2. Bureau of International Labor Affairs, Washington, D.C.
3. Bangkok Post   07/24/03
4. Bureau of International Labor Affairs, Washington, D.C.
5. Ekachai, Sanitsuda, *Shattered Dreams, "The Cruelty of the Rich,"* Bangkok Post, 08/07/03

6.	Bangkok Post	05/29/03
7.	Bangkok Post	06/04/03
8.	Washington Post	09/10/95

Pedophiles
1.	Bangkok Post	05/28/03 & 06/15/03
2.	Bangkok Post	05/12/03
3.	Bangkok Post	7/05/03
4.	Bangkok Post	04/05/96
5.	Bangkok Post	06/05/03
6.	SANE Newsletter	02/2003
7.	Bangkok Post	09/01/05

Chapter 7: *The Creation of Poverty in Thailand: The Setting for My Future*
1.	Bangkok Post	05/07/03
2.	Bangkok Post	09/17/03
3.	Bangkok Post	06/24/03
4.	Bangkok Post	05/12/03

Chapter 10: *Pattaya: A Sex-Tourist's Paradise*
1. CATW Fact Book, Ibid

SELECTED READINGS

Bello, Walden F., Shea Cummingham and Li Kheng Poh
A Siamese Tragedy: Development and Disintegration in Modern Thailand, White Lotus, Bangkok, 1998

Bello, Waldon F., Shea Cunningham and Bill Rau
Dark Victory, Pluto Press, London, 1994

Botte, Marie-France and Jean-Paul Mari
The Price of a Child: Four Years in the Hell of Child Prostitution in Bangkok, Robert Laffont Publishing, Paris, 1993

Brown Louise
Sex Slaves: The Trafficking of Women in Asia
Virago Press—Little, Brown and Company, London, 2000

Heilbroner, Robert L.
The Great Ascent: The Struggle for Economic Development in Our Time, Harper and Row, New York, 1963

Jeffrey, Leslie Ann
Sex and Borders: Gender, National Identity, and Prostitution Policy in Thailand, University of British Columbia Press, Canada, 2002

Mahbubani, Kishore
Can Asians Think? Times Books International, Singapore, 1998

Nartsupha, Chatthip
The Thai Village Economy in the Past, Silkworm Books, Chiang Mai, Thailand, 2000

O'Grady, Ron
The Child and The Tourist: The Story Behind the Escalation of Child Prostitution in Asia: Rape of the Innocent , ECPAT

Phongpaichit, Pasuk, Sungsidh Piriyarangsan and Nualnoi Treerat.
Guns, Girls, Gambling, Ganja: Thailand's Illegal Economy and Public Policy, Corruption and Democracy in Thailand
Silkworm Books, Chiang Mai, Thailand, 1998

Sakhrobanek, Siriphon, Nataya Boonpakdee and Chutima Chanathop,
The Traffic in Women: Human Realities of the International Sex Trade, Zed Books, London, 1997

Seabrook, Jeremy
Travels in the Skin Trade: Tourism and the Sex Industry
Pluto Press, London, 2001

Sorajjakool, Siroj
Child Prostitution in Thailand: Listening to Rahab
Haworth Press, New York, 2002

Sudham Pira
People of Esarn, Breakwater Books, St. John's, Canada, 1987

Sudham Pira
Monsoon Country, Breakwater Books, St. John's,Canada. 1988

INTERNATIONAL ORGANIZATIONS
To contribute to these organizations, please contact them directly.

AMNESTY INTERNATIONAL: Child Soldiers
The Campaign to Stop Child Soldiers
The international community has become increasingly concerned about the devastating problem of child soldiers forcibly abducted to fight in adult wars. Over 300,000 children and young people around the world are soldiers. The 10th anniversary of the UN Convention on the Rights of the Child in November provides an opportunity to put an end to this practice of using children and young people as soldiers.
www.amnesty.org.uk/childrights/soldier.htm

ANTI-SLAVERY
Today's Fight for Tomorrow's Freedom
Anti-Slavery was set up in 1839 with the specific objective of ending slavery throughout the world.
www.antislavery.org

CAPTIVE DAUGHTERS
Captive Daughters is dedicated to ending the sex trafficking of children, with a particular focus on girls and women.
3500 Overland Avenue #110-108,
Los Angeles, CA 90034-5696
TEL: (310) 669-4400
FAX: (310) 815-9197
E-Mail: captivedaughters@earthink.net
www.captivedaughters.org/Index.htm

CHILD WISE (ECPAT)
The Australian division of ECPAT working in Australia and overseas to end child sexual exploitation and abuse
www.childwise.net/our-vision.php

COALITION AGAINST TRAFFICKING IN WOMEN (CATW)
A non-governmental organization that promotes women's human rights by working internationally to combat sexual exploitation
www.catwinternational.org/about/index.php

328

COALITION TO ABOLISH SLAVERY AND TRAFFICKING (CAST)
ADDRESS: 5042 Wilshire Blvd., #586, Los Angeles, CA 90036
TEL: (213) 365 1906, (213) 365-5257
www.castla.org

END CHILD PROSTITUTION, CHILD PORNOGRAPHY AND TRAFFICKING OF CHILDREN FOR SEXUAL PURPOSES/END CHILD PROSTITUTION IN ASIAN TOURISM (ECPAT)
A network of organizations and individuals working together to eliminate the commercial sexual exploitation of children: It seeks to encourage the world community to ensure that children everywhere enjoy their fundamental rights free from all forms of commercial sexual exploitation.
www.ecpat.com

FONDAZIONE UMANITARIA ARCOBALENO
FUA is a non-governmental organization devoted to developmental, educational and medical projects. *Developmental*: It gives children the chance to free themselves from poverty and helps them to grow. *Educational:* It provides children with a good education and intellectual background. *Medical:* It gives preventive and curative help, where needed. "FONDAZIONE ARCOBALENO is currently operating projects in 3 Asian countries: Nepal, India and Thailand"
ADDRESS: Via Clemente Maraini 22, 6900 Lugano, Switzerland
TEL: (0041) 79-211-9324 Switzerland (0066) 7-106-4468 Thailand
www.fondarco.ch

GLOBAL FUND FOR WOMEN
An international network of women and men committed to a world of equality and social justice. It advocates for and defends women's human rights by making grants to support women's groups around the world.
www.globalfundforwomen.org/1work

GLOBAL MARCH AGAINST CHILD LABOR
Giving every child a chance to live and grow without the burden of exploitative work. Millions of child laborers around the world live a life of servitude. Get involved in its elimination!
www.globalmarch.org

HUMAN RIGHTS WATCH
An independent, non-governmental organization dedicated to protecting the human rights of people around the world. It is supported by contributions from private individuals and foundations worldwide. It accepts no government funds, directly or indirectly.
www.hrw.org

MADRE
Demanding Human Rights for Women and Families around the World
www.madre.org/press/pr/nationsex.html

POLARIS PROJECT – Combat Human Trafficking
A multi-cultural grassroots organization combating human trafficking and modern-day slavery
www.polarisproject.org

PROTECTION PROJECT
Establishing an international framework for the elimination of trafficking in persons, especially women and children
ADDRESS: 1717 Massachusetts Avenue, Washington DC 20036.
www.protectionproject.org

SAVE THE CHILDREN
The leading independent organization creating lasting change for children in need in the United States and around the world: It is a member of the International Save the Children Alliance, comprising 27 national Save the Children organizations working in more than 100 countries to ensure the well-being of children.
ADDRESS: 54 Wilton Road, Westport, CT 06880
TEL: 1-800-SAVETHECHILDREN
www.savethechildren.org

STANDING AGAINST GLOBAL EXPLOITATION PROJECT (SAGE)
A non-profit organization with one primary aim: bringing an end to the commercial sexual exploitation of children and adults.
ADDRESS: 1385 Mission Street, Suite 300,
San Francisco, CA 94103
TEL: (415) 905-5050   FAX: (415) 554-9981
www.sageprojectinc.org

"STOLEN CHILDHOODS:" The film
THE INTERNATIONAL LABOR RIGHTS FUND, an NGO
ADDRESS: 733 15th Street, N.W., Suite 920,
Washington, D.C. 20005
E-Mail: trina.tocco@ilrf.org
www.stolenchildhoods.org

STOP DEMAND
Vision: To live in a world free of sexual violence and sexual exploitation   *Mission:* To promote a world free of all forms of sexual violence against, and sexual exploitation of, children with a particular focus on challenging the demand for sex with children
www.stopdemand.com

THE CODE
Code of Conduct for the Protection of Children from Sexual Exploitation in Travel and Tourism
www.thecode.org

UNITED NATION'S CHILDREN'S FUND: Changing the World with Children
Created by the United Nations General Assembly in 1946 to help children after World War II in Europe, UNICEF was first known as the United Nations International Children's Emergency Fund. In 1953, UNICEF became a permanent part of the United Nations system, its task being to help children living in poverty in developing countries. Its name was shortened to the United Nations Children's Fund, but it retained the acronym "UNICEF."
www.unicef.org

WORLD VISION
A Christian relief and development organization dedicated to helping children and their communities worldwide reach their full potential by tackling the causes of poverty. World Vision serves the world's poor—regardless of a person's religion, race, ethnicity, or gender.
www.worldvision.org

WOMEN'S AND CHILDREN'S ORGANIZATIONS
THAILAND AND SOUTHEAST ASIA
To contribute to these organizations, please contact them directly.

ASIAN CONFEDERATION OF WOMEN'S ORGANIZATIONS
127/1 Sukumvit 79, Bangkok, 10250, Thailand

ASIA PACIFIC FORUM ON WOMEN'S LAW AND DEVELOPMENT (APWLD)
Santhitham YMCA Bldg, 3rd Floor, 11 Sermsuk Rd, Mengrairasmi, Chiang Mai, 50300, Thailand
TEL: 66-53-404-613/404-614   FAX: 66-53-404-615
E-Mail: apwld@loxinfo.co.th

ASSOCIATION FOR THE PROMOTION OF THE STATUS OF WOMEN
501/1 Moo 3 Dechatungka Rd., Sikan, Don Muang,
Bangkok, 10210, Thailand
E-Mail: may-fai@linethai.co.th or apsw2002@ksc.th.com

BURMESE WOMEN'S UNION
P.O. Box 42, Mae Hong Son 58000, Thailand
TEL/FAX: 66-53-611-146 or 66-53-612-361
E-Mail: caroline@ksc15.th.com

COALITION TO FIGHT AGAINST CHILD EXPLOITATION (FACE)
Post Office Box 178, Klong Chan
Bangkok, 10240, Thailand
TEL: (66) (2) 6522-2607
E-Mail: facesudabkk@yahoo.com
www.un.or.th/TraffickingProject/FACE/face_home.html

DEVELOPMENT AND EDUCATION PROGRAMME FOR DAUGHTERS AND COMMUNITIES CENTER (DEP)
P.O. Box 10, Mae Sai, Chiang Rai, 57130, Thailand

EMPOWER FOUNDATION: Supports women in the sex industry
57/60 Tivanond Road, Nontburi, 11000, Thailand
TEL: 02-526-8311, 02-968-8021, 02-968-8022
FAX: 02-526-3294
E-Mail: empower@cm.ksc.co.th, empower@cm-sun.cm.ksc.co.th

FOUNDATION FOR WOMEN
35/267 Charansanitwongse Road 62, Soi Wat Paorohit, Bangkoknoi, Bangkok, 10700, Thailand or
P.O. Box 47, Bangkoknoi, Bangkok, 10700, Thailand
TEL: 66-2-433 5149   FAX: 66-2-434 6774
E-Mail: FFW@mozart.inet.co.th

FOUNDATION FOR WOMEN, LAW AND RURAL DEVELOPMENT (FORWARD)
Chiang Mai University, Chiang Mai, 50200, Thailand

FRIENDS-INTERNATIONAL
Since 1994, Friends-International has been working with street children to develop creative projects that effectively support them to become independent and productive actors of their society.
9A, Street 178, Phnom Penh, Cambodia
TEL: +855-23 986 601
E-Mail: info@friends-international.org
www.friends-international.org / www.childsafe-cambodia.org

FRIENDS OF WOMEN FOUNDATION
Works for legal protection of women's human rights
(Grassroots Women's Network-GROWNET)
218/16 Soi Pradipat 18, Phayathai, Bangkok, 10400, Thailand
TEL: (66) 279-0867, (66) 278-3551

GENDER DEVELOPMENT AND RESEARCH INSTITUTE
501/1 Moo 3 Dechatungka Road, Sikan, Donmuagn, Bangkok, 10210, Thailand

GLOBAL ALLIANCE AGAINST TRAFFIC IN WOMEN (GAATW)

An international alliance to improve the coordination of national/global actions against the traffic in women: GAATW offers training, research, networking, and publishes handbooks.
191 Sivalai Condominium, Issaraphap Road, Soi 33, Bangkok Yai, Bangkok, 10600, Thailand or
P.O. Box 1281, Bangkok Post Office, Bangkok, 10500, Thailand
TEL: (66) (2) 864-1427/28 FAX: (66) (2) 864-1637
E-Mail: gaatw@mozart.inet.co.th
www.gaatw.net

GOODWILL GROUP FOUNDATION

(See below for more information)
2nd Floor Ruam Rudee Bldg. III, 51/2 Soi Ruam Rudee, Ploenchit Road, Lumpini, Phatumwan, Bangkok, Thailand
TEL: (66) (2) 253-8493 or (66) (2) 255-4176

HARBOR HOUSE

Kritsana Wankham, Manager
61 Moo 7 Baan Ta Sala
Sri Muang Chiem, Mae Sai, Chiang Rai, 51730 Thailand
TEL: 66-53-668-068
www.hhfthailand.org

HIGHLAND PEOPLE EDUCATION AND DEVELOPMENT FOUNDATION

Supports alternative livelihood projects for women and community organizing
658 Moo 15, Watmai Naakhai Road, T. Robwiang, A. Muang, Chiang Rai, 57000, Thailand
TEL: 66-53-714-772   FAX: 66-53-717-098

KAREN HUMAN RIGHTS GROUPS
KAREN WOMEN'S ORGANIZATION

P.O. Box 5, Mae Sot, Tak, 63110 Thailand

LANNA WOMEN'S CENTER

Chiang Mai University, Faculty of Education,
Chiang Mai, 50200, Thailand
TEL: 66 05 2 221699

THE LAWYER'S COUNCIL OF THAILAND
7/89 Mansion 10, Rajdamnoen Avenue,
Pranakorn District, Bangkok, 10200, Thailand
TEL: (66) (2) 629-1430   FAX: (66) (2) 282-9907-8
E-Mail: legalaid@lawyerscouncil.or.th
www.lawyerscouncil.or.th

MITH SAMLANH
#215, Street 13, Phnom Penh, Cambodia
TEL: +855-23 426 748
E-Mail: friends@everyday.com.kh
www.streetfriends.org

MLOP TAPANG
7, Makara St., Sihanoukville, Cambodia
TEL: +855-12 587 407
E-Mail: info@mloptapang.org
www.mloptapang.org

NATIONAL COUNCIL FOR WOMEN OF THAILAND
Umbrella Organization, Manangkasila Mansion, Lanluang Road,
Bangkok, 10300, Thailand
TEL: (02) 281 0081   FAX: (02) 281 2189

NATIONAL COUNCIL OF WOMEN
Clearinghouse and Information Centre
Bangkok, 10200, Thailand

NATIONAL HUMAN RIGHTS COMMISSION OF THAILAND
422 AMLO Building Phya Thai Rd., Pathum wan District,
Bangkok, 10330, Thailand
TEL: (66) 2-2219-2980   FAX: (66) 2-2219-2940
E-Mail: interhr@nhrc.or.th

NEW LIFE CENTER
Aids girls who are at-risk for being trafficked into the sex industry
P.O. Box 29,
Chiang Mai, 50000, Thailand
TEL/FAX: 66-53-244-569

OPÉRATIONS ENFANTS DE BATTAMBANG (OEB)
#229 Group 11 Sophy I village, Rattanak commune,
Battambang, Cambodia
TEL: +855-53 952 752
E-Mail: oeb@worldmail.com.kh

PAVENA FOUNDATION
A Site to Learn More About Child Abuse, Where to Go to Get Help
www.pavena.thai.com

PEUAN MIT
Phai Nam Road, Vientiane Capital, Lao PDR
TEL: +856-21 261 389
E-Mail: peuanmit@etllao.com

WOMEN IN DEVELOPMENT CONSORTIUM (WIDCIT)
Network for women in development
Thammasat University, Office of the Rector, Bangkok, Thailand

**WOMEN'S EDUCATION FOR ADVANCEMENT AND
EMPOWERMENT (WEAVE)**
Chiang Mai University, P.O. Box 58, Chiang Mai 50202 Thailand
TEL/FAX: 66-53-278-945 or 66-53-260-193

WOMEN'S INFORMATION CENTRE
2/3 Soi Wang Lang, Arunamarin Road, Bangkok, 10700, Thailand

WOMEN'S INFORMATION CENTRE AND FOUNDATION
P.O. Box 7-47, Bangkok, 10700, Thailand

WOMEN'S RESEARCH AND DEVELOPMENT CENTER
Prince of Songkla University, Faculty of Management Science,
Had Yai, 90112, Thailand

WOMEN'S STUDIES CENTER
Chiang Mai University, Faculty of Social Sciences,
Chiang Mai, 50200, Thailand
TEL: (66) (53) 943-572, (66) (53) 943-592-3
FAX: (66) (53) 219-245, (66) (53) 892-464
E-Mail: wsc@chiangmai.ac.th
www.soc.cmu.ac.th

GOODWILL GROUP FOUNDATION

2nd Floor Ruam Rudee Bldg. III, 51/2 Soi Ruam Rudee,
Ploenchit Road, Lumpini, Phatumwan, Bangkok
Phone: 66-2-253-8493 or 66-2-255-4176

Goodwill Group is a school for disadvantaged Thai women. We are a private, non-religious Thai foundation whose mission is to improve the quality of life of Thai women via free skills training and career services. The scope of our services includes English language classes, computer skills training and job placement services. We are nearly always in need of reliable, dedicated volunteer teachers and generally seek commitments of at least 3 months. Unfortunately, we are not in the position of being able to offer financial, work permit or visa procurement assistance to our non-Thai volunteers, who typically are working elsewhere under valid Thai work permits. Prior experience teaching English is preferred, but not required. Teaching a class requires a 10-week commitment of three hours a week. If interested in volunteering, please mail us at info@goodwillbangkok.com to arrange to visit the school for an interview. Goodwill Group is open every day except Friday from 9:30am until 8:00pm. We invite you to visit our website www.goodwillbangkok.com and subscribe to our newsletter.

Goodwill Group also desperately needs funding, and we would appreciate any and all donations, no matter how small. We are able to operate on a shoestring budget thanks to the help of our many unpaid volunteers, but we still need funds to pay our operating expenses. If you can help - our bank details are:

Thai Farmer's Bank,
Wireless Road Branch,
Bangkok, Thailand,
I/F/O: Goodwill Group Foundation,
Account number: 7092-308418,
Swift Code: KASITHBK

US citizens can send tax-deductible donations
(our Federal tax ID Number is 58-2667052) to:
Bank of America, CHIPS ID: 0032bankofamerica,
I/F/O: Goodwill Group Foundation Inc
Account number: 94209 35372,
Swift Code: FNBBUS33.

Julia Manzanares has served as an English-As-A-Foreign Language/ Intercultural Communication Instructor and Teacher-Trainer for the past 18 years with 12 years spent teaching abroad in Asia, Southeast Asia, and the Middle East. She earned an M.A. in Psychology/Drama Therapy from California State University, Los Angeles and holds Certificates in TESOL and Neuro-Linguistics.

Derek Kent earned his B.A. from U.C.L.A. and has been an English-As-A-Foreign Language Instructor in the Middle East and Thailand for 15 years. He is now involved in providing educational opportunities, developing job and career training, and establishing a support center for disadvantaged young girls in Thailand.

DATE DUE

8/6/19			
			PRINTED IN U.S.A.